D1798916

The Macdonald Guide to Trees

The Macdonald Guide to Trees

Marcello Goldstein   Gualtiero Simonetti
Marta Watschinger

*With over 1000 illustrations in colour
by Aldo Ripamonti and Lino Simeoni*

Macdonald

A **Macdonald** BOOK
© 1983 Arnoldo Mondadori Editore S.p.A., Milan
© 1984 in the English translation Arnoldo Mondadori Editore S.p.A., Milan

English translation by John Gilbert

First published in Great Britain in 1984
by Macdonald & Co (Publishers) Ltd
London & Sydney

A member of BPCC plc

All rights reserved
No part of this publication may be reproduced, stored in a
retrieval system, or transmitted, in any form or by any
means without the prior permission in writing of the
publisher, nor be otherwise circulated in any form of
binding or cover other than that in which it is published
and without a similar condition including this condition
being imposed on the subsequent purchaser.

British Library Cataloguing in Publication Data

Goldstein,Marcello
    The Macdonald guide to trees.
    1.Trees——Europe
    I.Title   II.Simonetti,Gualtiero
    III.Watschinger,Marta   IV.Guida al
    riconoscimento degli alberi d'Europa. *English*
    582.16094   QK487

    ISBN 0-356-10492-3 hb
    ISBN 0-356-10493-1 pb

Printed and bound in Italy
by Officine Grafiche A. Mondadori Editore, Verona

Macdonald & Co (Publishers) Ltd
Maxwell House
74 Worship Street
London EC2A 2EN

Contents

Introduction

Trees in the living world

Almost all life is concentrated in the first few metres of the atmosphere and the very thin layer of living soil and oceans extending around the earth. This fragile zone has been termed the biosphere – life zone.

The quantity (concentration) and quality (complexity) of life forms in any given part of the biosphere depend on the local combination of many factors. In simple language, it might be defined as the result of the interaction between living creatures and physical and chemical factors such as light, heat, water, carbon dioxide and mineral salts.

In the oceans, life is most prolific in the surface layers, an ideal environment though one lacking in stimuli. Plants in the oceans, where the main limiting factor is the gradual extinction of light at increasing depths, exhibit few variations in terms either of concentration or complexity.

On dry land the concentration of living organisms (life) depends essentially on the framework of cellulose that plants manage to build to support themselves. Here the most important limiting factor by far is the availability of water.

Working our way from the poles towards the equator, it is noticeable how, as soon as water becomes available, the natural tendency is for the plant life to adopt the form of forests; and the smaller the effect of low temperatures, the richer and more complex are the species that constitute these forests. Close to the equator, this effect is cancelled out entirely; and with abundant rainfall, distributed regularly throughout the year, a situation is reached where there are virtually no factors to restrict plant growth. Maximum concentration and complexity are thus to be found in the tropical rain forest.

In the temperate forest areas, trees are the dominant form of vegetation in terms of sheer numbers, but there is a much greater variety of shrub and

Above: trees constituting the temperate forest. The number of tree species is always very small and the same composition is repeated unvaryingly over large areas.
Opposite: trees constituting the tropical rain forest. The number of tree species is very high and the composition will not be repeated over vast areas, even liable to change in zones situated quite close to one another.

herbaceous plant species. Although these forests cover very large areas, the trees do not normally number more than two or three principal species, with perhaps a dozen or so secondary types.

In any single forest in the temperate zone there will not as a rule be more than 20 tree species. By comparison, the tropical rain forest displays a truly extraordinary wealth of trees belonging to a very considerable number of species, genera and families. In one forest in Malaysia, covering 23 hectares (58 acres), no fewer than 376 different tree species

were counted, divided into 139 genera representing 52 families.

The Brazilian rain forest probably contains more than 100 tree species per square kilometre. Such trees chiefly belong to typically tropical families, but there are many examples of tropical trees which have relatives in temperate regions, where they may assume herbaceous forms; this is the case with the Violet family (Violaceae), represented in France by 13 herbaceous species and not a single tree, but in the West African forests by a mere three herbaceous species and about 37 different tree species!

The structure of a tree: parts and functions

There is no equivalent organ in a tree to the heart or brain of the more highly evolved animals. The secret of a tree's growth and development is not locked away and protected inside the trunk, but centres around a very specific organ. This consists of a very thin zone, measuring only some thousandths of a millimetre in thickness, made up of a single layer of tiny cells, running between the bark and the wood from roots to crown, and present in every part of the tree down to the smallest branches. In relation to the overall size of the tree, this remarkable generative organ is minute, yet it determines the tree's entire structure. This covering of cells is called the cambium.

The function of the cambium is to generate new tissues to replace those which have exhausted their primary function. The tissues generated by the cambium are designed to carry the plant liquids.

Wood is deposited on the inner side of the cambium. The vessels of the wood carry the water and mineral salts extracted from the soil by the roots. Water is thus moved to the crown of the tree and here the vital functions of growth, photosynthesis and respiration, flowering and fruiting occur – activities which trees share with all other plants.

The young woody tissue remains active for a limited time (it varies from one species to another). As it ages it becomes lignified, imbued with lignin and tannic substances, resins and oils which help to preserve it. The dead inner part of the wood provides structural support and in some species it can be clearly distinguished by colour from the living, physiologically active outer ring of wood. These darker and lighter parts are known respectively as heartwood and sapwood.

The layer inside the cambium is known as xylem and the outside layer as bast or phloem. Circulating through the phloem vessels is a solution rich in organic substances produced by photosynthesis in the leaves. This solution carries food to all living parts of the tree, from roots to leaves, and is transformed into storage substances accumulated in the wood and roots or in the fruits and seeds.

When their own functions are exhausted, the tissues of the phloem collect on the inner side of the bark to form a thick fibrous layer which assumes the guise of thin scales, like the pages of a book.

The bark protects the underlying vascular layers as well as the cambium; and it is formed not only by phloem but also by another type of generative tissue, very like the cambium, called phellogen. The latter forms the outer side of the bark, the cells of which are impregnated with suberin, changing it into cork. The phellogen, or cork cambium, assumes different forms in diverse species, determining the peculiar outward appearance of the bark. In general, a cylindrical and continuous phellogen, parallel to the cambium, produces a smooth bark, whereas a discontinuous phellogen, with outward-curving layers, gives rise to a rough bark.

Whereas outward growth (the increasing girth of the trunk and breadth of the branches) is determined by the cambium, upward growth depends on rather more complex structures in the form of small bundles of generative cells which create leaf- and flower-bearing shoots above ground and root-bearing shoots below ground.

These bundles of cells, known as meristem, are situated both at the tips of shoots or roots and in the axils of the leaves (i.e. the points where the leaves are attached to the stem). In deciduous trees, by the end of summer they have already laid down the rudiments of future shoots and flowers. These are the buds, which are protected from the rigours of winter by a covering of bud scales or perules. In some species, however, there are no bud scales and rudimentary leaves are visible with a covering of down. The latter is known as a naked bud.

There are two types of bud: those that produce shoots are leaf or vegetative buds, those giving rise to flowers, flower buds. Buds may be apical (at the tip) or lateral (supported by a leaf or leaf scar).

The living world of trees

Where rainfall is plentiful, the temperature constant and hot and nutrients sufficiently available, trees are the dominant plant form. These 'ideal' conditions for tree growth are found in the tropical rain forests, where temperature ranges between 21°C and 34°C (70°–93°F) and the uniformly distributed rainfall annually exceeds 150 cm (59 in).

In zones where such ideal conditions for tree growth do not exist, as in temperate regions where cold or dry periods intervene, plant life, if undisturbed, is still largely made up of trees, and trees are the dominant and determining factor in the entire community of living things.

Even under extremely severe conditions, near and sometimes beyond the Arctic polar circle, the biosphere still accommodates a massive tree population: the boreal forest or taiga, of which spruces (*Picea*) make up the dominant species.

In areas that are subject to extreme dryness and which are characterized by grasses and herbaceous plants, such as the North American prairies, the Eurasian steppes and the African savannahs, the introduction of fire-prevention programmes is often enough to stimulate a natural process of afforestation.

Trees in the botanical hierarchy

Trees are capable of living for thousands of years – about 5000 in the case of Ancient Pine (*Pinus longaeva*), and can move water and nutrients from the roots at ground level to a height of over 100 m (327 ft), e.g. in the Coastal Redwood (*Sequoia sempervirens*). It might be thought that the trees capable of these feats would be structurally complex. However, this is not so and many trees are only placed part-way along the botanical hierarchy.

Ferns are the first plant group with living tree-like members. Tree-ferns are found in tropical and warm temperate regions, excluding Europe, and are rarely cultivated here. Ferns are characterized by the production of spores on the underside of the leaf-like fronds. In the past, tree-ferns were more widely distributed.

Conifers are one of the two principal tree groups. Botanically, they are 'Gymnosperms' which translated from the original Greek means 'naked seed'. They are so called because during the growth and maturity of the seed it is technically naked, not enclosed in a womb. If you look at the female flower of a cypress (*Cupressus* or *Chamaecyparis*, pp 91–97) during the winter, you can see between the scales a number of minute specks; these are the naked seeds.

Fortunately, a number of generally more useful characters also distinguish conifers. These include seeds usually in woody cones, leaves which are scale- or needle-like, a monopodal (i.e. single stem) growth habit and simple wood structure. Of these the scale- or needle-like leaves are most useful but, be on the lookout, as *Ginkgo* (p 89), has rather broad fan-shaped leaves yet is a Gymnosperm, and *Tamarix* (pp 217–218) has scale-like leaves but belongs in the next group.

The second principal group of trees belongs to the 'Angiosperms'. This word translates as 'hidden seeds' and the egg cells are never exposed and naked but are always enclosed in an ovary. Fertilization is effected by the pollen growing through the mother plant's tissue to join with the egg cell, whereas in the Gymnosperms it just lands on the egg cell from outside.

The Angiosperms divide into two groups, based upon the number of seed leaves, or cotyledons, the germinating seed has. Most Angiosperm trees are in the Dicotyledons, or Dicots, with two cotyledons, although a few are in the Monocotyledons, or Monocots, with only one seed leaf.

Dicotyledonous (broadleaved) trees differ from the conifers in their broad-bladed leaves with branched

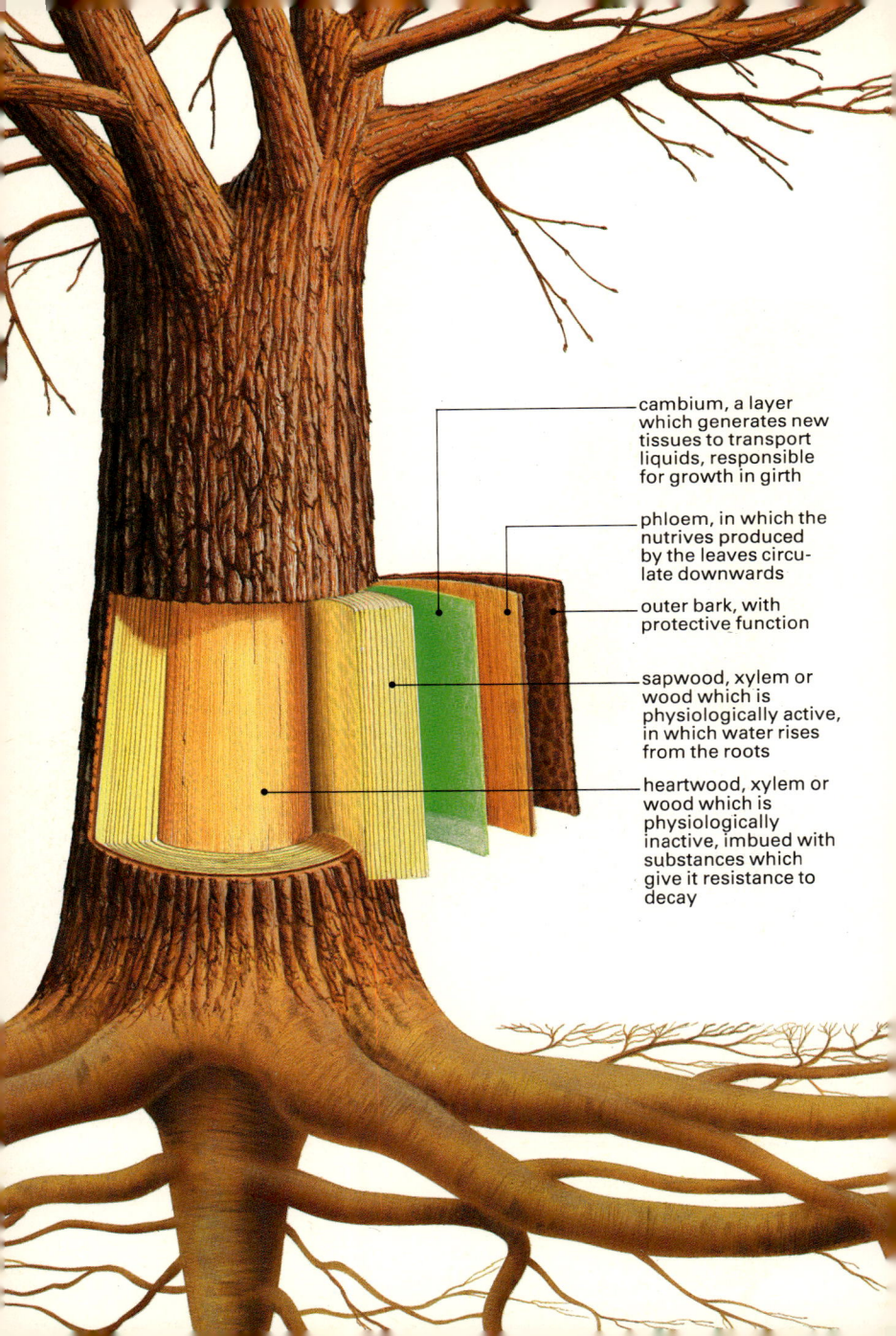

cambium, a layer which generates new tissues to transport liquids, responsible for growth in girth

phloem, in which the nutrives produced by the leaves circulate downwards

outer bark, with protective function

sapwood, xylem or wood which is physiologically active, in which water rises from the roots

heartwood, xylem or wood which is physiologically inactive, imbued with substances which give it resistance to decay

the bundle of embryonic or meristematic cells, ▶
small and cubical, distinguishable at the base of
this cross-section of leaf bud, responsible for
the growth of a shoot

◀ the layer of cells which forms the cambium runs
through the entire structure of the tree, down to
the smallest twigs, generating wood (xylem) on
the inside, phloem on the outside

the bundle of small, cubical ▶
embryonic cells,
distinguishable at the tip of
this cross-section of root
apex, is responsible for the
growth of the root which
anchors the tree to the
ground, finds water there
and absorbs it together with
dissolved mineral salts

veins, fruits in a variety of shapes and sizes (only rarely in woody, cone-like structures – see Alders, pp 140–142), in complex wood structure and in their frequently heavily branched crowns. The Dicotyledons also include most of our flowering plants and vegetables.

Monocotyledons include only a few trees. Most Monocots are grasses, orchids, or bulbs. Palms and bamboos, which are woody grasses, are the principal tree members.

Palms are characterized by their leaves having linear segments in which the veins are parallel, as in the grasses. They are usually monopodal, like conifers. The stem does not possess a cambium and is without the ability to produce secondary thickening. Instead the wood (xylem) and bast (phloem) elements are in a series of bundles. Young palm trees therefore have to establish a base as wide as the trunk will be before height growth is begun.

Trees and man

Centuries of scientific and technological development have coincided with the most widespread destruction of forests ever recorded in history. The most striking example of this, in terms of sheer extent of damage inflicted on a natural environment within a short period of time, has without doubt been the destruction, over just a few decades, of the forests which once stretched uninterruptedly across the eastern half of the United States. Out of more than one million square kilometres (386,100 square miles), only fragments (not exceeding 5,000 square kilometres in total – 1,930 square miles) of this forest region survive today. In Europe, too, vast areas of formerly prolific forest have likewise vanished.

Can damage to our natural heritage on such an immense scale ever be repaired? Fortunately there has developed a consciousness in industrialized countries, that the tide of destruction should at least be stemmed and that our forest resources must be safeguarded.

At the very time the worst destruction was taking place, Europe saw the genesis of the science of forestry and the introduction of more rational and less destructive methods of exploiting the forest environment. Today, in Europe, many of the surviving areas are under the management and protection of forest services. In many parts of the world outside Europe, economic self-interest is frequently too powerful, and good intentions and legal prohibitions are of little avail, so that every year sees vast tracts of forest irreversibly lost before there is a chance of introducing systems of rational management or safeguards. This occurs above all in the tropics as a result of human wantonness so that the extent of rain forest is continually reduced to make way for cultivation; these areas are subsequently abandoned, to be transformed into scrub or open savannah thus exposed to the risk of fires, or fated to become deserts.

Man needs forests and forest products to survive, but all too often he is squandering these resources. It is estimated that at present-day rates of destruction, tropical rain forests will scarcely exist by the year 2000, to be replaced by vegetation forms much less capable of sustaining life.

How to use this guide

The species encompassed in this guide are the principal tree species of the British Isles, central and southern Europe. All the common native trees and the commonest of the planted trees are featured. With experience and practice little difficulty should be met in identifying nearly every tree encountered.

Many of the native tree species have maps showing their native distribution. These maps are botanical in origin, which means that they show the areas where the tree is believed to be native, not where it may now be found growing wild – an example here is Sycamore (*Acer pseudoplatanus*, p 204) which is not native to Britain but, as many gardeners know, springs up as a rapacious weed and is now a constituent of our national woodlands. Another point to be remembered with the maps is that they show gross areas where the plant may be found. Local factors may make it absent, rare or plentiful in any single locality.

The illustrations provide faithful reproduction of the appearance of the leaves, etc., but the reader must remember that trees are living things. There is therefore variation through the year, from spring to autumn, in features such as colour and texture.

Measurements given throughout the book are ranges of average measurements. If the leaf in question is three times as large as the measurement in the book it is very unlikely to be that species, but if it is a centimetre or two larger or smaller, other features should be checked to see if it is indeed that species.

Identifying trees

The book consists of two separate parts to make the identification of any tree logical and simple.

The first part consists of the 'Guide to Identification', in which features of leaves, flowers and fruits are illustrated with short notes. This section is intended to point to the family, genus, or species involved and should always be consulted first when a new tree is met.

The second part features a detailed guide to individual species, in which further information and factual data are presented. This section includes the distribution maps and illustrations showing leaves, flowers, fruits, etc. together. With experience, this section can be used independently of the first part, either to check facts or to confirm a vaguely remembered identification.

The book should be used by comparing the illustration and descrip-

tion with the plant to be identified. Unless you have the owner's permission, specimens of leaf, flower or fruit should *not* be removed from the tree. However, this usually presents no difficulty as either foliage may be bent over to compare with the illustration, or wind- or animal-torn twigs and leaves can be found lying around beneath the tree. During the winter period, fallen leaves from beneath the tree can be very useful – but use other features to make sure they have not blown over from the neighbouring tree.

In the 'Guide to Species' are a number of botanical keys. These are often called dichotomous keys as they feature a series of choices each with two possible answers. Two main propositions, usually describing the leaf-shape, are followed by a series of alternatives. Determine which of the statements indicated by a single dash corresponds to your specimen, then repeat this process for successive pairs of distinguishing features, until you arrive at the name of the tree you are trying to identify. The number of dashes corresponds to the number of steps in the identification process.

Keys are quick and efficient methods of identifying trees but are not foolproof. The names obtained should always be checked against the description in the text. Errors are often due to using an unusual specimen, perhaps one in which the leaves are smaller than usual, or in which an obliging caterpillar has reshaped the outline.

Do not be afraid to use the keys. However, put some effort into understanding how they work. A simple way to do this is to start with a tree you know and work backwards through the key. If you do not end up at the correct initial proposition, either the tree is not what you thought it was or you have misinterpreted a statement at some point. Check each description against the leaf or twig. It should only take a little experience of this kind to make the keys useful and relevant.

Botanical and Latin names

Although all the trees listed in the guide have common or English names, they are arranged according to a botanical sequence. The botanical hierarchy adopted here starts with the family. Nearly all family names end in -aceae and a family includes one or more related genera of plants. A genus is a group of plants with many characters in common, e.g. all the maples have fruits which are in pairs, each with a flat wing, whilst the leaves are in opposite pairs on the shoot. In a genus are one or more species, differing from each other by a number of unique characters. A species may itself show a degree of variation. There are three botanical levels at which this variation may be described. A subspecies is a variation which has a morphological and geographical or ecological basis. Varieties and forma are lower orders of variation.

Many cultivated plants are selections from within a species or hybrids between two species. These are not part of the botanical variation. They are called 'cultivars', which is short for cultivated variety.

The system which has been adopted should simplify identification for the following reasons:

1) Identification is not based on the characteristics of flowers, which are all too often absent or inaccessible, except as shown on pp 56–57 where for a brief period in the year the flowers are very obvious and flowering precedes the new leaves. In all other cases, identification is based upon the character of the leaf, the shoots and the fruits. With the use of pp 51–55 winter identification is possible.

2) Identification can thus be made by comparing the fragment from the plant (leaf, twig or fruit) with the colour drawings in the relevant section of the 'Guide to Identification'. In this way identification is possible at a glance. This system is far easier than using written descriptions in dichoto-

mous keys alone and has the great advantage of being intelligible to beginners lacking detailed knowledge of botanical terminology. Such terms are nevertheless provided in the captions to these illustrations and in the glossary.

In cases where the use of a single element (say, the leaf) cannot positively establish identification when compared with a single drawing in the guide, i.e. if there is some doubt between two or three similar illustrations, it is almost always possible to verify matters by examining one of the other parts (fruits or twigs). The exception may be a short period during spring, from the opening of the buds to the first blossoms, when the plant exhibits leaves and flowers, or flowers alone. In the latter instance it is still possible to arrive at a conclusion by consulting the illustrations following those of the twigs, in the first part of the guide, which show the spring-like appearance of those species in which flowers precede leaves.

More frequently, however, identification during this brief period has to be based only on the leaves, and this can be done by looking at the second part of the book, the 'Guide to Species', where all are illustrated in flower. At other times of year it is often possible to utilize two or even three of the parts described in the first part of the guide. In fact, during summer both leaves and fruits are available, in autumn, leaves, fruits and buds, in winter fruits (at least at the foot of the tree) and twigs with buds.

Native British trees

Only a small number of the species frequently found in the United Kingdom are considered by botanists to have arrived by natural means after the last Ice Age. Nearly all have been introduced by man. Native trees are marked with one asterisk * after the common name and the commonest of the introduced trees with two asterisks **.

Guide to
Identification

BROADLEAVES **TABLES I–X**

evergreen or persistent leaves, stiff and heavy, leathery or prickly, often shiny above
L1–L20

Simple leaves L1–L108

deciduous leaves, herbaceous, soft and delicate, especially between veins, often hairy beneath
L21–L129

Compound leaves L109–L129

palmate leaves **L109–L110**

pinnate leaves **L111–L129**

elongate leaves, mostly entire margins **L1–L9**

elliptic leaves, variously toothed margins **L10–L15**

elliptic leaves, entire margins **L16–L20**

leaves with linear margins
L21–L36

leaves broadest in upper third
L21–L22

leaves elliptic, arranged in increasing
length **L23–L29**

leaves broadest in lower third
L30–L36

leaves with toothed or
serrate margins **L37–L78**

leaves elliptic, arranged in increasing
breadth **L37–L47**

leaves broadest in upper third
L48–L53

leaves more or less rounded **L54–L64**

leaves heart-shaped **L65–L71**

leaves broadest in lower third, or
triangular **L72–L78**

lobed leaves
L79–L108

lobed, pinnately veined leaves
L79–L91

two-lobed leaves (ginkgo leaves) **L92**

three-lobed or trifoliate leaves
L93–L99

four-lobed leaves (tulip tree leaves)
L100

five-lobed leaves, markedly palmate
L101–L108

SCALE-LIKE OR NEEDLE-LIKE LEAVES **TABLES XI–XII**

Scale-like leaves, covering the twigs **table XI, S1–S5**

Acicular (needle-shaped) leaves, directly attached to twigs **tables XI–XII**

short, sharp needles, radiating from twig in all directions **A1–A4**

short, flattened needles, radiating from twig mainly in two directions **A5–A12**

Acicular leaves, forming bundles on shortest twigs **table XII**

needles usually longer than 5 cm, sharp, in bundles of 2, 3 or 5 **A13–A15**

short needles, not longer than 5 cm, in large bundles (more than 10) **A16–A18**

TABLE I

Leaves 21

L1
L2
L3
L4
L5
L6
L7
L8
L9
L10
L11
L12
L13
L14
L15
L16
L17
L18
L19
L20

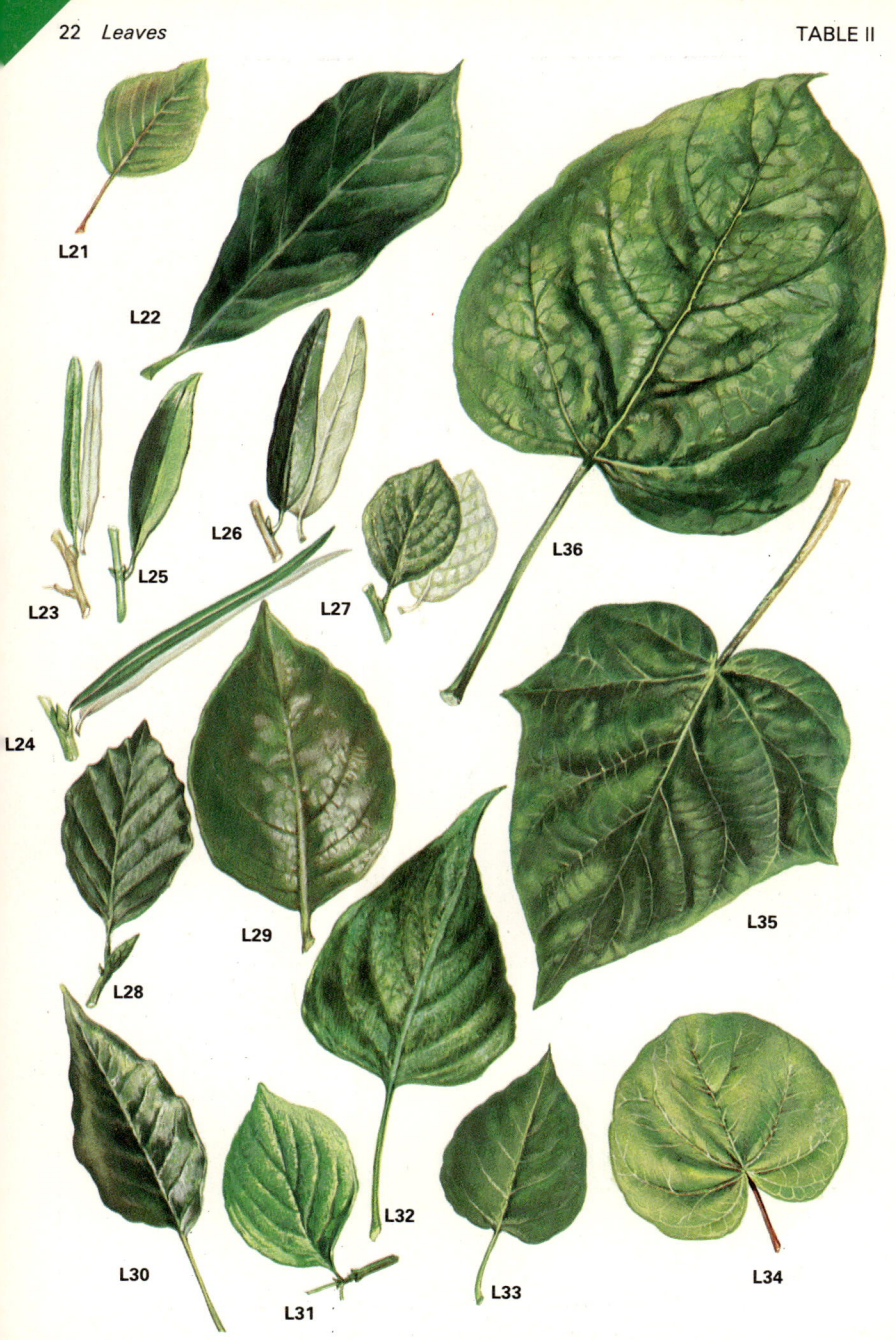

L21

L22

L23

L24

L25

L26

L27

L28

L29

L30

L31

L32

L33

L34

L35

L36

TABLE III

Leaves 23

L37

L38

L39

L40

L41

L47

L42

L43

L45

L46

L44

L50

L48

L52

L53

L49

L51

L54

L55

L56

L57

L58

L59

L60

L61

L62

L63

L64

L65

L66

L67

L68

L69

L70

L71

TABLE V   *Leaves* 25

L72

L73

L74

L75

L76

L77

L78

L79

L80

L81

L82

L83

L84

L85

L86

L87

L88

L89

L90

L91

L92

L93

L94

L95

L97

L96

L98

L99

L100

TABLE VII

Leaves 27

L101

L102

L103

L104

L105

L106

L107

L108

TABLE VIII

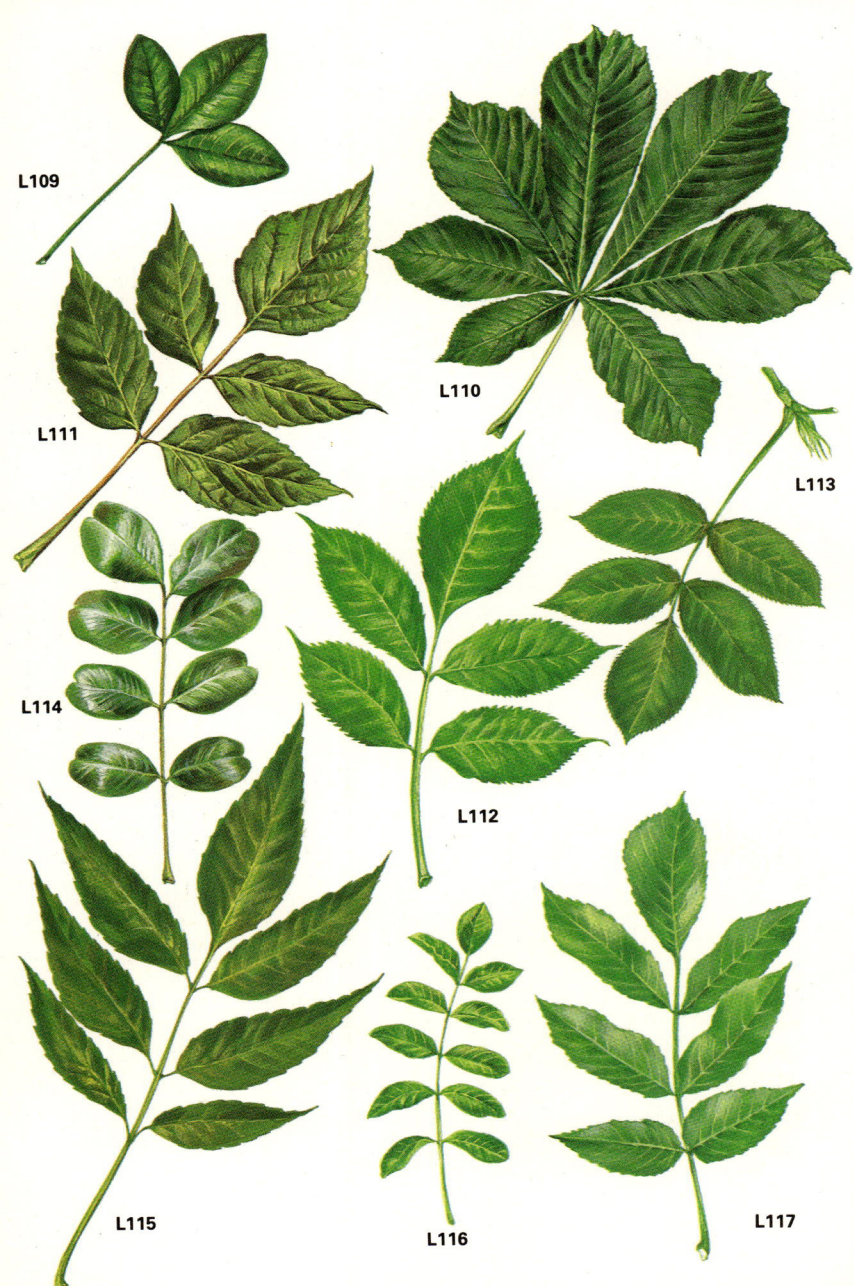

L109

L110

L111

L113

L114

L112

L115

L116

L117

TABLE IX

Leaves 29

L118

L119

L121

L120

L122

L124

L123

L125

L126

L127

L128

L129

TABLE XI

Leaves 31

S1

S2

S3

S4

S5

A1

A2

A3

A4

A5

A6

A7

A8

A9
A10
A11
A12
A13
A14
A15
A16
A17
A18

TABLE XIII

Leaves 33

P1

P2

P3

P4

P5

P6

L1 Box (**Buxus sempervirens** L., p 210). Typically revolute margins beneath. Rounded, sometimes slightly concave emarginate, i.e. notched tip. Unmistakable.
Fruit: **F59**

L2 Olive (**Olea europaea** L., p 226). Entire margin, lower edge slightly revolute and covered with thick silvery hair. Not to be confused with **L3** (*Quercus ilex*), **L23** (*Hippophae rhamnoides*) and **L26** (*Elaeagnus angustifolia*).
Fruit: **F26**

L3 Holm Oak (**Quercus ilex** L., p 154). The leaves with entire margins are often accompanied, even on the same branch, by leaves of the **L13** and **L14** type. Not to be confused with **L2** (*Olea europaea*), **L10** (*Phillyrea latifolia*), **L23** (*Hippophae rhamnoides*) and **L26** (*Elaeagnus angustifolia*).
Fruit: similar to **F79**
Similar species: *Quercus suber, Quercus coccifera.*

L4 Sweet Bay (**Laurus nobilis** L., p 168). Entire, undulate margins. The wrinkled leaf gives out a characteristic aroma. Not to be confused with **L15** (*Arbutus unedo*), **L18** (*Citrus limon*) and **L8** (*Prunus laurocerasus*).
Fruit: **F31**

L5 Pittosporum (**Pittosporum tobira** Ait., p 173). Margins entire, revolute beneath, tip truncate and slightly concave (notched). Upper side shiny. Unmistakable.
Fruit: **F63**

L6 Oleander (**Nerium oleander** L., p 231). Secondary veins numerous and parallel to one another, almost perpendicular to principal vein. Petiole very short or almost absent. May resemble **L9** (*Eucalyptus* sp.) in shape and venation, but latter is curved, glaucous in colour and furnished with a petiole.
Fruit: **F54**

L7 Loquat (**Eriobotrya japonica** Lindl., p 175). Slightly toothed margins. Secondary veins incurved upwards before reaching margins. Reddish-brown hair beneath. Unmistakable.
Fruit: **F13**

L8 Cherry Laurel (**Prunus laurocerasus** L., p 183). Slightly toothed margins. Glossy upper surface. In adult leaves maximum breadth tends to be in upper third. The young leaves may be mistaken for **L4** (*Laurus nobilis*), which are much stiffer.
Fruit: **F40**

L9 Blue Gum (**Eucalyptus globulus** Labill., p 219). Typically sickle-like, curving. Numerous secondary veins converging in a line that runs along the leaf margin. The leaves, both sides alike, hang down from the tree. Not to be confused with **L6** (*Nerium oleander*).
Fruit: **F58**
Similar species: *Eucalyptus viminalis, Eucalyptus camaldulensis*

L10 Phillyrea (**Phillyrea latifolia** L., p 228). Finely toothed margins. Leaf blade thick and stiffly flattened. Not to be confused with **L11** (*Rhamnus alaternus*), which is broader, glossy and with finer teeth.
Fruit: **F27**

L11 Mediterranean Buckthorn (**Rhamnus alaternus** L., p 212). Finely toothed margins. Glossy, leathery leaf blade. Not to be confused with **L10** (*Phillyrea latifolia*), not so finely toothed, narrower and opaque.
Fruit: **F4**

L12 Cork Oak (***Quercus suber*** L., p 155). Spiny, toothed margins. Leaf blade tends to be rounded, almost as broad as it is long, green above, grey woolly beneath. Not to be confused with **L3**, **L14** (*Quercus ilex*), which is larger and generally more oblong.
Fruit: similar to **F79**
Similar species: *Quercus ilex, Quercus coccifera*

L13 Holly (***Ilex aquifolium*** L., p 208). Undulate margins and spine-tipped teeth alongside and leaves with entire or asymmetrically toothed margins. Leaf blade glossy on both sides; this and dimensions distinguish it from **L3**, **L14** (*Quercus ilex*) and **L12** (*Quercus suber*), both of which are grey woolly beneath.
Fruit: **F11**

L14 Holm Oak (***Quercus ilex*** L., p 154). Spiny, toothed margin. Leaf blade broadly elliptic, green above, grey woolly beneath. Regularly found alongside forms with narrower blade and entire margins of type **L3**. Not to be confused with **L13** (*Ilex aquifolium*), which is glossy on both sides, and **L12** (*Quercus suber*), smaller and rounded.
Fruit: similar to **F79**
Similar species: *Quercus suber, Quercus coccifera*

L15 Strawberry Tree (***Arbutus unedo*** L., p 223). Serrate margin. Leaf blade elliptic, elongate, broadest in upper third, glossy mainly on upper surface. Not to be confused with **L11** (*Rhamnus alaternus*), which is smaller, broader and stiffer, or with **L4** (*Laurus nobilis*), which is comparatively opaque, with entire or undulate margins; aromatic to the touch.
Fruit: **F9**

L16 Myrtle (***Myrtus communis*** L., p 219). Leaf blade elliptic with sharp-pointed tip. Not to be confused with

L10 (*Phillyrea latifolia*), which is toothed and stiffer, or with **L1** (*Buxus sempervirens*), which has a rounded, slightly concave tip with its blade revolute along the margin beneath.
Fruit: **F12**

L17 Phytolacca (***Phytolacca dioica*** L., p 167). Leaf blade broadly elliptic, with very pointed (acuminate) tip. Slender petiole half as long as blade. Not to be confused with **L18** (*Citrus limon*) and **L19** (*Ligustrum lucidum*) which have a much shorter petiole.
Fruit: **F6**

L18 Lemon (***Citrus limon*** (L.) Burm., p 195). Minutely toothed margin. Leaf blade broadly elliptic, transparent. Not to be confused with **L15** (*Arbutus unedo*), which is smaller and stiffer, or with **L29** (*Diospyros kaki*), which has an entire margin and is deciduous, and opaque and greyish beneath.
Fruit: **F23**
Similar species: *Citrus sinensis*

L19 Chinese or Glossy Privet (***Ligustrum lucidum*** Ait., p 229). Perfectly entire margin. Leaf blade stiff, incurved and with the two lateral parts not arranged on the same plane (V-section), dark and glossy above. Not to be confused with **L17** (*Phytolacca dioica*) which has a petiole half as long as the blade and is also flat.
Fruit: **F5**

L20 Evergreen Magnolia (***Magnolia grandiflora*** L., p 169). Leaf blade large, dark green, glossy, leathery, reddish-brown beneath. The size, too, is unmistakable, markedly bigger than other leaves represented in this group.
Fruit: **F67**

L21 Alder Buckthorn (***Frangula alnus*** Miller, p 213). Leaf blade broadest in

upper third, light green. Leaf up to 5 cm long, petiole 1 cm.
Bud: **B23**
Fruit: **F7**

L22 Magnolia (***Magnolia x soulangiana*** Soul. Bod., p 170). Leaf blade broadest in upper third (obovate). Leaf over 8 cm long, with very short petiole. Differs from **L21** (*Frangula alnus*) in being markedly larger.
Bud: **B56**
Spring appearance: **Sp16**
Fruit: **F67**

L23 Sea Buckthorn (***Hippophae rhamnoides*** L., p 216). Leaf blade long and narrow, green above, silver beneath. Not to be confused with **L26** (*Elaeagnus angustifolia*), **L2** (*Olea europaea*) or **L24**, **L37** (*Salix elaeagnos*).
Bud: **B44**
Fruit: **F28**

L24 Hoary Willow (***Salix elaeagnos*** Scop., p 129). See description for **L37**.

L25 Pomegranate (***Punica granatum*** L., p 221). Leaf blade small and shiny, glabrous, with yellow-pinkish tints. The leaves, non-persistent and with entire margins, are unmistakable.
Bud: **B50**
Fruit: **F20**

L26 Oleaster (***Elaeagnus angustifolia*** L., p 216). Leaf blade long and elliptic, silver-grey, especially beneath. Not to be confused with **L23** (*Hippophae rhamnoides*) or **L39** (*Salix alba*), which has slightly toothed margins.
Bud: **B32**
Fruit: **F29**

L27 Storax (***Styrax officinalis*** L., p 226). Leaf blade broad and elliptic with unpronounced tip, hairy and whitish beneath. Leaves, with entire margins, unmistakable.
Fruit: **F36**

L28 Common Beech (***Fagus sylvatica*** L., p 146). Undulate or wavy margins with soft hairs, often joined on secondary veins which end in a small tooth. Leaves, with entire margins, unmistakable.
Bud: **B15**
Fruit: **F78**

L29 Chinese Persimmon (***Diospyros kaki*** L., p 225). Leaf blade large, broadly elliptic, green and shiny above, greyish and opaque beneath. In consistency and glossiness it resembles the persistent leaves with entire margins of types **L17** (*Phytolacca*), **L18** (*Citrus*) and **L19** (*Ligustrum*) which, however, are stiffer.
Bud: **B29**
Fruit: **F10**

L30 Osage Orange (***Maclura pomifera*** (Raf.) Schneid., p 166). Leaf blade pointed, with long stem. Not to be confused with **L29** (*Diospyros kaki*) which is broader, unpointed and with a shorter petiole.
Bud: **B41**
Fruit: **F74**

L31 Cornelian Cherry (***Cornus mas*** L., p 222). Leaf blade broadened in lower third or half, sharply pointed (acuminate), with secondary veins typically curved and running almost parallel to the leaf margin towards the tip.
Bud: **B3**
Spring appearance: **Sp11**
Fruit: **F32**
Similar species: *Cornus sanguinea*

Note also ***Lagerstroemia indica*** L., (p 218), with elliptic-lanceolate, acute leaves, 7 × 3 cm, more or less sessile, with entire and glabrous margin; leaves opposite, sometimes alternate or in threes.
Fruit: **F60**

L32 Clerodendrum (***Clerodendrum trichotomum*** Thunb., p 232). Leaf

blade broadly elliptic, broadest in lower third, sharply pointed tip; downy, dark green. Leaf very large with long petiole. Unmistakable.
Bud: **B7**
Fruit: **F8**

L33 Common Lilac (***Syringa vulgaris*** L., p 228). Leaf blade heart-shaped, glabrous and shining. Not to be confused with **L17** (*Phytolacca dioica*), which is stiffer with a longer petiole.
Bud: **B4**
Fruit: **F62**

L34 Judas Tree (***Cercis siliquastrum*** L., p 188). Leaf blade round with deeply heart-shaped (cordate) base and rounded tip; faint pink-violet tints beneath. Not to be confused with **L71** (*Cercidiphyllum japonicum*), which has a margin with rounded teeth (crenate), the leaves being opposite.
Bud: **B69**
Spring appearance: **Sp14**
Fruit: **F44**

L35 Foxglove Tree (***Paulownia tomentosa*** (Thunb.) Steud., p 232). Leaf blade very large, fundamentally cordate, but often with pointed, more or less pronounced, basal lobes. The smaller leaves may resemble **L36** (*Catalpa bignonioides*).
Bud: **B9**
Fruit: **F64**

L36 Indian Bean Tree (***Catalpa bignonioides*** Walt., p 233). Leaf blade very large, cordate, with sharply pointed tip; when crushed it gives off a pungent smell. It may exhibit lobation as in **L35** (*Paulownia tomentosa*), but in less pronounced form.
Bud: **B10**
Fruit: **F45**

L37 Hoary Willow (***Salix elaeagnos*** Scop., p 129). Leaf blade very narrow

with margins revolute beneath. Upper surface green, lower side covered with thick silvery down. Not to be confused with **L23** (*Hippophae rhamnoides*) or **L26** (*Elaeagnus angustifolia*), which are shorter, with non-revolute margins and the lower surface covered with scales instead of hairs.
Bud: similar to **B24**
Fruit: similar to **F55** and **F56**
Similar species: *Salix viminalis*

L38 Chinese Weeping Willow (***Salix babylonica*** L., p 128). Leaf blade very narrow, long and soft, pale green, with finely serrated margins. Unmistakable by reason of pendent, drooping appearance.
Bud: similar to **B24**
Fruit: similar to **F55** and **F56**
Similar species: *Salix alba* f. *vitellina* Rehd. 'tristis'

L39 White Willow (***Salix alba*** L., p 128). Finely serrated margins, leaf blade long and pointed, grey-green above, whitish beneath. Not to be confused with **L26** (*Elaeagnus angustifolia*), which has entire margin and less pointed tip.
Bud: similar to **B24**
Fruit: **F55**
Similar species: *Salix alba* f. *vitellina* 'tristis'

L40 Crack Willow (***Salix fragilis*** L., p 131). Margins roughly toothed. Leaf blade elongated-elliptic and pointed, shiny green above, opaque beneath. Unmistakable.
Bud: similar to **B24**
Fruit: similar to **F55** and **F56**

L41 Bay Willow (***Salix pentandra*** L., p 127). Margins finely toothed. Leaf blade elliptic, markedly broader than most other willows, dark green and shiny. Not to be confused with **L44** (*Prunus serotina*), which has a pair of small glands on the petiole at the

base of the blade, or with **L45** (*Salix caprea*), which has the lower surface covered with greyish down.
Bud: similar to **B24**
Fruit: **F56**
Similar species: *Salix triandra, Salix daphnoides*

L42 Hornbeam (***Carpinus betulus*** L., p 144). Margins doubly serrate. The secondary veins, parallel to one another, run straight through to the margin. Leaf blade elliptic, broad and pointed. Maximum breadth sometimes in lower third, but this is more frequent in **L73** (*Ostrya carpinifolia*).
Bud: **B14**
Fruit: **F87**
Similar species: *Carpinus orientalis*

L43 Crab Apple (***Malus sylvestris*** Mill., p 176). Margins with sharp, obtuse teeth, broad-based (crenate-serrate). Elliptic leaf blade dark green above, lighter and covered with fine hairs (pubescent) beneath. Petiole half as long as the blade and dark red near base. The smaller leaves are hard to distinguish from **L55** (*Pyrus communis*). See also **L60** (*Malus sylvestris* second form).
Bud: **B49**
Fruit: **F21**

L44 Black Cherry (***Prunus serotina*** Ehrh., p 184). Margins markedly toothed. Leaf blade broadly elliptic and unexpectedly pointed (acuminate), the base sometimes tapering (cuneate). Leaf dark green above, opaque beneath. The petiole, at the joint with the leaf blade, exhibits a pair of glands, sometimes enlarged into tiny green lobes. On this basis it differs from willows of the type **L40** and **L41**; and on the basis of its cuneate tendency from other *Prunus* species **L50, L52, L57, L58**.
Bud: similar to **B47** and **B53**
Fruit: similar to **F38**

L45 Pussy Willow (***Salix caprea*** L., p 126). Margins slightly crenate or almost entire (undulate). Leaf blade broadly elliptic, sometimes with maximum breadth in upper third (obovate), sometimes with a rounded base, terminating in a tip that is pointed and oblique on one side. Leaf green and glabrous above, with thick greyish hairs beneath. Petiole pubescent, dark red and often with two broad, green laminar expansions at the base. In general, unmistakable.
Bud: **B24**
Fruit: similar to **F55** and **F56**

L46 Whitebeam (***Sorbus aria*** (L.) Crantz, p 180). Margins irregularly toothed and with small, irregularly distributed lobes. Leaf blade thick, broadly elliptic, upper surface initially hairy then dark green, lower surface white as a result of thick silvery down and with very raised veining. In general, unmistakable.
Bud: similar to **B60** and **B61**
Fruit: **F17**

L47 Grey Alder (***Aldus incana*** (L.) Moench, p 141). Margins sharply toothed and with small, regularly distributed lobes, especially in the two upper thirds. Leaf blade broadly elliptic and rounded (cf **L63**), terminating, though not always, in a sharply pointed tip. Leaf green above and greyish beneath. May be easily distinguished from **L64** (*Alnus glutinosa*), which has neither regular lobes nor pointed tip, and from **L86** (*Sorbus intermedia*), which has much more pronounced lobation.
Bud: similar to **B66**
Fruit: **F84**

L48 European White Elm (***Ulmus laevis*** Pall., p 160). Margins doubly toothed. Leaf blade strongly asymmetric at base, rounded on one side and obliquely tapering on the other. Such characteristics are generally found in all the elms.
Bud: **B68**
Spring appearance: similar to **Sp9**

and **Sp10**
Fruit: **F97**
Similar species: *Ulmus minor*

L49 Wych Elm (***Ulmus glabra*** Huds.,
p 158). Like preceding species but the
base is asymmetrical with a lobe
covering the petiole; rough to the
touch, like emery paper.
Bud: **B68**
Spring appearance: **Sp10**
Fruit: **F96**
Similar species: *Ulmus minor*

L50 Bird Cherry (***Prunus padus*** L.,
p 183). Margins finely toothed. Leaf
blade with rounded base. It is to be
distinguished from **L52** (*Prunus
avium*) which is, on average, bigger
and has larger, double-toothed margins. Glands on petiole and at base of
leaf blade.
Bud: similar to **B47**, **B52** and **B53**
Fruit: **F38**

L51 Medlar (***Mespilus germanica*** L.,
p 174). Margins almost entire and
with irregular, very fine teeth, limited
to upper third. Leaf blade elongated,
terminating in a sometimes sharp tip.
Leaf whitish beneath. In comparison
L45 (*Salix caprea*) has margins with
rounded teeth (crenate), maximum
breadth in central or lower section, a
longer petiole, pubescent and dark
red.
Bud: **B33**
Fruit: **F19**

L52 Gean (***Prunus avium*** L., p 185).
Margins deeply and double toothed.
Leaf blade broadly elliptic, relatively
large, terminating in a pointed tip.
Red glands stand out on petiole near
leaf base. In comparison **L44** (*Prunus
serotina*) and **L50** (*Prunus padus*) are
slightly smaller and have finer teeth.
Bud: **B52**
Fruit: **F39**

L53 Sweet Chestnut (***Castanea sativa***
Miller, p 147). Margins with twenty or

so teeth terminating in a slender filament corresponding to secondary
veins. Leaf blade elongate-elliptic,
acuminate, usually slightly heart-
shaped at base, shiny and consistent.
Usually unmistakable.
Bud: **B11**
Fruit: **F81**
Similar species: *Castanea crenata*

L54 Eastern Hornbeam (***Carpinus
orientalis*** Miller, p 144). Generally
similar to, though smaller than **L42**
(*Carpinus betulus*), and like latter un-
mistakable overall.
Bud: similar to **B14**
Fruit: **F88**
Similar species: *Carpinus betulus*

L55 Common Pear (***Pyrus communis***
L., p 177). Margins with rounded
(finely crenate) teeth. Small leaf
blade, round to broadly elliptic, heart-
shaped or rounded at base, shiny,
with stem as long as the blade. Hard
to distinguish from smaller leaves of
crab apple (**L43**, **L60**) which tend to
have the base tapering to the petiole
(cuneate), deeper teeth, petiole dark
red at base.
Bud: **B48**, **B58**
Spring appearance: **Sp15**
Fruit: **F22**

L56 Christ's Thorn (***Paliurus spina-
christi*** Miller, p 211). Margins finely
toothed or entire. Leaf blade broadly
elliptic, with two secondary veins
which, from the point of junction to
the petiole, cross it almost to the tip;
short petiole. Similar overall to **L72**
(*Ziziphus jujuba*), which, however, is
broadest in lower third.
Bud: **B43**
Fruit: **F98**

L57 Sour Cherry (***Prunus cerasus*** L.,
p 185). Margins with rounded teeth.
Small leaf blade, broadly elliptic,
glabrous, with basal glands. Short,
dark red petiole. To be distinguished

from **L55** (*Pyrus communis*) and **L60** (*Malus sylvestris*) which have much longer petioles, from other *Prunus* species (**L44, L50, L52**) which have a bigger blade, and from **L58** (*P. mahaleb*) which has a shiny and much more rounded blade.
Bud: similar to **B47, B52** and **B53**
Fruit: similar to **F38** and **F39**
Similar species: *Prunus domestica*

L58 Saint Lucie Cherry (***Prunus mahaleb*** L., p 181). Finely toothed margins. Leaf blade round, with short pointed or blunted tip. Petiole with two glands at junction with blade. It is distinguished from **L60** (*Malus sylvestris*) which is opaque, and has a longer petiole without glands.
Bud: **B37**
Fruit: **F37**

L59 Aspen (***Populus tremula*** L., p 133). Margins with small, irregular, spaced teeth. Leaf blade round or as broad as it is long. Petiole longer than blade and laterally flattened. To be distinguished from **L61** (*Populus canescens*) which has fewer rounded teeth and a petiole shorter than the blade.
Bud: **B57**
Spring appearance: **Sp6**
Fruit: **F57**
Similar species: *Populus canescens*

L60 Crab Apple (***Malus sylvestris*** Miller, p 176). Margins finely toothed, leaf blade round with short, sometimes sharp, tip. Long petiole, dark red at base. To be distinguished from **L58** (*Prunus mahaleb*), which has a shinier blade and a short petiole with glands, and from **L55** (*Pyrus communis*), which has a less rounded blade, cordate or rounded at base.
Bud: **B49**
Fruit: **F21**

L61 Grey Poplar (***Populus canescens*** (Aiton) Sm., p 132). Margins with few

teeth, but broad and rounded, almost forming small lobes. Leaf blade rounded with lower surface covered in greyish down which disappears at maturity. Petiole a little over half as long as blade. It is found also in a three-lobed form (**L94**). To be distinguished from **L62** (*Populus tremula*), which is broader, has a much longer petiole and more numerous, pointed teeth.
Bud: similar to **B55**
Spring appearance: similar to **Sp1, Sp2, Sp5** and **Sp6**
Fruit: similar to **F57**
Similar species: *Populus tremula*

L62 Aspen (***Populus tremula*** L., p 133). Leaf blade almost elliptic; numerous teeth and long petiole. Other characteristics as **L59**.
Similar species: *Populus canescens*

L63 Grey Alder (***Alnus incana*** (L.) Moench, p 141). Margins which, corresponding to secondary veins, are divided into small pointed lobes, in their turn serrate. Leaf blade broadly elliptic, with sharp tip, covered with grey wool beneath. To be distinguished from **L65** (*Corylus avellana*) and **L66** (*Corylus colurna*) which have less regular margins, are broadest in the upper third, and have a cordate base; and from **L86** (*Sorbus intermedia*) which has much more pronounced lobation. It is also found in the form **L47**.
Bud: similar to **B66**
Spring appearance: similar to **Sp3**
Fruit: **F84**
Similar species: *Alnus cordata, Alnus glutinosa*

L64 Common Alder (***Alnus glutinosa*** (L.) Gaertner, p 140). Margins deeply and irregularly toothed. Leaf blade rounded, with maximum breadth in upper third; cuneate base, tip truncate or slightly concave. Unmistakable.
Bud: **B66**

Spring appearance: **Sp3**
Fruit: **C14**; similar to **F84**
Similar species: *Alnus cordata, Alnus incana*

L65 Common Hazel (***Corylus avellana*** L., p 142). Margins irregularly serrate-dentate. Leaf blade rounded with maximum breadth in central or upper third, short tip sharply pointed, base cordate, petiole very short. Leaf coarsely hairy, dark green above. To be distinguished from **L66** (*Corylus colurna*) which is larger and has a marked tendency to double teeth.
Bud: **B67**
Spring appearance: **Sp4**
Fruit: **F82**
Similar species: *Corylus colurna*

L66 Turkish Hazel (***Corylus colurna*** L., p 143). Compare description for **L65**. Leaf blade double toothed, often lobate, green and glossy above.
Bud: similar to **B67**
Spring appearance: similar to **Sp4**
Fruit: similar to **F82**
Similar species: *Corylus avellana*

L67 Italian Alder (***Alnus cordata*** (Loisel.) Desf., p 142). Margins with small rounded teeth (crenate). Leaf blade dark green and shiny above, lighter beneath. To be distinguished from **L68** (*Tilia* sp.), which has an asymmetrical base, narrower teeth and a tapering tip.
Bud: similar to **B66**
Spring appearance: similar to **Sp3**
Fruit: **C13**
Similar species: *Alnus glutinosa, Alnus incana*

L68 Large-leaved Lime (***Tilia platyphyllos*** Scop., p 215). Margins dentate-serrate. Leaf blade rounded and broad, with sharply pointed tip, base cordate and asymmetrical. Long petiole, obliquely attached to blade. To be distinguished from **L67** (*Alnus cordata*), which has a symmetrical base and a not-pronounced tip, and

from **L69** (*Morus alba*), which has a symmetrical base and deeper teeth.
Bud: similar to **B12**
Fruit: similar to **F94**
Similar species: *Tilia cordata, Tilia x vulgaris*

L69 White Mulberry (***Morus alba*** L., p 163). Margins deeply toothed. Leaf blade more or less heart-shaped, sometimes with deep incisions, co-existing with lobate forms of the type **L89** and **L96**, and oval forms of the type **L75**. To be distinguished from **L68** (*Tilia platyphyllos*), which has dentate-serrate margins, an asymmetrical base and the petiole obliquely attached to the blade.
Bud: similar to **B30**
Fruit: **F70**
Similar species: *Morus nigra*

L70 Paper Mulberry (***Broussonetia papyrifera*** (L.) L'Hér., p 166). Leaf blade velvety, cordate, with a fairly deep asymmetrical base. Not to be confused with the mulberries, which are less hairy. See also **L99**.
Bud: **B31**
Fruit: **F69**

L71 Katsura Tree (***Cercidiphyllum japonicum*** Sieb. & Zucc., p 167). Margins with rounded teeth (crenate). Heart-shaped blade with fan-like veins very prominent beneath. Leaves opposite, bright red when young. Reddish petiole. Not to be confused with **L34** (*Cercis siliquastrum*), with alternate leaves.
Spring appearance: **Sp8**
Fruit: **F47**

L72 Jujube (***Zizyphus jujuba*** Miller, p 211). Compare description for **L56** (*Paliurus spina-christi*).
Bud: **B42**
Fruit: **F30**

L73 Hop Hornbeam (***Ostrya carpinifolia*** Scop., p 145). Similar in all respects to **L42** (*Carpinus betulus*), except that it tends to be broadest in the lower third.

Bud: similar to **B14**
Fruit: **F86**
Similar species: *Carpinus betulus, Carpinus orientalis*

L74 Southern Nettle-tree (***Celtis australis*** L., p 161). Base of leaf blade asymmetrical with two long secondary veins originating from attachment to petiole, more obvious on lower surface. Unmistakable.
Bud: **B36**
Fruit: **F33**

L75 Black Mulberry (***Morus nigra*** L., p 163). Distinguishable from **L69** (*Morus alba*) in that the leaves are more leathery, margins more clearly toothed; leaf blade with deeply cordate base and with less tendency to show lobate forms of the type **L89** and **L96**.
Bud: **B30**
Fruit: **F70**
Similar species: *Morus alba*

L76 Black Poplar (***Populus nigra*** L., p 134). Margins with rounded teeth (crenate). Rhomboid blade. To be distinguished from **L78** (*Populus x euroamericana*), which has a triangular blade, and from **L77** (*Betula pubescens*), which has straight secondary veins which reach the finely toothed margins.
Bud: **B54**
Spring appearance: similar to **Sp1, Sp2, Sp5** and **Sp6**
Fruit: similar to **F57**
Similar species: *Populus x euroamericana*

L77 Downy or Brown Birch (***Betula pubescens*** Ehrh., p 139). Margins finely toothed. Leaf blade triangular, sometimes rhomboid, secondary veins straight and undivided to margins. Petiole half as long as blade. Not to be confused with **L76** (*Populus nigra*) and **L78** (*Populus x euroamericana*).
Bud: **B65**
Fruit: similar to **F85**
Similar species: *Betula pendula* Roth., with double-toothed margins

L78 Hybrid Black Poplar (***Populus x euroamericana*** Guiner, p 135). Margins with rounded teeth (crenate). Triangular leaf blade. Petiole one-quarter the length of blade. Not to be confused with **L76** (*Populus nigra*) and **L77** (*Betula pubescens*).
Bud: similar to **B54**
Spring appearance: **Sp1**
Fruit: similar to **F37**
Similar species: *Populus nigra*

L79 Caucasian Elm (***Zelkova carpinifolia*** (Pall.) K. Koch, p 162). Margins almost crenate, divided into small lobes corresponding to secondary veins, which terminate in a point (mucro). Elliptic leaf blade. Not to be confused with **L80** (*Quercus trojana*).
Bud: **B34**
Fruit: **F83**

L80 Macedonian Oak (***Quercus trojana*** Webb, p 157). Margins divided into small pointed lobes corresponding to secondary veins, which terminate in a point (mucro). Elliptic-elongate blade. Not to be confused with **L79** (*Zelkova carpinifolia*) which has more rounded and more regularly arranged lobes.
Bud: similar to **B39**
Fruit: similar to **F80**
Similar species: *Quercus ilex, Quercus suber*

L81 Turkey Oak (***Quercus cerris*** L., p 149). Blade divided into lobes terminating in a clear mucro, separated by grooves up to two-thirds as long as the whole blade, which is broadest in the upper third. Unmistakable among forms represented.
Bud: **B39**
Fruit: **F80**
Similar species: *Quercus robur*

L82 Sessile or Durmast Oak (***Quercus petraea*** (Mattuschka) Liebl, p 153). Leaf blade broadest in upper third, divided into rounded, shallow lobes and rounded sinuses which reach one-third way to midrib. Cuneate

base. Unmistakable among forms represented.
Bud: **B38**
Fruit: **F79**
Similar species: *Quercus pubescens, Quercus frainetto*

L83 English or Pedunculate Oak (***Quercus robur*** L., p 153). Similar to preceding species, but with two distinct ear lobes (aurioles) at the leaf base.
Bud: similar to **B38**
Fruit: similar to **F79**
Similar species: *Quercus pubescens*

L84 Red Oak (***Quercus rubra*** L., p 150). Leaf blade divided into shallow pointed lobes, sometimes themselves incised, with rounded grooves, making up to half the whole breadth of the blade. The latter is broadest in the upper third. Unmistakable among forms represented.
Bud: similar to **B38**
Fruit: similar to **F79**
Similar species: *Quercus palustris*

L85 Valonia Oak (***Quercus macrolepis*** Kotschy, p 157). Leaf blade divided into many small sharp, bristle-tipped, triangular lobes, themselves toothed. Lobes separated by sharp sinuses which are up to one-third the breadth of the whole blade. The latter is broadest in lower third. Not to be confused with **L80** (*Quercus trojana*) and **L84** (*Quercus rubra*).
Fruit: similar to **F80**

L86 Swedish Whitebeam (***Sorbus intermedia*** (Ehrh.) Pers., p 181). Leaf blade broadly elliptic, divided in correspondence with secondary veins which are lobed with toothed margins in the form of acute, shallow incisions. Not to be confused with **L47** and **L63** (*Alnus incana*).
Bud: similar to **B60** and **B61**
Fruit: similar to **F15**
Similar species: *Sorbus aria*

L87 Midland Hawthorn (***Crataegus laevigata*** (Poir.) DC., p 174). Leaf blade with entire margins or with a few teeth, subdivided into five rounded lobes formed of shallow incisions only in the upper third of the blade. A number of leaves should be examined.
Bud: similar to **B46**
Fruit: similar to **F18**
Similar species: *Crataegus monogyna*

L88 Common Hawthorn (***Crataegus monogyna*** Jacq., p 173). Leaf blade subdivided into five pointed and irregularly toothed lobes, formed by sharp, deep incisions which extend up to two-thirds of the whole breadth of the blade. A number of leaves should be examined.
Bud: **B46**
Fruit: **F18**
Similar species: *Crataegus laevigata*

L89 White Mulberry (***Morus alba*** L., p 163). Leaf blade subdivided into five lobes by means of deep, rounded sinuses. Coexists with forms **L69** and **L96**. Not to be confused with **L99** (*Broussonetia papyrifera*).
Bud: **B30**
Fruit: **F70**
Similar species: *Morus nigra*

L90 Wild Service Tree (***Sorbus torminalis*** (L.) Crantz, p 180). Leaf blade subdivided into seven to nine pointed, toothed lobes formed by sharp incisions that extend up to one-half of the whole length of the blade. Not to be confused with **L88** (*Crataegus monogyna*) which is smaller and has fewer, less sharp lobes.
Bud: **B61**
Fruit: **F14**

L91 Finnish Whitebeam (***Sorbus hybrida*** L., p 181). Leaf blade subdivided by incisions, which in the basal part extend to the principal vein/midrib, giving place to a certain number (three to five) of free leaflets, while on the upper portion they become shallower towards the tip, being replaced by a series of dentate lobes. Unmistakable.

Bud: similar to **B61**
Fruit: similar to **F15**
Similar species: *Sorbus aucuparia, Sorbus intermedia*

L92 Maidenhair Tree (***Ginkgo biloba*** L., p 89). Leaf blade fan-shaped, with a sinus of varying depth in the upper semi-circular part of the margin, but usually divided into two, irregularly grooved lobes. Unmistakable.
Bud: **B64**
Fruit: **F25**

L93 Montpellier Maple (***Acer monspessulanum*** L., p 201). Entire margins. Blade divided by sharp and very large sinuses into three rounded, divergent lobes. Unmistakable.
Bud: similar to **B5**
Fruit: **F92**

L94 Grey Poplar (***Populus canescens*** (Aiton) Sm., p 132). Basal lobes not very pronounced. Other characteristics as in entire form **L61**. Not to be confused with **L95** (*Populus alba*).
Bud: similar to **B55**
Spring appearance: similar to **Sp1**, **Sp2**, **Sp5** and **Sp6**
Fruit: similar to **F57**
Similar species: *Populus alba*

L95 White Poplar (***Populas alba*** L., p 131). Margins almost entire. Blade divided into three large triangular lobes and two smaller basal lobes, sometimes well developed as in **L102**; lower surface covered with dense white down and very prominent veins. Not to be confused with **L94** (*Populus canescens*).
Bud: **B55**
Spring appearance: **Sp5**
Fruit: similar to **F57**
Similar species: *Populus canescens*

L96 Black Mulberry (***Morus nigra*** L., p 163). Trilobate form coexisting with entire form **L75** and sometimes with

forms possessing more lobes, similar to **L89** (*Morus alba*). Not to be confused with **L89** (*Morus alba*), **L97** (*Ficus carica*) and **L99** (*Broussonetia papyrifera*).
Bud: **B30**
Fruit: similar to **F70**
Similar species: *Morus alba*

L97 Fig (***Ficus carica*** L., p 164). Rough, thick leaf blade, subdivided into three to five rounded lobes, with irregularly sinuate margins and heart-shaped base. Not to be confused with **L89** (*Morus alba*) and **L96** (*Morus nigra*).
Bud: **B25**
Fruit: **F71**

L98 London Plane (***Platanus hispanica*** Prot., p 171). Leaf blade subdivided by deep, rounded sinuses into three large triangular, pointed lobes and, especially in basal part, with irregularly distributed teeth. Not to be confused with **L106** (*Acer platanoides*) and **L107** (*Platanus orientalis*).
Bud: **B28**
Fruit: **F72**
Similar species: *Platanus orientalis*

L99 Paper Mulberry (***Broussonetia papyrifera*** (L.) L'Hér., p 166). Leaf blade hairy, subdivided by deep, rounded sinuses, asymmetrically distributed into pointed lobes. Coexists with forms similar to **L70**. Not to be confused with **L89** (*Morus alba*) and **L96** (*Morus nigra*).
Bud: **B31**
Fruit: **F69**

L100 Tulip Tree (***Liriodendron tulipifera*** L., p 170). Blade divided into four triangular lobes. Unmistakable.
Bud: **B26**
Fruit: **F66**

L101 Field Maple (***Acer campestre*** L., p 202). Entire margins. Small leaf blade subdivided into three to five obtuse lobes, themselves lobate as a result of broad, deep sinuses. Cor-

date base. Opposite leaves. Not to be confused with **L105** (*Liquidambar styraciflua*), with alternate leaves and of larger dimensions.
Bud: similar to **B5**
Fruit: **F90**
Similar species: *Acer obtusatum*

L102 White Poplar (***Populus alba*** L., p 131). Five-lobed form coexisting with three-lobed form **L95**. Leaf base truncate. Leaf blade white and hairy beneath. Alternate leaves.
Bud: **B55**
Spring appearance: **Sp5**
Fruit: similar to **F57**

L103 Italian Maple (***Acer opalus*** Miller, p 203). Leaf blade divided by sharp, shallow sinuses into three to five rounded lobes. Cordate base.
Bud: similar to **B5**
Fruit: similar to **F90** and **F91**
Similar species: *Acer obtusatum*

L104 Sycamore (***Acer pseudoplatanus*** L., p 204). Margins toothed. Blade subdivided by narrow, sharp sinuses into five pointed lobes. Cordate base. Not to be confused with **L106** (*Acer platanoides*).
Bud: **B5**
Fruit: **F91**
Similar species: *Acer platanoides*

L105 Sweet Gum (***Liquidambar styraciflua*** L., p 170). Finely toothed margins. Leaf blade subdivided by sharp, deep sinuses into five pointed lobes. Cordate base. Alternate leaves. Not to be confused with **L101** (*Acer campestre*) and **L104** (*Acer pseudoplatanus*) which have opposite leaves.
Bud: **B35**
Fruit: **F73**

L106 Norway Maple (***Acer platanoides*** L., p 205). Margins with a few teeth separated by broad sinuses. Leaf blade subdivided into five sharp lobes by broad, obtuse, shallow sinuses. Cordate base. Opposite leaves. Not to be confused with **L104**

(*Acer pseudoplatanus*) and **L98** (*Platanus hispanica*), the latter with alternate leaves.
Bud: similar to **B5**
Fruit: similar to **F90**
Similar species: *Acer pseudoplatanus*

L107 Oriental Plane (***Platanus orientalis*** L., p 171). Margins entire and with a few large teeth, almost small pointed lobes, irregularly arranged. Blade subdivided into five small pointed lobes by deep, narrow sinuses. Leaf base truncate. Not to be confused with **L108** (*Acer saccharinum*) which has opposite leaves.
Bud: similar to **B28**
Fruit: similar to **F72**
Similar species: *Platanus hispanica*

L108 Silver Maple (***Acer saccharinum*** L., p 205). Blade subdivided by narrow, deep, obtuse sinuses into five pointed lobes, themselves lobate and dentate. Leaf base truncate. Not to be confused with **L107** (*Platanus orientalis*), with alternate leaves.
Bud: similar to **B5**
Fruit: similar to **F91**

L109 Scotch Laburnum (***Laburnum alpinum*** (Mill.) Bercht. & J. Presl, p 192). Leaf made up of three elliptic sessile leaflets with entire margins. In general, unmistakable.
Bud: similar to **B51**
Fruit: **F53**
Similar species: *Laburnum anagyroides*

L110 Horse Chestnut (***Aesculus hippocastanum*** L., p 206). Leaf with long stem, blade divided into seven toothed segments, broadened in upper third, with sharply narrowing, sessile tip. Unmistakable.
Bud: **B8**
Fruit: **F77**
Similar species: *Aesculus pavia*

L111 Box-elder (***Acer negundo*** L., p 200). Leaf made up of five (sometimes three or seven) elliptic leaflets, irregularly and markedly toothed,

stalked, the lateral ones broadest in lower third, the apical one broadest in upper third. Petiole longer than the rachis bearing the leaflets. Opposite leaves. Unmistakable.
Bud: similar to **B5**
Spring appearance: **Sp12**
Fruit: similar to **F91**

L112 Elder (***Sambucus nigra*** L., p 234). Leaf composed of five (sometimes seven) dentate leaflets, broadly elliptic with a sharply pointed tip, and a short petiolule. The petiole is shorter than the rachis bearing the leaflets, but both are large. Opposite leaves. Not to be confused with **L113** (*Staphylea pinnata*) and **L117** (*Fraxinus ornus*).
Bud: **B1**
Fruit: **F3**

L113 Bladder-nut (***Staphylea pinnata*** L., p 209). Leaf composed of five toothed, elliptic, sessile leaflets with short pointed appendage at point of attachment to axis. Stalk as long as rachis. Opposite leaves. Not to be confused with **L112** (*Sambucus nigra*) and **L117** (*Fraxinus ornus*).
Bud: **B2**
Fruit: **F65**

It should be remembered that ***Melia azedarach*** L. (p 197) has bipinnate leaves with seven leaflets.

L114 Carob (***Ceratonia siliqua*** L., p 189). Compound, even-pinnate leaves with six to eight leaflets with entire, rounded margins and very short stalk. Stalk shorter than rachis. Persistent, leathery leaves. Unmistakable.
Fruit: **F42**

L115 Narrow-leaved Ash (***Fraxinus angustifolia*** Vahl., p 230). Leaves made up of seven narrow, elongate, sessile leaflets with serrate margins. Unmistakable.
Bud: similar to **B6**
Spring appearance: similar to **Sp13**
Fruit: similar to **F93**

L116 Turpentine Tree (***Pistacia terebinthus*** L., p 198). Leaf composed of seven elliptic leaflets terminating in a small point (mucro), with entire, rounded margins. Alternate leaves. Not to be confused with **L117** (*Fraxinus ornus*).
Fruit: **F34**
Similar species: *Pistacia lentiscus* L. (p 198) which, however, has evergreen, equally pinnate leaves.
Fruit: **F35**

L117 Manna Ash (***Fraxinus ornus*** L., p 229). Leaf composed of seven elliptic leaflets, broadest in central or lower third, with toothed margins and pointed tip, and very short stalk. Opposite leaves. Not to be confused with **L112** (*Sambucus nigra*), **L113** (*Staphylea pinnata*), with opposite leaves, and **L116** (*Pistacia terebinthus*), with alternate leaves.
Bud: similar to **B6**
Fruit: similar to **F93**
Similar species: *Fraxinus angustifolia, Fraxinus excelsior*

L118 Common Walnut (***Juglans regia*** L., p 135). Leaf composed of six to nine elliptic leaflets, margins entire, with sharply pointed tip and very short stalk. Alternate leaves, relatively large and with a characteristic smell if rubbed. Unmistakable.
Bud: **B27**
Spring appearance: **Sp7**
Fruit: **F75**
Similar species: *Juglans nigra*

L119 Shagbark Hickory (***Carya ovata*** (Mill.) p 137). Leaf composed of five to seven elliptic, pointed leaflets, broadest in central or upper third, with toothed, sessile margins. Alternate leaves. Not to be confused with **L115** (*Fraxinus angustifolia*) and **L117** (*Fraxinus ornus*).
Fruit: **F76**

L120 Robinia or Black Locust (***Robinia pseudacacia*** L., p 193). Leaf composed of 15–17 elliptic leaflets with entire margins and rounded tip,

short-stalked. Alternate leaves. Not to be confused with L124 (*Gleditsia triacanthos*).
Bud: **B16**
Fruit: **F52**

L121 Stag's Horn Sumach (***Rhus typhina*** L., p 199). Leaf made up of 13–15 leaflets, elliptic-elongate, pointed, toothed, sessile. Stalk and rachis covered with velvety hairs. Alternate leaves. Not to be confused with **L122** (*Fraxinus excelsior*) and **L123** (*Sorbus aucuparia*).
Bud: **B18**
Fruit: **F68**

L122 Ash (***Fraxinus excelsior*** L., p 230). Leaves composed of 11–13 elliptic, pointed, toothed, short-stalked and glabrous leaflets. Opposite leaves. Not to be confused with **L121** (*Rhus typhina*) and **L123** (*Sorbus aucuparia*), which are hairy.
Bud: **B6**
Spring appearance: **Sp13**
Fruit: **F93**
Similar species: *Fraxinus angustifolia, Fraxinus ornus*

Note, too, **Koelreuteria paniculata** Lax. (p 207), with 13–17 oval leaflets which have deep, rounded teeth.

L123 Rowan or Mountain Ash (***Sorbus aucuparia*** L., p 178). Leaf composed of 13–15 leaflets, elliptic, deeply toothed, sessile and hairy beneath. Alternate leaves. Not to be confused with **L121** (*Rhus typhina*) and **L122** (*Fraxinus excelsior*).
Bud: similar to **B60** and **B61**
Fruit: **F15**
Similar species: *Sorbus domestica*

L124 Honey Locust (***Gleditsia triacanthos*** L., p 190). Leaf composed of 21–25 elliptic-elongate leaflets, sessile, along with simply- or doubly-pinnate leaves. Alternate leaves. Not to be confused with **L120** (*Robinia pseudacacia*).
Bud: **B19**, **B40**
Fruit: **F43**

Note, too, **Cladrastis lutea** Koch (p 195), which, however, has sharp leaflets.
Bud: **B22**
Fruit: **F48**

Note, too, **Schinus molle** L. (p 200), with evergreen, pendant leaves and lanceolate, crescent-curved leaflets.

L125 Black Walnut (***Juglans nigra*** L., p 136). Leaf composed of 16–18 elliptic leaflets, more or less asymmetrical, pointed, toothed, sessile. Alternate leaves. Apical leaflet may be missing (even-pinnate). Not to be confused with **L126** (*Pterocarya fraxinifolia*).
Bud: similar to **B27**
Fruit: similar to **F75**
Similar species: *Juglans regia*

L126 Caucasian Wing-nut (***Pterocarya fraxinifolia*** (Lam.) Spach., p 138). Leaf composed of 13–19 leaflets, elliptic-elongate, pointed, finely toothed, sessile. Leaflets more or less asymmetrical, sickle-shaped towards tip. Apical leaf sometimes missing. Alternate leaves. Not to be confused with **L125** (*Juglans nigra*).
Fruit: **F89**

L127 Tree of Heaven (***Ailanthus altissima*** (Mill.) Swingle, p 196). Leaf composed of (13) 15–17 elliptic leaflets, with entire, pointed margins, expanded at base into two or more triangular, short-stalked lobes. Opposite leaves. Unmistakable.
Bud: **B21**
Fruit: **F99**

L128 Pink Siris (***Albizzia julibrissin*** Durazzo, p 191). Leaf sometimes finely divided (tripinnate) with actual leaves sessile and even-pinnate; leaflets mucronate, about 5 mm wide. Not to be confused with **L129** (*Acacia dealbata*).
Bud: **B20**
Fruit: **F51**

L129 Mimosa or Silver Wattle (*Acacia dealbata* Link, p 190). Leaves finely divided, with narrow, elongated, sessile leaflets, formed of linear segments about 1 mm wide. Leaves and leaflets even-pinnate. Evergreen. Not to be confused with **L128** (*Albizzia julibrissin*).
Fruit: **F49**

S1 Branch of White Cedar (*Thuja occidentalis* L., p 97). Flattened shoot covered with pointed scale-leaves which are adherent and which partially cover one another like roof tiles. Dorsal scale has a prominent gland. Branch grows horizontally. Not to be confused with **S2** (*Cupressus sempervirens*) and **S3** (*Chamaecyparis lawsoniana*).
Cone: **C24**
Similar species: *Thuja orientalis, Thuja plicata*

Note, too, *Calocedrus decurrens* (Torrey) Florin (p 96).
Fruit: **C23**

S2 Branch of Italian Cypress (*Cupressus sempervirens* L., p 91). Shoot four-angled, covered with scale-leaves which are adherent and which partially cover one another. Branches not set on the same plane. Not to be confused with **S1** (*Thuja occidentalis*) and **S3** (*Chamaecyparis lawsoniana*).
Cone: **C16**
Similar species: *Cupressus glabra, Cupressus lusitanica, Cupressus macrocarpa, Cupressocyparis leylandii*

S3 Branch of Lawson Cypress (*Chamaecyparis lawsoniana* Parl., p 96). Flattened shoot covered with pointed scale-leaves, adherent and partially covering one another, but with divergent tips. Branches arranged more or less horizontally. Not to be confused with **S1** (*Thuja occidentalis*) and **S2** (*Cupressus sempervirens*).
Cone: **C17**
Similar species: *Chamaecyparis nootkatensis, Cupressocyparis leylandii*

S4 Branch of French Tamarisk (*Tamarix gallica* L., p 217). Cylindrical shoot with delicate, deciduous, triangular scale-leaves, partially covering one another and decreasing in size towards the tip. Main branches brown, shiny, with few scales. Unmistakable.
Bud: **B17**
Fruit: **F61**
Similar species: *Tamarix africana*

S5 Branch of Monkey Puzzle (*Araucaria araucana* K. Koch, p 90). Large scale-leaves (3–4 cm long and 1 cm wide), very stiff, elliptic, broadest in central third and terminating in a spine. Scales sessile, spirally set on shoot and diverging outwards. Unmistakable.
Cone: **C4**

A1 Branch of Tree Heath (*Erica arborea* L., p 224). Acicular leaves, persistent, attached to shoot in whorls of three to four. Needles neither stiff nor sharp. Unmistakable.

A2 Branch of Wellingtonia (*Sequoiadendron giganteum* (Lindl.) Buchholz, p 123). Sessile needles with broad base, pointed and curving outwards at the tip. Not to be confused with those of **A3** (*Cryptomeria japonica*), which are similar, but curving inwards.
Cone: **C18**

A3 Shoot of Japanese Red Cedar (*Cryptomeria japonica* Don, p 123). Sessile needles with broad base, pointed and curving inwards at the tip. Not to be confused with those of **A2** (*Sequoiadendron giganteum*), which are similar, but curving outwards.
Cone: **C20**

A4 Branch of Common Juniper (*Juniperus communis* L., p 93). Stiff, sharp needles, sessile, attached to shoot, triangular in section, in whorls of three. White grooving on lower surface. Unmistakable.
Fruit: **F2**
Similar species: *Juniperus virginiana*

A5 Shoot of Coast Redwood (***Sequoia sempervirens*** (Lamb.) Endl., p 122). Flat, sessile needles, growing together with shoot in basal part. Exist simultaneously in two lengths: large and broad on lateral branches, in two opposite rows; small and narrow on apical shoots, facing in all directions. Not to be confused with **A6** (*Taxodium distichum*) and **A8** (*Taxus baccata*).
Cone: **C21**

A6 Branch of Swamp Cypress (***Taxodium distichum*** Rich., p 124). Needles flat, alternate, sessile and growing together with shoot in basal part. Needles delicate, deciduous, flexible, light green and herbaceous in consistency, arranged alternately on shoot in two rows; length up to 18 mm, smaller on apical shoots. Tree deciduous. Not to be confused with **A5** (*Sequoia sempervirens*), **A7** (*Metasequoia glyptostroboides*) and **A8** (*Taxus baccata*).
Bud: **B62**
Cone: **C19**

A7 Branch of Dawn Redwood (***Metasequoia glyptostroboides*** Hu & Cheng, p 125). Opposite needles, similar to **A6** (*Taxodium distichum*), but up to 25 mm long. Likewise deciduous. Not to be confused with **A5** (*Sequoia sempervirens*), **A6** (*Taxodium distichum*) and **A8** (*Taxus baccata*).
Cone: **C22**

A8 Branch of Yew (***Taxus baccata*** L., p 89). Needles flat, leathery, flexible and slightly crescent-shaped, attached spirally to shoots with the basal part tapering to very short petiole. Nevertheless they take on a secondary arrangement in opposite rows as the petioles twist at the shoots. Two light lines on lower surface. Not to be confused with **A5** (*Sequoia sempervirens*), **A6** (*Taxodium distichum*), **A7** (*Metasequoia Glyptostroboides*) and **A10** (*Abies alba*).
Fruit: **F1**

A9 Branch of Eastern Hemlock (***Tsuga canadensis*** (L.) Carr., p 107). Flattened needles, short and obtuse at tip, with two white lines on lower surface, attached by a short petiole to a cushion-like extension of the shoot. Needles 1 cm or a little longer. Not to be confused with **A10** (*Abies alba*), **A11** (*Pseudotsuga menziesii*) and **A12** (*Picea abies*).
Cone: **C7**
Similar species: *Tsuga heterophylla*

A10 Branch of Common Silver Fir (***Abies alba*** Mill., p 99). Needles flattened, with obtuse or slightly concave tip, with two very prominent white lines on lower surface, attached to the cylindrical shoot by a short petiole spreading from a kind of round pad. Needles up to 2 cm long. Not to be confused with **A9** (*Tsuga canadensis*), **A11** (*Pseudotsuga menziesii*) and **A12** (*Picea abies*).
Cone: **C1**
Similar species: all other *Abies*

A11 Branch of Douglas Fir (***Pseudotsuga menziesii*** (Mirb.) Franco, p 106). Needles flattened, soft and more than 2 cm long, with rounded tip attached by a short petiole to a cushion-like expansion of the shoot. Not to be confused with **A9** (*Tsuga canadensis*), **A10** (*Abies alba*) and **A12** (*Picea abies*).
Cone: **C6**

A12 Branch of Norway Spruce (***Picea abies*** (L.) Karst., p 103). Needles stiff and sharp, attached by a short petiole to an elongated expansion of the shoot. Needles not flat but prismatic. Not to be confused with **A9** (*Tsuga canadensis*), **A10** (*Abies alba*) and **A11** (*Pseudotsuga menziesii*).
Cone: **C5**
Similar species: all other *Abies*

A13 Shoot of Austrian or Corsican Pine (***Pinus nigra*** Arn., p 112). Needles pointed, semi-circular in section, 8–18 cm long, attached in pairs to very short shoots (fascicles).
Cone: **C9**
Similar species: *Pinus brutia, P. con-*

torta, *P. halepensis, P. leucodermis, P. uncinata, P. pinaster, P. pinea, P. rigida, P. sylvestris*

A14 Branch of Monterey Pine (***Pinus radiata*** Don, p 117). Needles soft, triangular in cross-section, 10–20 cm long, attached in threes to very short shoots (fascicles).
Cone: similar to **C9**
Similar species: *Pinus ponderosa*

A15 Branch of Weymouth Pine (***Pinus strobus*** L., p 117). Needles flexible, glaucous, 5–14 cm long, attached in fives to very short shoots (fascicles).
Cone: **C10**
Similar species: *Pinus cembra, P. peuce, P. wallichiana*

A16 Branch of Atlas Cedar (***Cedrus atlantica*** (Endl.) Carr., p 120). Needles 2 cm long, stiff, green-blue, joined in tufts (more than 20) on very short shoots. Needles are also attached singly to new shoots. Not to be confused with **A17** (*Cedrus deodara*).
Cone: similar to **C2**
Similar species: *Cedrus deodara, Cedrus libani*

A17 Branch of Deodar or Himalayan Cedar (***Cedrus deodara*** G. Don, p 122). Needles flexible, pale green, 3.5–5 cm long, joined in tufts (more than 20) on very short shoots. Needles are also attached singly to new shoots. Not to be confused with **A16** (*Cedrus atlantica*) and **A18** (*Larix decidua*).
Cone: **C2**
Similar species: *Cedrus atlantica, Cedrus libani*

A18 Branch of European Larch (***Larix decidua*** Mill., p 118). Soft, flexible needles, herbaceous in colour and consistency, deciduous, sparse on apical branches of previous year and joined in tufts on very short shoots. Tree deciduous. Not to be confused with **A17** (*Cedrus deodara*).
Bud: **B63**
Cone: **C3**
Similar species: *Larix kaempferi*

P1 Chusan (or Chinese Windmill) Palm (***Trachycarpus fortunei*** Wendl., p 236). Petiole long and without spines, bearing a circular lamina divided into numerous long, pointed segments, spreading out like a fan at the tip of the petiole. Not to be confused with **P2** (*Washingtonia filifera*) and **P3** (*Chamaerops humilis*).

P2 Petticoat Palm (***Washingtonia filifera*** Wendl., p 236). Upper half of petiole furnished with inward-pointing spines, bearing a triangular or rhomboidal fan-shaped lamina composed of segments radiating from a short expanded rachis. Fibrous threads, from which the name of the species derives, are attached to the margins and tip of the segments. Not to be confused with **P1** (*Trachycarpus fortunei*) and **P3** (*Chamaerops humilis*).

P3 European Fan Palm (***Chamaerops humilis*** L., p 235). Leaves formed from a long spiny petiole bearing a semi-circular lamina made up of straight segments, sometimes divided in two at the tip (bifid). Not to be confused with **P1** (*Trachycarpus fortunei*) and **P2** (*Washingtonia filifera*).

P4 Canary Islands Date Palm (***Phoenix canariensis*** Chabaud, p 236). Pinnate leaves up to 5–7 m long, constituted of a long rachis from which stem straight, pointed segments, transformed at the base into spines, their length decreasing towards the tip, which give the lamina an overall pointed shape. Not to be confused with **P5** (*Phoenix dactylifera*).

P5 Date Palm (***Phoenix dactylifera*** L., p 237). Leaves as for **P4**, but larger in size and more rounded in shape. Not to be confused with **P4** (*Phoenix canariensis*).

P6 Cabbage Palm (***Cordyline australis*** (Forst.) Hook., f., p 238). Entire, sessile leaves, with tapering, pointed laminae, drooping outwards, joined in clusters at tips of branches.

BUDS AND TWIGS: **B**

Buds opposite, in pairs, on planes perpendicular to one another
table XIV, B1–B10

Buds alternate, arranged on same plane
table XIV, B11–B15

Spiny shoots
tables XVI–XVII, B40–B50

Shoots with short shoots (many leaf scars close together)
table XVII, B51–B61

Leaf buds clearly distinguishable from flower buds, which are long and spherical or cylindrical
tables XVIII–XIX, B65–B70

Buds alternate, arranged in spirals
tables XV–XVI

small, showing large leaf scar
B16–B22

without bud scales or with one or two bud scales
B23–B32

with many small bud scales
B33–B39

Buds small, conical, sometimes difficult to distinguish
table XVII

isolated **B62**

on very short shoots **B63–B64**

SPRING APPEARANCE: **Sp**

Spring shoots which flower before sprouting leaves
tables XVIII–XIX

with long, drooping catkins
Sp1–Sp7

with clusters of flowers, sometimes difficult to distinguish as such, small and numerous **Sp8–Sp13**

with clusters of large flowers, numerous to single **Sp14–Sp16**

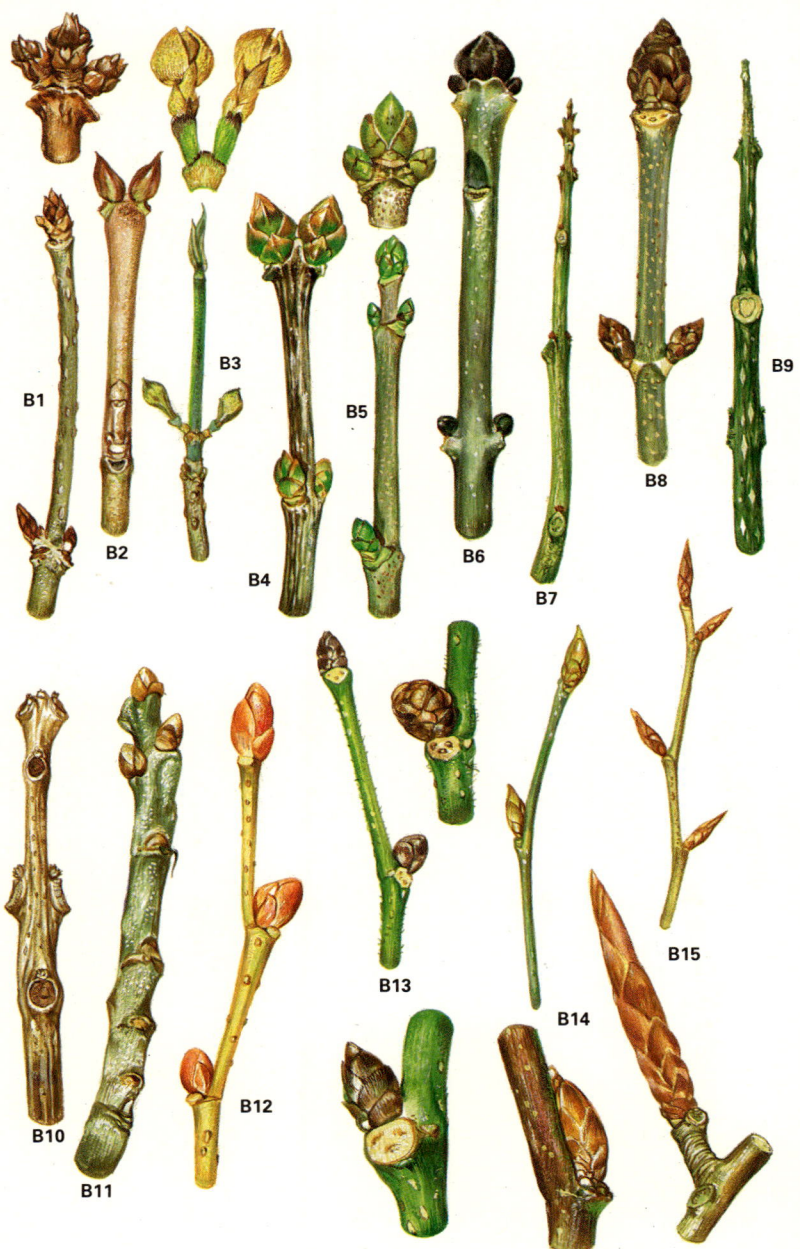

B1

B2

B3

B4

B5

B6

B7

B8

B9

B10

B11

B12

B13

B14

B15

TABLE XV

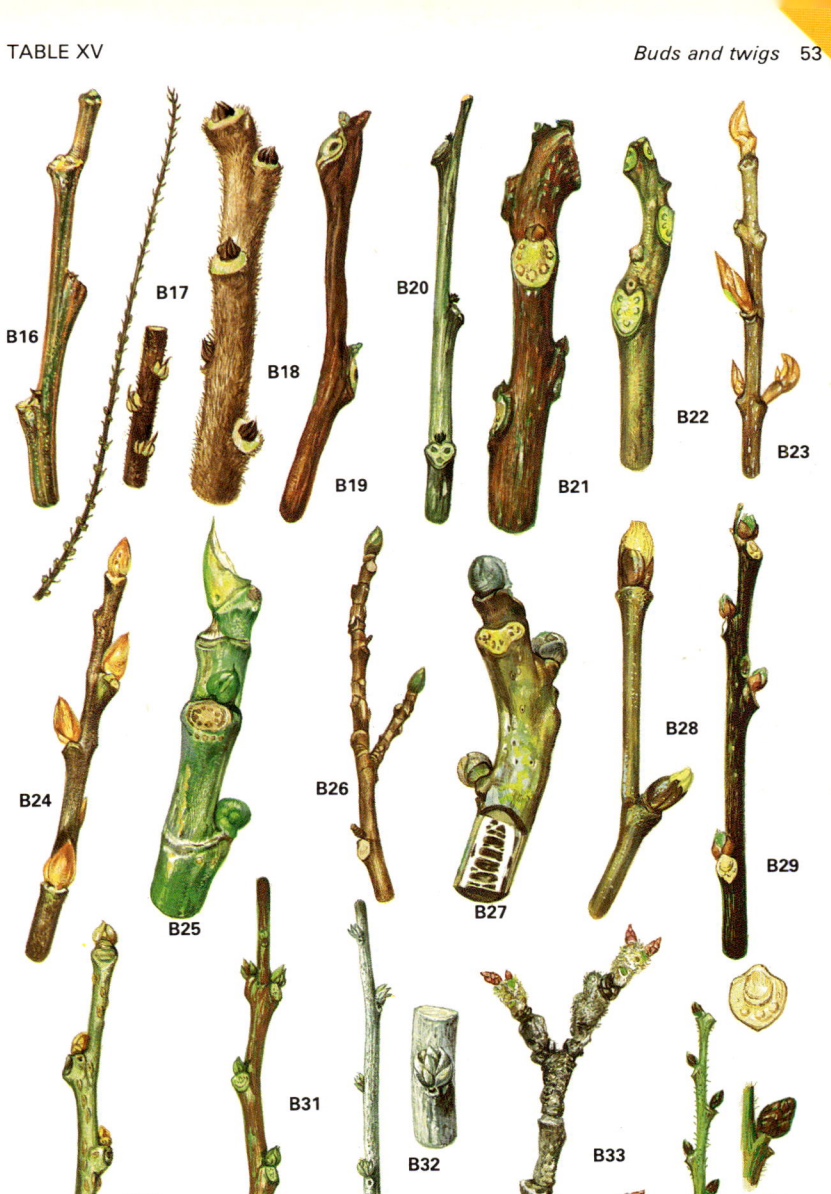

B16

B17

B18

B19

B20

B21

B22

B23

B24

B25

B26

B27

B28

B29

B30

B31

B32

B33

B34

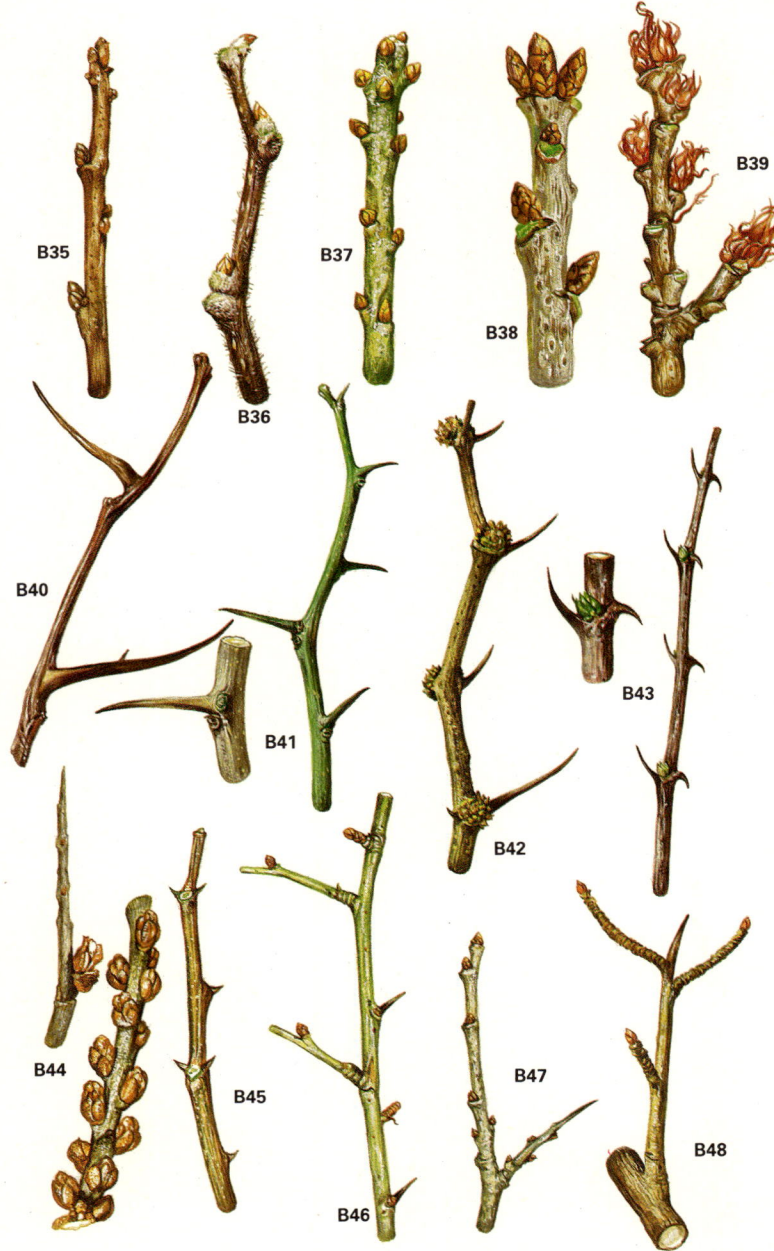

B35

B36

B37

B38

B39

B40

B41

B42

B43

B44

B45

B46

B47

B48

TABLE XVII

Buds and twigs 55

B49

B50

B51

B52

B53

B54

B55

B56

B57

B58

B59

B60

B61

B62

B63

B64

TABLE XVIII

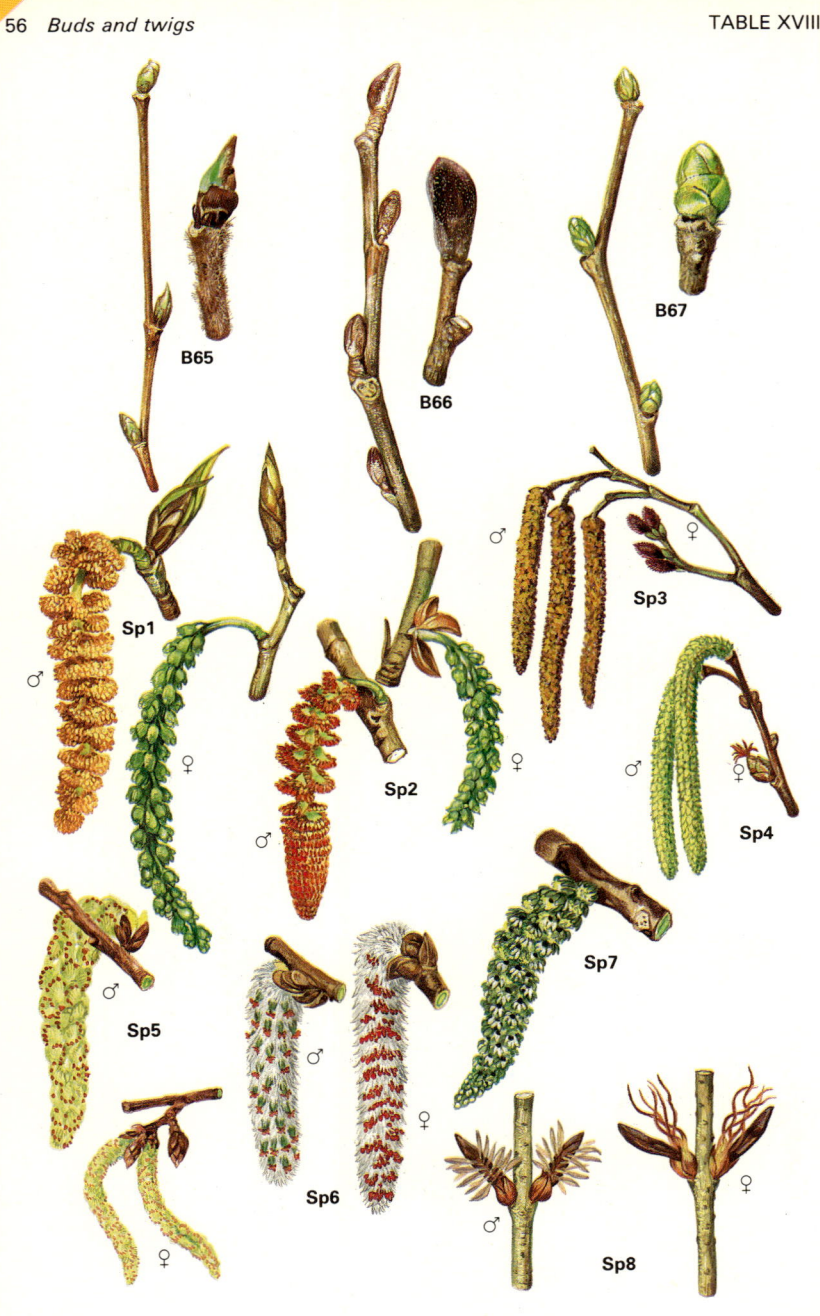

B65

B66

B67

♂ Sp3 ♀

Sp1

♂

♀

Sp2

♂

♀

♂ Sp4 ♀⚥

♂ Sp5

Sp7

♂ Sp6 ♀

♀

♂ Sp8 ♀

TABLE XIX

Buds and twigs 57

B1 Twig of *Sambucus nigra*.
Buds opposite, in pairs, perpendicular to one another, ovoid, with four to six soft, not closely adherent, greenish or reddish perulae (bud scales). Twig large, light grey-green, with many warty lenticels. Large white pith.
Leaf: **L112**
Fruit: **F3**

B2 Twig of *Staphylea pinnata*.
Buds opposite, in pairs, perpendicular to one another, ovoid, divergent, covered by a single large, green to reddish-brown, glabrous scale. Twig terminates in two large paired buds, of which often only one lasts.
Leaf: **L113**
Fruit: **F65**

B3 Twig of *Cornus mas* (see also **B70**).
Buds opposite, in pairs, perpendicular to one another, divergent on youngest branches, clearly differentiated into two types: leaf buds, elliptic and pointed, with two brown, hairy scales; flower buds, round and pedunculate, with two yellowish-green scales.
Leaf: **L31**
Fruit: **F32**
Spring appearance: **Sp11**

B4 Twig of *Syringa vulgaris*.
Buds opposite, in pairs, perpendicular to one another, divergent, with 4–6 green to brown scales, fringed with white, paired at tip of twig.
Leaf: **L33**
Fruit: **F62**

B5 Twig of *Acer pseudoplatanus*.
Buds opposite, in pairs, perpendicular to one another, divergent, pointed and ovoid, with 4–6 greenish-yellow and glabrous scales, the brown fringes of which are slightly ciliate. Terminal bud larger, flanked by two lateral buds. Twig with numerous light, elongated lenticels.
Leaf: **L104**
Fruit: **F91**

B6 Twig of *Fraxinus excelsior*.
Buds opposite, in pairs, perpendicular to one another, divergent, hemispherical, with 2–4 opaque black scales. Terminal bud larger than lateral buds and usually longer and pointed. Twig grey-green, glabrous, with occasional lenticels.
Leaf: **L122**
Fruit: **F93**
Spring appearance: **Sp13**

B7 Twig of *Clerodendrum trichotomum*.
Buds opposite, in pairs, perpendicular to one another, very small, red, on large oval leaf scar. Twig covered in dense hair.
Leaf: **L32**
Fruit: **F8**

B8 Twig of *Aesculus hippocastanum*.
Buds opposite, in pairs, perpendicular to one another, outstandingly large, with reddish-brown, shiny and sticky scales. Large leaf scar, white against brown of twig.
Leaf: **L110**
Fruit: **F77**

B9 Twig of *Paulownia tomentosa*.
Buds opposite, in pairs, perpendicular to one another, in form of a tiny reddish protuberance, pointed, on very large circular leaf scar. Terminal bud missing. Sturdy twig with prominent rhomboidal lenticels.
Leaf: **L35**
Fruit: **F64**

B10 Twig of *Catalpa bignonioides*.
Buds opposite, in pairs, perpendicular to one another, in the form of tiny orange-brown protuberance, on very large, ovate leaf scar. Terminal bud missing. Sturdy twig, smooth, enlarged at site of leaf scars.
Leaf: **L36**
Fruit: **F45**

B11 Twig of *Castanea sativa*.
Buds alternate, on same plane, ovoid

and pointed, with two large unequal scales, yellow-brown to reddish-brown, with fine hairs, fringed in black. Angular twig with numerous pale lenticels and a roughly pentagonal pith.
Leaf: **L53**
Fruit: **F81**

B12 Twig of *Tilia cordata*.
Buds alternate, on same plane, divergent, ovoid and obtuse, with two green to purple-red scales, a small one which covers half the bud, and a large one which covers it entirely. Twig soft, glabrous, with a few dark lenticels.
Leaf: similar to **L68**
Fruit: **F94**

Cf also **B28** (*Platanus hispanica*).

Cf also **B67** (*Corylus avellana*).

B13 Twig of *Ulmus* sp. (see also **B68**).
Buds alternate, on same plane, divergent, ovoid and pointed, attached obliquely to leaf scar. Numerous brown-black, hairy scales. Flower buds larger and round. Twig soft, slightly hairy at tip, sometimes furnished with corky ridges.
Leaf: **L48, L49**
Fruit: **F95, F96, F97**
Spring appearance: **Sp9, Sp10**

B14 Twig of *Carpinus betulus*.
Buds alternate, on same plane, appressed, fusiform and pointed, with many small dark brown, black-fringed scales. Male flower buds larger and divergent. Twig brown, hairy, with light lenticels.
Leaf: **L42**
Fruit: **F87**

B15 Twig of *Fagus sylvatica*.
Buds alternate, on same plane, divergent, tapering, up to 2 cm long, with numerous small light brown, black-fringed scales with hairy tips. Flower buds slightly larger. Twig soft, more or less hairy.
Leaf: **L28**
Fruit: **F78**

B16 Twig of *Robinia pseudacacia* (see also **B45**).
Buds not visible, buried in leaf scar, which may exhibit two large triangular spines at sides. Twig reddish-brown, angular, glabrous.
Leaf: **L120**
Fruit: **F52**

B17 Twig of *Tamarix gallica*.
Buds in form of tiny protrusions at the axil of the now inactive scale-like leaves on twigs of previous years.
Leaf: **S4**
Fruit: **F61**
Compare, too, **B62** (*Taxodium distichum*).

B18 Twig of *Rhus typhina*.
Buds alternate, in spirals, like small round projections, downy, almost wholly surrounded by a horseshoe-shaped, soft leaf scar. Terminal buds missing. Strong twig, covered by thick, velvety hairs; if broken in spring, it emits latex and reveals large, yellow-brown pith.
Leaf: **L121**
Fruit: **F68**

B19 Twig of *Gleditsia triacanthos*.
See description for **B40**.

B20 Twig of *Albizzia julibrissin*.
Tiny buds on prominent leaf scars, sprouting crosswise. Twigs brown or grey-green, with many lenticels.
Leaf: **L128**
Fruit: **F51**

B21 Twig of *Ailanthus altissima*.
Small, ovoid and obtuse buds, reddish-brown, on large grey leaf scar.

Strong, orange-brown twig, with many lenticels.
Leaf: **L127**
Fruit: **F99**

B22 Twig of ***Cladrastis lutea***.
Buds alternate, in spirals, small and covered in thick down, almost completely surrounded by large leaf scars. Terminal bud missing. Sturdy twig.
Leaf: similar to **L122**
Fruit: **F48**

B23 Twig of ***Frangula alnus***.
Buds alternate, in spirals, appressed, without scales, solidly enveloped in rudimentary leaves and covered with brown hair. Terminal bud larger, woolly. Twig covered with numerous long, pale lenticels.
Leaf: **L21**
Fruit: **F7**

B24 Twig of ***Salix caprea***.
Buds alternate, in spirals, divergent, ovoid and pointed, with a single reddish-brown scale covering each bud like a hood; buds initially hairy, then glabrous, leaf buds clearly distinguishable from flower buds; dark red twig.
Leaf: **L45**
Fruit: similar to **F55**, **F56**

B25 Twig of ***Ficus carica***.
Lateral buds alternate, in spirals, divergent, ovoid to round; terminal buds pointed, wrapped in a single greenish-yellow scale. Twig green with large white pith, exuding sticky latex.
Leaf: **L97**
Fruit: **F71**

B26 Twig of ***Liriodendron tulipifera***.
Buds broad and rounded above (obovoid); terminal buds large (more than 1 cm), flattened, with two scales; lateral buds much smaller, slightly hairy. Twig sturdy, shiny brown, with large circular or oval leaf scars.
Leaf: **L100**
Fruit: **F66**

B27 Twig of ***Juglans regia***.
Lateral buds alternate, in spirals, terminal bud larger than laterals; they are round, covered with two grey-brown scales, black-fringed and glabrous. Twig sturdy, brown and glabrous, with large heart-shaped leaf scars, the pith step-like in longitudinal cross-section.
Leaf: **L118**
Fruit: **F75**
Spring appearance: **Sp7**

B28 Twig of ***Platanus hispanica***.
Buds alternate, on same plane, divergent, conical, wrapped in a single reddish-brown glabrous scale. Twig reddish-brown with numerous prominent pale lenticels. Leaf scars surround the buds.
Leaf: **L98**
Fruit: **F72**

B29 Twig of ***Diospyros kaki***.
Lateral buds alternate, in spirals; terminal bud scarcely larger than lateral buds; buds are ovoid, covered by two scales, brown with a black transverse stripe, and glabrous. Brown twig with numerous pale lenticels and yellowish-green pith.
Leaf: **L29**
Fruit: **F10**

B30 Twig of ***Morus*** sp.
Buds alternate, in spirals, ovoid and obtuse, with three light brown, black-fringed scales. Twig greyish-brown with a few pale lenticels.
Leaf: **L69**, **L75**, **L89**, **L96**
Fruit: **F70**

B31 Twig of ***Broussonetia papyrifera***.
Buds alternate or in spirals, ovoid and obtuse, with 2–3 scales of varying

size. Twig pale brown with lenticels.
Leaf: **L70**, **L99**
Fruit: **F69**
Compare also **B69** (*Cercis siliquastrum*).

B32 Twig of ***Elaeagnus angustifolia***.
Buds alternate, in spirals, divergent, ovoid and conical, with 4–5 greyish-green bud scales, covered with silvery scales. Twig initially covered as well with such scales, later reddish-brown, shiny. Spines and short shoots present.
Leaf: **L26**
Fruit: **F29**

B33 Twig of ***Mespilus germanica***.
Buds alternate, in spirals, ovoid and pointed, small, with many tiny dark red, black-fringed and ciliated scales. Twig reddish, woolly, with pale lenticels.
Leaf: **L51**
Fruit: **F19**

B34 Twig of ***Zelkova carpinifolia***.
Buds alternate, on same plane, divergent, small, ovoid and obtuse, with dark reddish-brown scales covered in white down. Twig soft, grey-green, covered with fine hairs.
Leaf: **L79**
Fruit: **F83**

B35 Twig of ***Liquidambar styraciflua***.
Buds alternate, in spirals, divergent, ovoid and conical, with a few orange-brown scales. Twig green to brownish-yellow, shiny, often with corky growths.
Leaf: **L105**
Fruit: **F73**

B36 Twig of ***Celtis australis***.
Buds alternate, on same plane, appressed, small, ovoid and elongate, with 6–8 tiny reddish-brown hairy scales. Apical bud twisted outwards. Twig soft, dark, downy, with pale lenticels.
Leaf: **L74**
Fruit: **F33**

B37 Twig of ***Prunus mahaleb***.
Buds alternate, in spirals, divergent, ovoid, with 8–10 reddish-brown, pale-fringed scales. Terminal buds clustered at tip of twig, not larger than lateral buds. The epidermis, which flakes off, gives the twig a silver-grey colour. Many large lenticels.
Leaf: **L58**
Fruit: **F37**

B38 Twig of ***Quercus petraea***.
Buds alternate, in spirals, divergent, conical and pointed, more or less angular; they are clustered at tip of twig, around the terminal bud, similar in size to the rest. Scales small and numerous, light brown with dark, hairy margins. Twig glabrous, grey-brown, with many pale, pointed lenticels.
Leaf: **L82**
Fruit: **F79**

B39 Twig of ***Quercus cerris***.
Buds alternate, in spirals, ovoid and pointed, with light brown, hairy scales; the basal buds terminate in long curly points which give the whole twig a characteristically ruffled look. Twig with long-persisting dry leaves. Numerous lenticels.
Leaf: **L81**
Fruit: **F80**

B40 Twig of ***Gleditsia triacanthos***.
Buds in form of small protuberances, often concealed beneath bark, surrounded by large leaf scar and surmounted by a long, often ramified bifid or trifid spine. Terminal bud missing.
Leaf: **L124**
Fruit: **F43**

B41 Twig of ***Maclura pomifera***.
Buds hardly visible, flanked on one side by a long spine (1 cm) below leaf scar. Twig green, glabrous, zigzag in shape, which exudes latex if broken off in spring.
Leaf: **L30**
Fruit: **F74**

B42 Twig of *Ziziphus jujuba*.
Buds hardly visible; alternate and on same plane, each with a short, dark, straight spine. Twig very soft, almost like the rachis of a compound leaf, green and glabrous, zigzag in shape.
Leaf: **L72**
Fruit: **F30**

B43 Twig of *Paliurus spina-christi*.
Buds alternate, on same plane, small, each with two spines, one straight, the other curved like a hook. Twig soft, with fine hairs, zigzag in shape.
Leaf: **L56**
Fruit: **F98**

B44 Twig of *Hippophae rhamnoides*.
Buds spherical, in clusters of three or four, covered by small rust-red scales. Twig sturdy, terminating in a spine and bearing lateral spines, hairy at beginning of season.
Leaf: **L23**
Fruit: **F28**

B45 Twig of *Robinia pseudacacia*.
See description for **B16**.

B46 Twig of *Crataegus monogyna*.
Buds alternate, in spirals, divergent, small, ovoid to round; they are sometimes paired, one small and the other large, surmounted by a long spine (2–3 cm); scales small, reddish-brown. Twig spiny or terminating in a spine, glabrous, grey-yellow to reddish-brown, shiny.
Leaf: **L88**
Fruit: **F18**

B47 Twig of *Prunus domestica*.
Buds alternate, in spirals, small, conical and pointed, without appreciable differences between lateral and terminal forms; covered by large brown scales with a broad pale border. Twig hairy at beginning, then glabrous with a few dark lenticels. Short shoots with many leaf scars present.
Leaf: similar to **L57**
Fruit: **F41**

B48 Twig of *Pyrus communis*.
Buds alternate, in spirals, divergent, ovoid to conical and pointed, with scales that are brown with pale specks and a fringed edge. Twig strong, brown and shiny, with lateral spurs terminating in a spine. Short shoots present.
Leaf: **L55**
Fruit: **F22**
Spring appearance: **Sp15**

B49 Twig of *Malus sylvestris*.
Buds alternate, in spirals, the laterals compressed and appressed, ovoid and obtuse, with 4–6 thick-haired scales. Twig strong, the terminal part hairy, with short shoots which are sometimes pointed.
Leaf: **L43**, **L60**
Fruit: **F21**

B50 Twig of *Punica granatum*.
Buds obliquely opposite, or opposed in pairs perpendicularly to one another; divergent, small, round and pointed, with 2–3 pinkish-brown scales. Pale, soft twig tapering towards tip, eventually often forming a spine. Short shoots present.
Leaf: **L25**
Fruit: **F20**

B51 Twig of *Laburnum anagyroides*.
Buds alternate, in spirals, mostly divergent, ovoid with rounded scales, greenish or brown, covered with silvery hairs. Twig green, covered with silvery down. Short shoots present.
Leaf: similar to **L109**
Fruit: similar to **F53**

B52 Twig of *Prunus avium*.
Buds alternate, in spirals, divergent, ovoid and pointed, often clustered in groups of 3–8 at tip of short shoots. Shiny reddish-brown, woolly edged scales, 8–10 in number. Twig glabrous, light brown or grey, eventually peeling slightly.
Leaf: **L52**
Fruit: **F39**

B53 Twig of *Prunus domestica*.
Similar to **B52** (see previous description).
Leaf: similar to **L57**
Fruit: **F41**

B54 Twig of *Populus nigra*.
Buds alternate, in spirals, divergent, conical, pointed and elongated, with tip curving backwards, especially in case of flower buds; with numerous reddish-brown, glabrous, sticky scales. Twig flexible, smooth and shiny, with short shoots.
Leaf: **L76**
Fruit: similar to **F57**
Spring appearance: **Sp2**

B55 Twig of *Populus alba*.
Leaf buds alternate, in spirals, divergent, conical and pointed; flower buds round, larger than leaf buds and less pointed. Pale, rounded, cottony scales. Twig likewise cottony initially, then light brown. Short shoots present.
Leaf: **L95, L102**
Fruit: similar to **F57**
Spring appearance: **Sp5**

B56 Twig of *Magnolia x soulangiana*.
Buds alternate, in spirals, ovoid and pointed; flower buds apical, ovoid, enclosed by two hairy scales (2–3 cm in size); leaf buds small (0.5 cm) and lateral. Twig light brown with green specks and few lenticels.
Leaf: **L22**
Fruit: **F67**
Spring appearance: **Sp16**

B57 Twig of *Populus tremula*.
Leaf buds alternate, in spirals, conical and pointed; flower buds ovoid to round, with brown, glabrous and slightly sticky borders, with ciliate borders. Twig grey-green, with many short shoots.
Leaf: **L59**
Fruit: **F57**
Spring appearance: **Sp6**

B58 Twig of *Pyrus communis*.
See description for **B48**.
Leaf: **L55**
Fruit: **F22**
Spring appearance: **Sp15**

B59 Twig of *Malus sylvestris*.
See description for **B49**.
Leaf: **L60**
Fruit: **F21**

B60 Twig of *Sorbus domestica*.
Buds alternate, in spirals, divergent, ovoid and elongate; more or less obtuse, covered by 5–6 scales, green with dark borders and with sparse hairs, glabrous, often sticky. Twig strong, glabrous, with short shoots.
Leaf: similar to **L123**
Fruit: **F16**

B61 Twig of *Sorbus torminalis*.
Buds alternate, in spirals, divergent; terminal buds larger than lateral ones, with 3–4 large scales, bright green with brown edge, slightly hairy or glabrous. Twig reddish-brown, initially hairy, then brown and smooth, with many short shoots.
Leaf: **L90**
Fruit: **F14**

B62 Twig of *Taxodium distichum*.
Buds identifiable as small protuberances on twig, which has no short shoots (they are shed with the leaves); the reddish-brown bark exhibits long cracks and flakes off in fibrous strips during winter.
Leaf: **A6**
Fruit: **C19**

B63 Twig of *Larix decidua*.
Buds almost spherical, slightly pointed, covered with tiny resinous scales. Twig pale yellow, bearing the cones and persistent short shoots in form of thick protrusions, a few millimetres long.
Leaf: **A18**
Fruit: **C3**

B64 Twig of ***Ginkgo biloba***.
Buds conical, at tip of large short shoots, with leaf scars very close together, diverging from main branch at right-angles. The twig is similar to that of a pear tree.
Leaf: **L92**
Fruit: **F25**

B65 Twig of ***Betula pubescens***.
Buds ovoid and conical, usually curved, with shiny, sticky reddish-brown scales. Twig brown, initially covered in fine down, then glabrous. Future male or pollen catkins only, already visible during winter.
Leaf: **L77**
Fruit: **F85**

B66 Twig of ***Alnus glutinosa***.
Buds ovoid, enlarged and rounded at tip, the lateral buds pedunculate and divergent, with two violet-brown scales covered by a waxy and often sticky layer. Twig reddish, hairy only at tip, visibly bearing female fruits of previous year (small cones) and also male (elongated catkins) and future female fruits.
Leaf: **L64**
Fruit: **C14**
Spring appearance: **Sp3**

B67 Twig of ***Corylus avellana***.
Buds ovoid, rounded at tip, laterally compressed, alternate and on same plane, with large green to light brown scales bearing white hairs along the edges. Twig has glandular hairs (hairs terminating in a tiny head) with future male inflorescences (cylindrical catkins) clearly visible in winter.
Leaf: **L65**
Fruit: **F82**
Spring appearance: **Sp4**

B68 Twig of ***Ulmus minor***.
See description for **B13**.

B69 Twig of ***Cercis siliquastrum***.
Leaf buds alternate, in spirals, appressed, small, ovoid and pointed; terminal buds twisted, with 2–3 dark, violet-brown scales. Flower buds much larger than leaf buds, ovoid and pointed, divergent. Twig reddish-brown, slightly grooved.
Leaf: **L34**
Fruit: **F44**
Spring appearance: **Sp14**

B70 Twig of ***Cornus mas***.
See description for **B3**.

Sp1 Spring appearance of ***Populus x euroamericana***.
Catkins 10–15 cm long, male with glabrous, reddish bracts and red anthers, female more fragile, green with yellow stigmas.
Leaf: **L78**
Fruit: similar to **F57**
Bud: similar to **B54**, **B57**

Sp2 Spring appearance of ***Populus nigra*** cultivar 'Italica'.
Similar in description to **Sp1**.
Leaf: **L76**
Fruit: similar to **F57**
Bud: **B54**

Sp3 Spring appearance of ***Alnus glutinosa***.
Female catkins, small, reddish and pedunculate (at maturity they resemble small cones); male, long, pendent and reddish-yellow.
Leaf: **L64**
Fruit: **C14**
Bud: **B66**

Sp4 Spring appearance of ***Corylus avellana***.
Female catkins, similar to ovoid buds but slightly bigger than leaf buds, are crowned by a cluster of red stigmas. Male catkins are long and drooping, with yellow anthers.
Leaf: **L65**
Fruit: **F82**
Bud: **B67**

Sp5 Spring appearance of ***Populus alba***.
Male catkins, 8–10 cm long, with soft hairs and anthers that are first purple and then yellow; female short (3–7 cm), greenish, with pink stigmas.
Leaf: **L95, L102**
Fruit: similar to **F57**
Bud: **B55**

Sp6 Spring appearance of ***Populus tremula***.
Male catkins short (8–10 cm), grey and silky, with purple anthers; female 12 cm long, green and silky, with red stigmas.
Leaf: **L59, L62**
Fruit: **F57**
Bud: **B57**

Sp7 Spring appearance of ***Juglans regia***.
Male catkins drooping, large, greenish-brown, with yellow stamens (female inflorescences barely visible at leaf axil).
Leaf: **L118**
Fruit: **F75**
Bud: **B27**

Sp8 Spring appearance of ***Cercidiphyllum japonicum***.
Clusters of red stamens on male plants, small bunches of erect, twisted dark red stigmas on female plants. Twigs slender, green, with small dark opposite buds; apical buds in pairs, prominent, larger than lateral buds.
Leaf: **L71**
Fruit: **F47**

Sp9 and **Sp10** Spring appearance of ***Ulmus minor*** and ***Ulmus glabra***.
Hemispherical bunches of small hermaphrodite flowers (with both anthers and stigmas), pinkish-purple, tightly clustered on most recent twigs.
Leaf: **L49**
Fruit: **F96**
Bud: **B13, B68**

Sp11 Spring appearance of ***Cornus mas***.
Hemispherical bunches of small hermaphrodite flowers (with both anthers and stigmas), yellow in colour; anthers yellow, following each other in pairs on most recent twigs.
Leaf: **L31**
Fruit: **F32**
Bud: **B3, B70**

Sp12 Spring appearance of ***Acer negundo***.
Drooping bunches of yellow flowers, with brown anthers, on male plants; bunches of greenish-yellow flowers, also drooping but longer, on female plants.
Leaf: **L111**
Fruit: similar to **F91**
Bud: similar to **B5**

Sp13 Spring appearance of ***Fraxinus excelsior***.
Thick clusters of stamens with red or violet anthers (male inflorescences) or ovaries (female inflorescences), first purple, then green, on twig of previous year.
Leaf: **L122**
Fruit: **F93**
Bud: **B6**

Sp14 Spring appearance of ***Cercis siliquastrum***.
Clusters or short bunches of 3–6 pink flowers, 2 cm long, similar to those of *Robinia*; pedunculate, also attached to old branches and even to trunk.
Leaf: **L34**
Fruit: **F44**
Bud: **B69**

Sp15 Spring appearance of ***Pyrus communis***.
Large hemispherical inflorescences (5–8 cm) of big hermaphrodite flowers (with both anthers and stigmas), white, with purple and woolly pedunculate anthers. They appear

before or at the same time as the leaves.
Leaf: **L55**
Fruit: **F22**
Bud: **B48**, **B58**

Sp16 Spring appearance of *Magnolia*

x soulangiana.
Large white terminal flowers, hermaphrodite (with stamens and pistils); petals 7.5–10 cm.
Leaf: **L22**
Fruit: **F67**
Bud: **B56**

FRUITS: **F**

 Berries – seeds enclosed in a juicy pulp – remains of flower at base of fruit
table XX, F1–F10

 Drupes of Walnut and Shagbark Hickory
table XXIV, F75–F76

Nuts **table XXIV**

 Pomes – seeds enclosed in a fleshy pulp – remains of floral involucre at apex of fruit
tables XX–XXI, F11–F24
(**F23–F24** Citrus fruits – seeds enclosed in a fleshy segmented pulp)

 seeds surrounded by a thin membranous covering, closed even at maturity, contained in various secondary involucres
F77–F83

 Drupes – seeds with woody (stony) layer, enclosed in a usually fleshy pulp
table XXI, F25–F41

 seeds surrounded by a thin membranous covering, closed even at maturity, with various wing expansions
F84–F99

Pods **table XXII**

 with fleshy valves which do not open even at maturity
F42–F43

 with valves which open at maturity
F44–F53

CONES: **C**

Capsules **tables XXII–XXIII**

Cones **table XXV**

 with two valves, containing seeds with long hairs
table XXII, F54–F57

 with thin, membranous scales which overlap one another
C1–C7

 with two or more valves, containing numerous seeds
table XXIII, F58–F65

 compact fruit clusters, sometimes resembling a single fruit, formed of numerous small fruits linked in a single body (syncarp)
table XXIII, F66–F74

 with hard, woody scales which at maturity diverge from one another
C8–C14

small and spherical, with few scales, fleshy, woody or membranous
C15–C26

TABLE XX

F1

F2

F3

F4

×1/5

F5

×1

F6

F7

F8

F9

F10

F11

F12

F13

F14

F15

F16

F17

F18

TABLE XXI

Fruits 69

F19

F21

F22

F23

F20

F27

F24

F25

F26

F29

F28

F30

F32

F31

F33

F34

F35

F36

F37

F40

F39

F38

F41

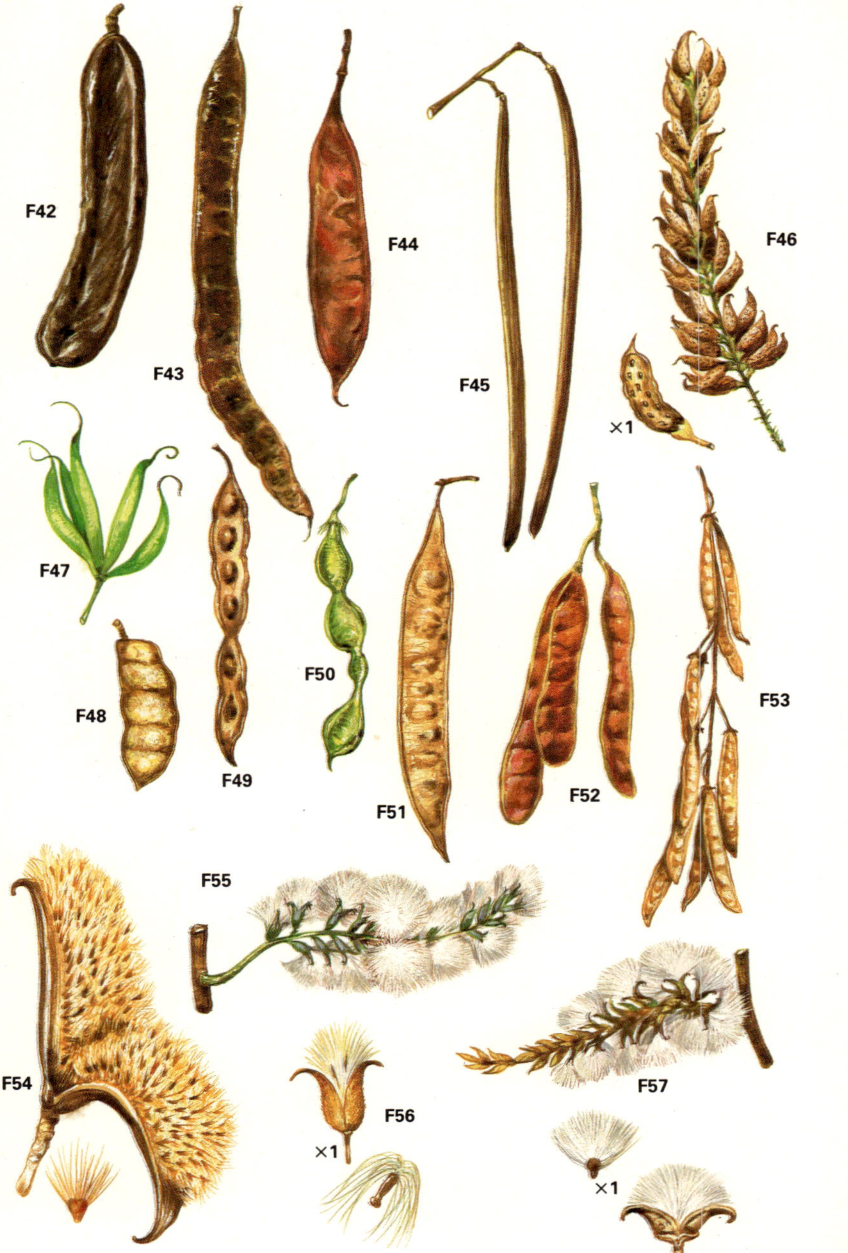

F42

F43

F44

F45

F46

×1

F47

F48

F49

F50

F51

F52

F53

F54

F55

F56

×1

F57

×1

TABLE XXIII

Fruits 71

F58

F59

F60

×3

F61

F62

F63

×2

F64

F65

F66

F67

F68

F69

F70

F71

F72

F73

F74

×2/3

F75

F76

F77

F78

F79

F80

F81

F82

F83

×2

F84

F85

×2

F86

F87

F88

F89

×2.5

F90

F91

F92

F93

F94

F95

F96

F97

F98

F99

TABLE XXV

C1

C2

C3

C4

C5

C6

C7

C8

C9

C10

C11

C12

C13

C14

C15

C16

C17

C18

C19

C20

C21

C22

C23

C24

C25

C26

F1 Fruit of ***Taxus baccata***.
Seed surrounded by red pulp, in shape of cup (aril). 1 cm.
Leaf: **A8**

F2 Fruit of ***Juniperus communis***.
Female cones with 3 fleshy, inter-linked scales, similar to berries, with 3 seeds. Green at beginning, blue and black when ripe. 0.6–0.8 cm.
Leaf: **A4**

F3 Fruit of ***Sambucus nigra***.
Berries black and juicy, abundant and drooping, with red stalks. 0.6–0.8 cm.
Leaf: **L112**
Bud: **B1**

F4 Fruit of ***Rhamnus alaternus***.
Berries red, black when ripe, with 3 seeds, in small clusters. 0.4–0.6 cm.
Leaf: **L11**

F5 Fruit of ***Ligustrum lucidum***.
Berries black, shiny, erect. 0.6–0.8 cm.
Leaf: **L19**

F6 Fruit of ***Phytolacca dioica***.
Berries black, fleshy, drooping. 0.3–0.7 cm.
Leaf: **L17**

F7 Fruit of ***Frangula alnus***.
Berries red, black when ripe, single or in small clusters. 0.6–1 cm.
Leaf: **L21**
Bud: **B23**

F8 Fruit of ***Clerodendrum trichotomum***.
Berries violet-red, with 5 bright red fleshy bracts at base; double-tipped terminal fruits. 0.6–0.8 cm.
Leaf: **L32**
Bud: **B7**

F9 Fruit of ***Arbutus unedo***.
Berries yellow, red when ripe, with grainy surface, hanging in clusters of 4–5. 1.5–2 cm.
Leaf: **L15**

F10 Fruit of ***Diospyros kaki***.
Berries globose, with sharp taste when immature, very sweet when ripe, with showy residues of flowers at base. 5–10 cm.
Leaf: **L29**
Bud: **B29**

F11 Fruit of ***Ilex aquifolium***.
Small spherical scarlet fruits with very evident residues of flowers at tip. 4 seeds. 0.7–1 cm.
Leaf: **L13**

F12 Fruit of ***Myrtus communis***.
Small spherical blue-black fruits when ripe, covered with bloom, and with very evident residues of flowers at tip. Long peduncle. 0.6–1 cm.
Leaf: **L16**

F13 Fruit of ***Eriobotrya japonica***.
Small yellow pomes, elongate, pear-shaped, edible. 2–3.5 cm.
Leaf: **L7**

F14 Fruit of ***Sorbus torminalis***.
Brown pomes, surface dotted with small raised lenticels, with long peduncles to small clusters. 1–1.5 cm.
Leaf: **L90**
Bud: **B61**

F15 Fruit of ***Sorbus aucuparia***.
Pomes orange-red when ripe, containing 3 seeds, in large clusters. 0.9–1.2 cm.
Leaf: **L123**
Bud: similar to **B60**

F16 Fruit of ***Sorbus domestica***.
Pomes brownish-green when ripe, in form of small pears. 2–4 cm.
Leaf: similar to **L123**
Bud: **B60**

F17 Fruit of ***Sorbus aria***.
Small red pomes, surface dotted with small raised lenticels, small clusters with woolly peduncles. 0.8–1.5 cm.
Leaf: **L46**
Bud: similar to **B60, B61**

F18 Fruit of ***Crataegus monogyna***.
Small, shiny dark red pomes, in clusters of 2 or 3; 1 seed. 0.8–1 cm.
Leaf: **L88**
Bud: **B46**

F19 Fruit of ***Mespilus germanica***.
Pomes brown-green, rusty, with large apical depression when ripe, surrounded by persistent residues of flowers (laciniate calyx). 5–6 cm in cultivated form, 1–3 cm in wild.
Leaf: **L51**
Bud: **B33**

F20 Fruit of ***Punica granatum***.
Pomes large, yellow-red, characterized by prominent floral residues in apical part (laciniate calyx); the outer layer of the fruit is leathery; contains numerous seeds, surrounded by juicy flesh, bright red in colour. 6–12 cm in cultivated plants, 3 cm in wild.
Leaf: **L25**
Bud: **B50**

F21 Fruit of ***Malus sylvestris***.
Green and very sour pomes, small in comparison with cultivated apple varieties. 5–15 cm in cultivated plants, 2.5–4 cm in wild.
Leaf: **L60**
Bud: **B49**

F22 Fruit of ***Pyrus communis***.
Large pomes of characteristic shape. Residues of flower involucre just visible at apex. 5–12 cm in cultivated plants, 1–4 cm in wild.
Leaf: **L55**
Bud: **B48**

F23 and **F24** Fruits of ***Citrus limon*** and ***Citrus sinensis***.
Characteristic (hesperid) type of fruits made up of a leathery skin, aromatic, enclosing a juicy flesh, divided into segments, in which the seeds are embedded. 5–10 cm.
Leaf: **L18**

F25 Fruit of ***Ginkgo biloba***.
Fruit drupaceous, consisting of a fleshy involucre, yellow and foul-smelling when ripe, which encloses a seed with a hard shell; edible. 2.5–3 cm.
Leaf: **L92**
Bud: **B64**

F26 Fruit of ***Olea europaea***.
Drupes green, black when ripe. 1–3.5 cm.
Leaf: **L2**

F27 Fruit of ***Phillyrea latifolia***.
Drupes blue-black when ripe. 0.6 cm.
Leaf: **L10**

F28 Fruit of ***Hippophae rhamnoides***.
Drupes oblong, surface slightly grainy, orange-red, sourish taste. 0.6–0.8 cm.
Leaf: **L23**
Bud: **B44**

F29 Fruit of ***Elaeagnus angustifolia***.
Drupes ellipsoid, surface dotted with silvery scales. 1.5–2 cm.
Leaf: **L26**
Bud: **B32**

F30 Fruit of ***Ziziphus jujuba***.
Drupes oblong, reddish-brown, with slightly acid flesh; edible (jujubes). 1.2–1.5 cm.
Leaf: **L72**
Bud: **B42**

F31 Fruit of ***Laurus nobilis***.
Fruits drupaceous (really berries), green, black when ripe. 1.5 cm.
Leaf: **L4**

F32 Fruit of ***Cornus mas***.
Drupes oblong, bright red when ripe. 1.5–2 cm.
Leaf: **L31**
Bud: **B3**

F33 Fruit of ***Celtis australis***.
Drupes spherical, long-stalked, reddish-black when ripe, sweet. 1 cm.
Leaf: **L74**
Bud: **B36**

F34 Fruit of *Pistacia terebinthus*.
Small bright red drupes, pedunculate, in large showy clusters,
ramified. 0.5–0.7 cm.
Leaf: **L116**

F35 Fruit of *Pistacia lentiscus*.
Small bright red drupes, pedunculate, in compact clusters. 0.3–0.5 cm.
Leaf: similar to **L116**, but even-
pinnate

F36 Fruit of *Styrax officinalis*.
Drupes of fibrous consistency, surface velvety, opening when ripe;
resinous and aromatic. 1.5–2 cm.
Leaf: **L27**

F37 Fruit of *Prunus mahaleb*.
Drupes fleshy, black when ripe, bitter.
0.6–1 cm.
Leaf: **L58**
Bud: **B37**

F38 Fruit of *Prunus padus*.
Drupes black and shiny, bitter, in long
clusters. 0.8 cm.
Leaf: **L50**
Bud: similar to **B61**

F39 Fruit of *Prunus avium*.
Shiny light or dark red drupes, sweet
or bitter depending on variety, single
or in clusters of 2–3. 1.5–2 cm.
Leaf: **L52**
Bud: **B52**

F40 Fruit of *Prunus laurocerasus*.
Drupes ovoid, at first green, reddish-
black when ripe, with very short
peduncles, in small clusters. 1–2 cm.
Leaf: **L8**

F41 Fruit of *Prunus domestica*.
Drupes large, ovoid, green at first,
and when ripe assuming different
colours according to variety and hybrids (yellow-green, red, bluish-
violet). 2–7 cm.
Leaf: similar to **L52** and **L57**
Bud: **B53**

F42 Fruit of *Ceratonia siliqua*.
Fleshy brown pods which do not

open when ripe. 10–20 cm.
Leaf: **L114**

F43 Fruit of *Gleditsia triacanthos*.
Large sickle-shaped pods, flattened
and twisted. They do not open when
ripe. 35–40 cm.
Leaf: **L124**
Bud: **B19** and **B40**

F44 Fruit of *Cercis siliquastrum*.
Pods flattened and elongated, purple
at beginning of season, then brown.
10–15 cm.
Leaf: **L34**
Bud: **B69**
Spring appearance: **Sp14**

F45 Fruit of *Catalpa bignonioides*.
Long, narrow, persistent pods, dark
brown. 15–40 cm.
Leaf: **L36**
Bud: **B10**

F46 Fruit of *Amorpha fruticosa*.
Short, stiff pods, curving and erect,
elongated, composed of numerous
parts. 0.7–0.9 cm.

F47 Fruit of *Cercidiphyllum japonicum*.
Pods erect, curved at tip, claw-
shaped, green, light yellow at base, in
clusters of 4–6. 1.5–5 cm.
Leaf: **L71**
Spring appearance: **Sp8**

F48 Fruit of *Cladrastis lutea*.
Tapering pods, with 4–6 seeds.
Length 7–10 cm, width 1–2 cm.
Leaf: similar to **L122**
Bud: **B22**

F49 Fruit of *Acacia dealbata*.
Pods brown and glabrous. Length 6–
12 cm, width 0.9–1.2 cm.
Leaf: **L129**

F50 Fruit of *Sophora japonica*.
Fleshy, undulating pods, contracted
in spaces between seeds. Length 8–
10 cm, width 0.8 cm.
Leaf: similar to **L120**
Bud: similar to **B16**

F51 Fruit of *Albizzia julibrissin*.
Pods flat and glabrous, with edges roughly parallel and valve surfaces enlarged by ripening seeds. Length 7–15 cm, width 1.5 cm.
Leaf: **L128**
Bud: **B20**

F52 Fruit of *Robinia pseudacacia*.
Pods elongated, reddish-brown, in drooping clusters. Length 5–10 cm, width 0.9–1.2 cm.
Leaf: **L120**
Bud: **B16** and **B45**

F53 Fruit of *Laburnum alpinum*.
Pods long and twisted, dark brown, in long, drooping clusters, made up of many parts. Length 5–8 cm, width 0.7 cm.
Leaf: **L109**
Bud: similar to **B51**

F54 Fruit of *Nerium oleander*.
Pairs of long follicles, which open along lines of juncture (in all similar to a pod), reddish-brown, containing many seeds, displaying a tuft of yellow-orange hairs. 10–18 cm.
Leaf: **L6**

F55 and **F56** Fruit of *Salix alba* and *Salix pentandra*.
Clusters of capsules which when ripe open in two valves, releasing numerous seeds, bearing a tuft of silky hairs.
Leaf: **L39** and **L41**
Bud: similar to **B24**

F57 Fruit of *Populus tremula*.
Long clusters of capsules which when ripe open in two valves, releasing numerous seeds bearing a tuft of silky hairs. Drooping fruits.
Leaf: **L59** and **L62**
Bud: **B57**
Spring appearance: **Sp6**

F58 Fruit of *Eucalyptus* sp.
Hemispherical, fibrous capsules which open at the top in three valves, releasing numerous small seeds. 1–2.5 cm.
Leaf: **L9**

F59 Fruit of *Buxus sempervirens*.
Oval, three-pointed capsule which opens in three valves, releasing shiny black seeds. 0.8 cm.
Leaf: **L1**

F60 Fruit of *Lagerstroemia indica*.
Fibrous capsule which opens in 3–6 valves, releasing winged seeds. 0.8–1.2 cm.

F61 Fruit of *Tamarix gallica*.
Elongated capsule which opens in three valves, releasing seeds bearing a tuft of long hairs. 0.2–0.4 cm.
Leaf: **S4**
Bud: **B17**

F62 Fruit of *Syringa vulgaris*.
Pointed, leathery capsule which opens in two valves, releasing winged seeds. 1.2–1.8 cm.
Leaf: **L33**
Bud: **B4**

F63 Fruit of *Pittosporum tobira*.
Spherical capsule, leathery, which opens in three valves, revealing large red seeds covered with a resinous layer, thus sticky. 1–1.2 cm.
Leaf: **L5**

F64 Fruit of *Paulownia tomentosa*.
Persistent capsules on axes of inflorescence, each opening in two valves, releasing winged seeds. 3–5 cm.
Leaf: **L35**
Bud: **B9**

F65 Fruit of *Staphylea pinnata*.
Pendulous clusters of swollen capsules, of papery consistency, with long peduncles, containing large brown seeds. 3–4 cm.
Leaf: **L113**
Bud: **B2**

F66 Fruit of *Liriodendron tulipifera*.
Brown, erect, pointed cone, persistent throughout winter, constituted of numerous papery winged carpels which eventually drop off, leaving the central axis bare. Overall length 5–8 cm.
Leaf: **L100**
Bud: **B26**

F67 Fruit of *Magnolia* sp.
Fruit reddish-brown, erect, composed of numerous oval-shaped fleshy parts around a central axis which open and release 1–2 seeds. Overall length 7–10 cm.
Leaf: **L20** and **L22**
Bud: **B56**
Spring appearance: **Sp16**

F68 Fruit of *Rhus typhina*.
Fruit crimson, erect, elongated, very hairy, composed of small dry drupes containing a single seed. Overall length 10–20 cm.
Leaf: **L121**
Bud: **B18**

F69 Fruit of *Broussonetia papyrifera*.
Spherical fruit composed of small drupes covered by an involucre of bracts (scale-like growths similar to leaves but more variably coloured and often with a consistency of a membrane or paper); orange-red. Overall diameter 1.8–2.5 cm.
Leaf: **L70** and **L99**
Bud: **B31**

F70 Fruit of *Morus alba*.
Fruit globose, whitish or dark red, edible, composed of interlinked drupes that represent the true fruits. Overall diameter 1–2 cm.
Leaf: **L69**, **L89** and **L96**
Bud: **B30**

F71 Fruit of *Ficus carica*.
Fruit globose or pear-shaped, composed of a fleshy involucre which contains a cavity inside which are the tiny nuts (achenes) representing the true fruits. 5–7 cm.
Leaf: **L97**
Bud: **B25**

F72 Fruit of *Platanus hispanica*.
Small nuts (achenes) with long hairs at the base, joining to form a spherical fruit in clusters of 3–5 on a long peduncle. Overall diameter 2–3 cm.
Leaf: **L98**
Bud: **B28**

F73 Fruit of *Liquidambar styraciflua*.
Small capsules with 1–2 seeds and a long point (style), linked to form a spherical fruit, themselves joined in drooping clusters which remain on the plant throughout the winter. Overall diameter 2.5–3 cm.
Leaf: **L105**
Bud: **B35**

F74 Fruit of *Maclura pomifera*.
Fleshy fruit, similar in size and appearance to an orange, the pulp of which contains small drupes representing the true fruits. Overall diameter 10–15 cm.
Leaf: **L30**
Bud: **B41**

F75 Fruit of *Juglans regia*.
Large drupes, comprising a fleshy rind that covers a large stone containing the edible seed, commonly called 'nuts'. The drupe of the Black Walnut differs from that of the Common Walnut in having a thicker rind and prominent ridges. 4–5 cm.
Leaf: **L118**
Bud: **B27**
Spring appearance: **Sp7**

F76 Fruit of *Carya ovata*.
Globose fruit with outer layer opening in four valves, and a hard, smooth inner layer divided into compartments containing the edible seed. 2–4 cm.
Leaf: **L119**

F77 Fruit of *Aesculus hippocastanum*.
Large capsule with leathery walls and sharp, conical spines, containing 1–3 large, shiny seeds. 3–5 cm.
Leaf: **L110**
Bud: **B8**

F78 Fruit of *Fagus sylvatica*.
Two nuts (seeds enclosed by a simple membranous wall), sharp and elongated, contained in a spiny involucre which opens in 4 valves. 1.5–2 cm.
Leaf: **L28**
Bud: **B15**

F79 Fruit of *Quercus petraea*.
Nut (seed enclosed by a simple membranous wall) surrounded at the base by a woody involucre or cupule, covered in small scales. 1.5–3 cm.
Leaf: **L82**
Bud: **B38**

F80 Fruit of *Quercus cerris*.
Nut (seed enclosed by a simple membranous wall) surrounded at the base by an involucre bearing long, pointed, curved scales. 2–3 cm.
Leaf: **L81**
Bud: **B39**

F81 Fruit of *Castanea sativa*.
2–3 nuts (seeds enclosed by a simple membranous wall), brown and shiny, inside an involucre with ramified and very sharp spines, which opens in 2–4 valves. 2–3 cm.
Leaf: **L53**
Bud: **B11**

F82 Fruit of *Corylus avellana*.
Clusters of 1–4 nuts (seeds enclosed by a woody wall), each surrounded at the base by a pair of green bracts (growths similar to leaves but more variously coloured and often of a membranous or papery consistency); toothed and hairy. 1.5–2 cm.
Leaf: **L65**
Bud: **B67**
Spring appearance: **Sp4**

F83 Fruit of *Zelkova carpinifolia*.
Small nuts (seeds enclosed by a simple membranous wall) about the size of peas, green and with fine hairs, with asymmetrical tips. 0.5–0.7 cm.
Leaf: **L79**
Bud: **B34**

F84 Fruit of *Alnus incana*.
Tiny nuts (seeds enclosed by a simple membranous wall), winged, contained in fruits resembling tiny woody cones, globose, in clusters of 2–4, on a long stalk. Nutlet 0.2 cm, overall diameter of fruit 1 cm.
Leaf: **L47**
Bud: similar to **B66**

F85 Fruit of *Betula* sp.
Very small nuts (seeds enclosed by a simple membranous wall), winged, contained in drooping, cylindrical fruits which split up when ripe. Nutlet 0.2 cm.
Leaf: **L77**
Bud: **B65**

F86 Fruit of *Ostrya carpinifolia*.
Tiny nuts (seeds enclosed by a simple membranous wall) contained in papery, inflated sacs, consisting of two adjoining bracts and joined to form a long, drooping fruit which remains for a long time on the plant. Nutlet 0.1–0.2 cm, papery sacs 1.5 cm.
Leaf: **L73**
Bud: similar to **B14**

F87 Fruit of *Carpinus betulus*.
Tiny nuts (seeds enclosed by a simple membranous wall) accompanied by three-lobed bracts and joined to form a long, drooping fruit, which remains for a long time on the plant. Nutlet 0.6 cm, bract 3 cm.
Leaf: **L42**
Bud: **B14**

F88 Fruit of *Carpinus orientalis*.
Tiny nuts (seeds enclosed by a simple membranous wall) accompanied by

bracts similar to small leaves, oval and finely toothed, joined to form a drooping fruit. Nutlet 0.2–0.4 cm, bract 1–1.5 cm.
Leaf: **L54**
Bud: similar to **B14**

F89 Fruit of *Pterocarya fraxinifolia*.
Small nuts (seeds enclosed by a simple membranous wall) with two large wings at the base, which are joined to form a very long, drooping fruit. Winged nut 2 cm, fruit 30–50 cm.
Leaf: **L126**

F90 Fruit of *Acer campestre*.
Pair of dry fruits, each with a wing (samara) which form an angle of about 180°. Overall length of samara 5–6 cm.
Leaf: **L101**
Bud: similar to **B5**

F91 Fruit of *Acer pseudoplatanus*.
Pair of dry fruits, each with a wing (samara) which form an angle of about 90°. Length of wing 5 cm.
Leaf: **L104**
Bud: **B5**

F92 Fruit of *Acer monspessulanum*.
Pair of dry fruits, each with two wings (samara) which are almost parallel to each other and partly overlap. Length of wing 1.2 cm.
Leaf: **L93**
Bud: similar to **B5**

F93 Fruit of *Fraxinus excelsior*.
Dry fruit with one wing (samara) in variable clusters, hanging from long stalks. Length of wing 4 cm.
Leaf: **L122**
Bud: **B6**
Spring appearance: **Sp13**

F94 Fruit of *Tilia cordata*.
Dry fruits similar to small nuts (seeds enclosed by a simple membranous wall), globose, joined to form drooping fruits, made up of 3–5 sections,

borne on long peduncles at the base of which is a broad membranous wing. 0.3–0.6 cm.
Leaf: similar to **L68**
Bud: **B12**

F95 Fruit of *Ulmus minor*.
Small samaras (seeds enclosed by a wall which expands sideways in a membranous wing) with seeds placed towards the wing tip, joined in large clusters. Length of wing 1–2 cm.
Leaf: similar to **L49**
Bud: similar to **B13** and **B68**

F96 Fruit of *Ulmus glabra*.
Samaras (seeds enclosed by a wall which expands sideways in a membranous wing), with short peduncle; glabrous, with seeds at the centre of the wing, joined in large clusters. Length of wing 1.5–2 cm.
Leaf: **L49**
Bud: **B13** and **B68**
Spring appearance: **Sp10**

F97 Fruit of *Ulmus laevis*.
Small samaras (seeds enclosed by a wall which expands sideways in a membranous wing), with long peduncle and provided with long, soft hairs (cilia), joined in large clusters. Length of wing 1–2 cm.
Leaf: **L48**
Bud: similar to **B13** and **B68**

F98 Fruit of *Paliurus spina-christi*.
Dry, woody fruit (nut) in form of an expanded disc in a circular, broad, undulating wing; in small clusters. 2–4 cm.
Leaf: **L56**
Bud: **B43**

F99 Fruit of *Ailanthus altissima*.
Fruit clusters with many oblong samaras, the wing twisted like a screw, each with a seed in the central part; colour of fruits from yellow to bright red. Length of wing 3–5 cm.
Leaf: **L127**
Bud: **B21**

C1 Cone of *Abies alba*.
Cylindrical, oblong, erect cones; when mature the cone disintegrates, releasing the large, thin scales, seeds and toothed bracts, leaving the central axis on the branch. 10–15 cm.
Leaf: **A10**

C2 Cone of *Cedrus deodara*.
Erect, short, thickset cones, with rounded tips, which flake off at maturity in large flakes, leaving the central axis on the branch. 8–14 cm.
Leaf: **A17**

C3 Cone of *Larix decidua*.
Small, globose, lightweight cones with large, rounded scales. Often numerous, interposed at brief intervals, on drooping twigs. 2–3.5 cm.
Leaf: **A18**
Bud: **B63**

C4 Cone of *Araucaria araucana*.
Large spherical-oval cone, woody and spinous, which breaks up to release the seeds. 10–18 cm.
Leaf: **S5**

C5 Cone of *Picea abies*.
Cylindrical, oblong, drooping cones, which at maturity do not break up but fall entire, after dissemination. Large, thin, undulating scales, with two teeth and an incision at tip. 10–18 cm.
Leaf: **A12**

C6 Cone of *Pseudotsuga menziesii*.
Oval-elongate cones, hanging from tip of branches; fall entire after dissemination. Round, thin scales, from which the trifid bracts sprout prominently, with a long central point and almost filiform, turning upwards. 5–8 cm.
Leaf: **A11**

C7 Cone of *Tsuga canadensis*.
Tiny, ovoid cones, hanging at tip of lateral shoots, with a few rounded scales with wavy edges. 2–2.5 cm.
Leaf: **A9**

C8 and **C9** Cones of *Pinus sylvestris* and *Pinus nigra*.
Conical-ovoid cones with stiff, woody scales which protrude externally, the central boss (apophysis) pyramidal with a short rostrum (umbo). 3–8 cm.
Leaf: **A13**

C10 Cone of *Pinus strobus*.
Oblong, drooping cones with woody scales but thinner than **C8** and **C9**, and with an unpointed terminal boss (umbo). 10–15 cm.
Leaf: **A15**

C11 Cone of *Pinus cembra*.
Globose-ovoid cones, with thin scales, leathery in consistency, thickened at tip, which when ripe turns outwards. Seeds large, in a very hard shell; edible. 5–8 cm.
Leaf: similar to **A15**

C12 Cone of *Pinus pinea*.
Very big cones with large, woody scales, thickening to a boss, convex and obtuse, at tip. Large seeds with hard shell; edible. Length 8–16 cm, width 7–12 cm.
Leaf: similar to **A13**

G13 Cone of *Alnus cordata*.
Fruits resembling small cones, woody, brown, ovoid, in groups of 2–4 on a long curved stalk. Length over 2 cm.
Leaf: **L67**
Bud: similar to **B66**

C14 Cone of *Alnus glutinosa*.
Fruits similar to tiny cones, woody, brownish-black, ovoid, in groups of 2–4 on a long curved stalk. Length 1 cm.
Leaf: **L64**
Bud: **B66**
Spring appearance: **Sp3**

C15 Cone of *Cupressus macrocarpa*.
Ovoid-cylindrical cones, formed of 8–14 polygonal scales with a large blunt central spine. Colour brown. 2.5–3.5 cm.
Leaf: similar to **S2**

C16 Cone of ***Cupressus semper-virens***.
Globose cones formed of 8–14 pentagonal scales with a central spine (mucro) or virtually flattened. Colour greyish. 2–3 cm.
Leaf: **S2**

C17 Cone of ***Chamaecyparis lawsoniana***.
Minute cones, formed of 8–10 hexagonal scales, provided in centre with small spine (mucro). 0.7–1 cm.
Leaf: **S3**

C18 Cone of ***Sequoiadendron giganteum***.
Ovoid, oblong cones formed of 25–45 scales, with rhomboidal boss; compressed spine set in a central depression from which a number of wrinkles radiate. Persistent for a long time on tree. 5.5–6.5 cm.
Leaf: **A2**

C19 Cone of ***Taxodium distichum***.
Globose, wrinkled cones formed of scales with rhomboidal boss, and a small pine (mucro) in centre. 2–3 cm.
Leaf: **A6**
Bud: **B62**

C20 Cone of ***Cryptomeria japonica***.
Globose cones, turned upwards, formed of 20–30 scales with a long spine (mucro) curved upwards and with an upper edge comprising 5–6 long, pointed teeth which give them a spiny appearance. 1.3–2 cm.
Leaf: **A3**

C21 Cone of ***Sequoia sempervirens***.

Ovoid cones, formed of 12–20 rhomboidal scales, and a central depression and small spine (mucro). 2–2.5 cm.
Leaf: **A5**

C22 Cone of ***Metasequoia glyptostroboides***.
Globose green cones, scales compressed, protruding outwards, scored by a long transverse groove. 1.2–2.5 cm.
Leaf: **A7**

C23 Cone of ***Calocedrus decurrens***.
Ovoid yellow or reddish-brown cones, formed of three pairs of scales, the side pairs diverging when mature. 1.8–2.5 cm.
Leaf: similar to **S1**

C24 Cone of ***Thuja occidentalis***.
Greenish-yellow cones, opening at maturity, formed of 8–10 scales with rounded tip, lacking a spine (mucro). 1–2 cm.
Leaf: **S1**

C25 Cone of ***Thuja orientalis***.
Ovoid, erect cones formed of 6–8 scales, the upper ones furnished with a spine (mucro) which is long and curved, galbulus, blue-green and fleshy at first, woody with divergent scales when mature. 1.3–2.5 cm.
Leaf: similar to **S1**

C26 Cone of ***Thuja plicata***.
Ovoid scales, brown when mature, formed of 5–6 pairs of leathery scales which open in divergent fashion, furnished with short spines at tip. 1–2 cm.
Leaf: similar to **S1**

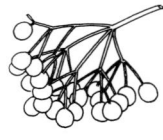

Guide to Species

Identification of species

The foregoing 'Guide to Identification' will identify most European trees as belonging to a group of two or three species; indeed it is often possible to arrive at a single species by comparative examination of several organs such as fruits, twigs and buds. But this may not always be possible, especially in some genera where the characteristics are not clearly in evidence, or where those that distinguish the constituent species are only available for a short period of time.

In order to ensure that your identification of a species is correct, you should refer to the rest of this section, which provides morphological and descriptive notes on all the trees under consideration.

The single entries are arranged so that the reader can make a quick comparison of factual details that are readily visible (height, crown, trunk, bark, foliage, leaf structure, leaf attachment, autumn coloration, flowers, blossom, fruits, etc.). Furthermore, in the case of genera comprising more than one species, and frequently not always capable of being identified by using the 'Guide to Identification', the following section also includes dichotomous keys to help determine the individual species.

These dichotomous keys deal only with the most obvious features and do not take into account anatomical and morphological characteristics of flowers (rarely present), as with traditional scientific keys; consequently they are based on a morphological feature that is usually always available or characteristic of a group of plants: in virtually all instances, the leaf.

Leaf shape, however, can be highly variable even within a species and may consequently lead to uncertainty. For this reason, other elements which are easily observable and persist for some time, such as the ripe fruits, are often included in order to ensure that a correct identification can be made.

Besides using the keys, it will be helpful to consult the facts contained in the description of the single species, as well as the maps and, it goes without saying, the illustrations.

The guide describes 150 European, 54 American and 30 Asiatic species which grow naturally or are cultivated for fruit – in all, including other brief references, over 240 species which are likely to be met in Britain, central and southern Europe.

The book covers species which are native, i.e. they occur in a region naturally without man's assistance, as well as those which are cultivated, e.g. for timber, fruit or ornament, and also plants which are not native but have become naturalized and now appear to be wild. Sycamore (*Acer pseudoplatanus*, p 204) and Horse Chestnut (*Aesculus hippocastanum*, p 206) are two such species.

The nomenclature adopted follows Tutin's *Flora Europaea* for Europe in general, Pignatti's *Flora d'Italia* for Italy, and the works of Krüssmann for exotic species.

The systematic arrangement is based on the most recent classifications, but has necessarily been adapted in places to the usage for which this book is designed.

Trees are grouped into their botanical families but without any general description; further information on tree families may be found in *Flora Europaea*.

Listed on the four following pages, under families and genera, are all the species subsequently discussed and the pages on which they are to be found.

How entries are listed

The scientific names (in Latin) are listed by 'genus' and 'species', followed by the name, abbreviated name or initial of the authority for the name (for example, L. = Linnaeus, D.C. = De Candolle, Jacq. = Jacquin, etc.). Synonyms are shown in parentheses, with the generic name abbreviated to the initial letter. The common name of the species is also given, where applicable.

    The following forms of measurement also require explanation:

height 10 (20) m indicates that the tree when fully grown is usually 10 metres high, but that in particular cases (by reason of isolation or some other cause) it may reach 20 metres;

height 10–20 m indicates that mature trees may be found varying in height from 10 to 20 metres;

leaves 10 cm indicates that this is the length of the leaf, the width may be estimated from the description of the shape: lanceolate, round, etc.;

leaves 10 × 5 cm indicates both the length and width of the leaf.

Symbols

∅   Indicates the diameter of a cylindrical or spherical object;
♂   Indicates a male flower or inflorescence;
♀   Indicates a female flower or inflorescence;
*   Indicates that a tree is native to the United Kingdom;
**   Indicates that a tree has been introduced to the United Kingdom (see p16).

GYMNOSPERMS

GINKGO BILOBA L.
(= *Salisburia adiantifolia* Sm.)
Maidenhair Tree **
Family *Ginkgoaceae*

height 25 (40) m
crown pyramidal, slender, few branches in ♂, more irregular in ♀
trunk erect, with straight, verticillate branches; bark grey with irregular fissures and ridges
foliage deciduous
leaves flabellate (fan-like), incised, 5 × 8 cm and more, attached to short shoots of 3–5 cm; autumn colour golden yellow; alternate arrangement
flowers dioecious; ♂ flowers catkins of 6–8 cm; ♀ flowers terminal, inconspicuous, on 4 cm short shoots; flowering period April
fruit similar to a drupe, yellow when ripe, 3 cm ∅, emitting an unpleasant odour when rotting

fruit
× ½

seed
× ½

♂

♀

Ginkgo biloba

The generic name is derived from a corruption of the Chinese Yin-Kuo-Tsu. A fast-growing ornamental tree, it is widely diffused in European park-

land, being adaptable to almost any climate. It is resistant to urban environments and does not exhibit serious parasitic diseases. The species comes from China, where it was grown in the vicinity of temples, and was introduced to Europe around 1730 and to England in 1759. It may no longer grow wild in China. It is very long-lived and indeed the original tree at Kew, planted in 1760, is still in fine health.

There are fossil remains of genus *Ginkgo* in Jurassic and Cretaceous rocks (195–65 million years ago).

The pale, easily worked wood is valued and used in joinery. Furthermore, in its countries of origin the seeds are roasted for eating, after removal of the fleshy involucre.

Cultivars: 'Fastigiata', columnar in form, with straight, clustered branches, suitable for planting along roads; 'Pendula', smaller in size, with branches bending downwards.

TAXUS BACCATA L.
Yew *
Family *Taxaceae*

height up to 20 (25) m
crown pyramidal, spreading
trunk erect, often divided at base, branchy; bark of mature tree reddish-brown to purple, flaking off in long strips
foliage evergreen
leaves needle-like, linear, slightly sickle-shaped, points not sharp, 1–3.5 cm; pectinate arrangement
flowers dioecious; ♂ flowers axillary oval yellow catkins; ♀ flowers solitary, similar to buds, green; flowering period February
fruit seed similar to small nut, covered by a fleshy bell-shaped aril, red when ripe, 0.7–1 cm

The Yew is widely distributed throughout Europe, where it grows wild in shady broadleaved woods

×1

♂

immature
fruit

♀

×1

Taxus baccata

from 300 to 1500 m in altitude, especially on calcareous soil. In Britain it is native throughout, although less frequent in Scotland. It is widely cultivated as an ornamental tree and for hedging; it can resist urban pollution and does not harbour serious parasites. Often seen in church yards.

The sapwood is white, the heartwood reddish, hard, heavy and homogeneous. It is used in turnery and for cabinet-making, because it turns black when treated with ferrates. The whole tree, with the exception of the red aril, is poisonous because of the presence of the alkaloid taxine, which affects the heart. The sweetish aril is edible, provided the poisonous seeds are avoided.

This very long-lived tree is some-

times credited with ages of 2000 years.

Cultivars: numerous, differing from one another in shape and in the colour of leaves and fruits.

ARAUCARIA ARAUCANA (Mol.) K. Koch
(= *A. imbricata* Pavon)
Monkey Puzzle **
Family *Araucariaceae*

height up to 30 m
crown oval-pyramidal, open
trunk straight, with verticillate, horizontal branches; bark grey and rough
foliage evergreen
leaves scale-like, green and glossy, pointed, 3–4 cm, triangular on main trunk, oval-elliptical on branches; spiral arrangement
flowers dioecious; ♂ and ♀ on separate trees; ♂ flowers terminal, oval, 10 × 6 cm; ♀ flowers spherical cones covered by bracts, 10–18 cm long, maturing in two years; flowering period June
fruits seeds 4 × 2 cm, edible

The Monkey Puzzle or Chile Pine (*araucana* is derived from the name of a Chilean Indian tribe) is found in its country of origin on the western

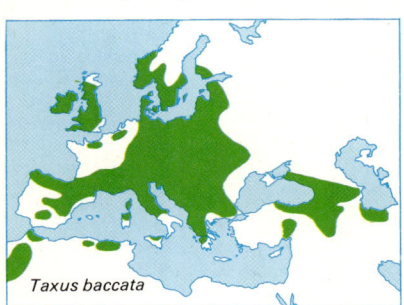

Taxus baccata

slopes of the Andes, up to considerable altitudes. It was introduced from South America to England in 1795 and can often be seen in front gardens in urban areas. In Europe it is widely grown as an ornamental tree, because of its strange appearance, in gardens and parks.

Related to the above is *Araucaria heterophylla* (Salisb.) Franco (= *A. excelsa* R. Br.). Originally from Norfolk Island in the Pacific, it has linear needles 1 cm long and dense, verticillate branches; although not hardy, it is widely grown as an ornamental in central and northern Europe. In southern Europe it grows to over 20 m in height, with twigs arranged in pairs at the tip of upward-turned projecting branches.

Araucaria araucana

♀ seed
♂
×½

Key to **CYPRESSES**

Leaves scale-like and obtuse, packed closely together; cones 3–4 cm

– mature cones grey, opaque; foliage, when crushed, not very aromatic:
 Cupressus sempervirens
– mature cones brown, shiny; foliage, when crushed, smells of lemon:
 Cupressus macrocarpa

Leaves scale-like and acute, divergent at apex; cones 1–3 cm

– young shoots grey, if crushed foul-smelling
–– bark greenish-brown, flaking off in short, thin strips:
 Cupressus arizonica

–– bark purple, flaking off in curled strips:
– shoots green or blue-green, with no unpleasant odour if crushed:
 Cupressus lusitanica

CUPRESSUS SEMPERVIRENS L.
Italian Cypress
Family *Cupressaceae*

height 20–30 m
crown columnar, variously spreading
trunk erect, branchy down to base, ridged; bark grey-brown, smooth

foliage evergreen
leaves scale-like, obtuse, imbricated (arranged like tiles); arranged two by two on twig
flowers unisexual; ♂ flowers oval, 3 mm, terminal, yellow; ♀ short-stemmed globose cones; flowering period February–May
fruits woody cones, more or less

Cupressus sempervirens

♂

×3

seed

×2

spherical, 3.5 cm ∅, formed of 8–14 scales, scarcely pointed, maturing in second year

The cypress originally came from the eastern Mediterranean and was introduced in cultivated form throughout southern Europe. Hardy, it is less common in the British Isles. It flourishes in a warm climate with dry summers, being harmed by prolonged frosts.

It adapts to various subsoils, even those which are shallow and not too compact, deriving sustenance from them by means of its surface root system. In the Mediterranean region it has been used in reafforestation of arid terrain in association with evergreens such as pines.

The cypress is threatened in Europe by a parasitic fungus, *Coryneum cardinale* Wag., which

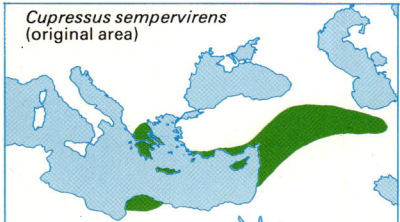

Cupressus sempervirens
(original area)

was discovered in Tuscany at the beginning of the 1950s and which has become widely diffused since then.

The species is used as an ornamental in parks and for lining roads. The wood is of excellent quality, pale yellow, sweet-smelling, hardy and resistant to parasites. It is particularly suitable for shutters and furniture. An essence known as 'cypress oil' is extracted from the shoots and can be used to cure coughs.

Varieties: *horizontalis*, with spreading crown; *stricta*, with columnar crown.

CUPRESSUS MACROCARPA
Hartweg
Monterey Cypress **
Family *Cupressaceae*

This cypress has shiny, brown, elongated cones, about 3 cm, arranged singly or in pairs. The leaves are dark green; when crushed, they give out a lemony smell. In other respects it is similar to the Italian Cypress.

Originally from a restricted area in California, it was introduced to Europe around 1840, finding wide distribution as an ornamental species and, more recently, for reafforestation in the Mediterranean region. In

Britain it is used as a hedging plant, particularly in coastal areas, but has been planted less since Leyland Cypress gained popularity in the 1960s. It grows very rapidly and is resistant to even salty winds, and is therefore planted to create windbreaks. The tree possesses a deep root system.

The wood is used for the same purposes as that of the Italian Cypress.

Varieties: *lambertiana*, with a spreading, flattened crown; *fastigiata*, with a columnar habit.

See also Leyland Cypress (*Cypressocyparis leylandii*, p 96, under *Chamaecyparis nootkatensis*).

CUPRESSUS LUSITANICA Miller
(= *C. glauca* Lam.)
Mexican Cypress
Family *Cupressaceae*

The branches are spreading and pendent, the shoots green or glaucous, emitting a disagreeable odour when crushed; the leaves are pointed and spreading at the apex; the cones are small, round, 1.2 cm ⌀.

For long it was not known where this tree originated: it was thought to be India (an alternative name is Cedar of Goa) but is now known to be Mexico. In Europe, the species has been planted for ornament and to form wind-breaking hedges. In Britain it is occasionally planted in the south.

CUPRESSUS ARIZONICA Greene
Arizona Cypress
Family *Cupressaceae*

The leaves are sharp and scale-like, spreading at the apex; the cones vary in size from 1–3 cm; the young branches, if rubbed, give off a disagreeable odour. The overall colour is pale green.

This cypress came originally from western regions of North America, from mountainous zones in Arizona and northern Mexico. Introduced into Britain in 1882, it is planted as an ornamental and has been used on the

continent for reafforestation. Adaptable to different soils, provided they are sufficiently deep, it tolerates drought and frost.

CUPRESSUS GLABRA Sudw.
(= *C. arizonica* var. *bonita* Lemmon)
Smooth Cypress
Family *Cupressaceae*

This conifer, originally from central Arizona, is often confused with the preceding species. It is distinguished by its purple bark, which flakes off in curled strips, whereas *C. arizonica* has greenish-brown bark which flakes off in short, soft strips.

Cupressus glabra is less used in sylviculture because it is more demanding in terms of environmental conditions and grows more slowly. Nevertheless it is widely planted as an ornamental species, because it can stand trimming, and for its unmistakable grey-green coloration and interesting bark.

JUNIPERUS COMMUNIS L.
Juniper *
Family *Cupressaceae*

height up to 5–6 m, more often a shrub
crown columnar, more or less spreading

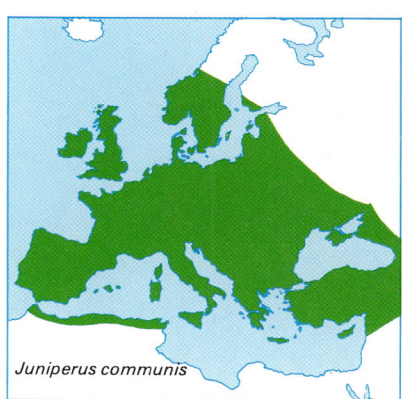

Juniperus communis

Key to **JUNIPERS**

Leaves all acicular, in whorls of 3

– needles with one white band above; cones dark blue, covered with down: *Juniperus communis*
– needles with two white bands above; cones from reddish-brown to black, shiny: *Juniperus oxycedrus*

Leaves scale-like, present on adult branches, sometimes together with acicular leaves on young branches

– acicular leaves in whorls of 3; cone reddish-brown: *Juniperus phoenicea*

– leaves in opposite pairs; cones 4–6 mm
–– acicular leaves present; cultivated species, tree or shrub: *Juniperus virginiana*
–– scale-leaves prevalent; wild species, usually shrubby: *Juniperus sabina*

trunk erect, divided from base, with ascendant branches; bark grey-brown, initially smooth, then flaking in long brown fibres
foliage evergreen
leaves needle-like, sharply pointed, 1–1.5 cm, with white bands above; verticillate arrangement in threes
flowers dioecious; ♂ flowers oval, axillary, formed of 3–6 pollen sacs; ♀ axillary, formed of 3–4 scales; flowering period February–April
fruits spherical cones, 4–8 mm, fleshy, blue-black when mature in second year

Juniperus communis

×2

The Juniper has a vast distribution in the northern hemisphere, growing wild from sea-level up to considerable altitudes – the shrubby, dwarf, prostrate form (subsp *nana*) is found at 3700 m in the Monte Rosa massif in the Italian-Swiss Alps.

It will adapt to virtually any conditions of climate or soil; it flourishes in bright open places, in both firm soil and shifting detritus, tolerating drought and strong winds. It is frequently found on pasture and waste land. Juniper is native throughout Britain, in the creeping form or as a small tree. It is found on both chalk downland and acidic soils.

The hard, compact, fine-grained wood is used in joinery and lathe-work, and also, because of its aromatic qualities, for smoking meat. The softer, more flexible branches are used for basket-making. The cones, which resemble berries, are used in food flavouring and in making gin. They contain a complex essence, with an anti-rheumatic and balsamic action, used in herbal medicines. The oil distilled from the leaves and wood is used to treat skin ailments.

Varieties: *hibernica*, of columnar habit; *compressa*, small in size.

JUNIPERUS OXYCEDRUS L.
Prickly Juniper
Family *Cupressaceae*

A tree or shrub with acicular leaves, found in coastal regions from Portugal to the Black Sea, characterized by reddish-brown cones; it is quite a rarity in cultivation in the U.K. Highly resistant to drought and saltiness, it is, of all coastal tree species, the one that grows closest to the sea. Its uses are the same as those of the Juniper.

Juniperus phoenicea

where it reaches a height of 3–8 m.

The pinkish wood has uses similar to those of the Juniper, and is also used for small marquetry work. The cones are used in industry for the extraction of alcohol and soap-making.

JUNIPERUS CHINENSIS L.
Chinese Juniper **
Family *Cupressiaceae*

The Chinese Juniper is more common as a small tree in Britain. It keys out here but is really closer to Pencil Cedar, from which it differs in the larger, rounded glaucous cones and acicular leaves in threes, not pairs.

JUNIPERUS SABINA L.
Savin
Family *Cupressaceae*

This juniper with its scale-leaves usually has the dimensions and habit of a shrub, seldom of a tree. It grows wild, though it is not common, on calcareous soil in mountain zones of southern Europe, sometimes under harsh conditions. Occasionally used as a ground cover plant, it is rare in cultivation in Britain.

The Savin is poisonous, in that it contains properties with an intense irritant action, which may be fatal.

×2.5

Juniperus oxycedrus

JUNIPERUS PHOENICEA L.
Phoenician Juniper
Family *Cupressaceae*

This juniper with scale-leaves grows wild in the Mediterranean basin, ranging from coastal zones to altitudes of 1300 m. It forms a constituent part of the evergreen maquis,

JUNIPERUS VIRGINIANA L.
Pencil Cedar **
Family *Cupressaceae*

The Pencil Cedar exhibits both scale-leaves, on adult branches, and acicular leaves, on terminal twigs, simultaneously. In parts of North America, where it originated, it may grow to 25 m tall. In Europe it is cultivated as an ornamental species, because it is rugged and adaptable to very varied conditions of terrain and climate.

The wood, of good quality, is used for joinery and for making pencils. It contains an essence used in medicine and perfumery.

CHAMAECYPARIS LAWSONIANA
(Murray) Parl.
Lawson Cypress **
Family *Cupressaceae*

height 10–30 m
crown pyramidal, with branches often pendent
trunk straight, thickly ramified from base; bark reddish-brown
foliage evergreen
leaves scale-like, pointed, 2 mm, with a transparent gland in middle; opposite arrangement in pairs
flowers unisexual; ♂ flowers terminal, 5 mm, before red blossoms; ♀ flowers spherical, 8 mm, blue-green; flowering period March–April
fruits woody, round cones, brown, 1 cm ⌀

Because of the small dimensions of many species and its resemblance to the cypress, the genus has been called *Chamaecyparis*, from the Greek *chamai* and *kyparissos* (false cypress).

Originally from California and Oregon, it was introduced to Britain in 1854 and is frequent as an ornamental. In its native region it flourishes in areas with a maritime climate, high humidity and minimal temperature fluctuations, forming mixed coniferous woods. In Europe it does well in similar habitats, in fresh,

Chamaecyparis lawsoniana

deep soil, protected from the wind.

The wood is of good quality and resistant to parasites; light and durable, it is pale brown and used in joinery.

The numerous varieties are subdivided according to particular characteristics of habit and leaf colour.

CHAMAECYPARIS NOOTKATENSIS
(D. Don) Spach
Nootka Cypress **
Family *Cupressaceae*

The species came originally from the mountainous zones of North America, along the Pacific coast, where it is an important forest species. Found in Europe since the middle of the 19th century, it is planted in Britain as an ornamental tree. In appearance it resembles the preceding species, but differs in shape, which is markedly conical, with drooping branches and pointed scales, turned slightly outwards, without translucent glands.

Nootka Cypress is, with *Cupressus macrocarpa*, one of the parents of Leyland Cypress (*Cupressocyparis leylandii*). This fast-growing, large tree is a frequent hedging plant. It can be distinguished from Nootka Cypress by its three-dimensional (not flat) foliage sprays and different cones. It differs from Monterey Cypress in its softer, flatter foliage and smaller cones.

CALOCEDRUS DECURRENS (Torrey) Florin
(= *Libocedrus decurrens* Torrey)
Incense Cedar **
Family *Cupressaceae*

height up to 30 m
crown narrowly pyramidal, columnar
trunk almost completely branched, sometimes bifurcate; bark reddish-brown, deflaking in plaques
foliage evergreen
leaves scale-like, pointed, 2 mm, on flattened twigs; the two lateral scales cover the central ones
flowers unisexual; ♂ flowers apical, oval, 5 mm, yellow and very numerous; ♀ flowers inconspicuous; flowering period January
fruits oval cones of 2 cm, with only two fertile scales, yellowish to

Calocedrus decurrens

brown; when mature the lateral scales spread out perpendicularly to the central ones

---

Key to **THUJA**

Twigs arranged vertically, fan-like; leaves scale-like, identically coloured above and below; ovoid cone with hooked scales: ***Thuja orientalis***

Twigs arranged more or less horizontally, fan-like; ovoid, elongated cone without hooks; leaves scale-like, differently coloured above and below

– scale-leaves yellow-green below: ***Thuja occidentalis***
– scale-leaves with two white bands below: ***Thuja plicata***

This tree originated in California and Oregon, where it grows on the Sierra Nevada up to an altitude of 2000 m, reaching a height of 30 m. In Europe it has been grown since around 1850 as an ornamental species, valued for its columnar habit. It has shown itself to be highly resistant climatically while indifferent to subsoil. In Britain it is fairly common and is noticeable for its columnar habit.

THUJA OCCIDENTALIS L.
White Cedar **
Family *Cupressaceae*

height up to 20 m
crown pyramidal, with rounded apex
trunk erect, thickly branched from base; bark orange-brown, longitudinally ridged
foliage evergreen
leaves scale-like, with conspicuous

gland in centre; colour of scales yellowish-green; twigs arranged horizontally, mostly pendent

flowers unisexual; ♂ flowers small, apical; ♀ flowers 10–20 mm, first yellow, brown when mature; flowering period March–April

fruits ovoid, brown cones, 15 mm

The name of the genus derives from the Greek *thyia* (resin, incense). *T. occidentalis* came originally from North America, from Nova Scotia to North Carolina. It was widely planted in Europe from the mid-19th century as an ornamental; it is adaptable to harsh climates, pollution and to drought. It is indifferent to subsoil.

The wood, pale in colour, very light and durable, can be used in joinery. The leaves contain oils that have medicinal properties.

Thuja orientalis

×1

×1

Thuja occidentalis

Cultivars: 'Aureo-spicata', with yellow striped shoots and, 'Fastigiata', with columnar habit, and 'Rheingold' with bronzy-gold foliage.

THUJA ORIENTALIS L.
Chinese Thuja **
Family *Cupressaceae*

Originally from Manchuria and Korea, this Thuja was imported into

Europe in 1752, being planted as an ornamental species, for hedges and boundaries, because of its tolerance to clipping. It is rugged, adapting to various, but well drained, subsoils, and in Britain is mostly found in urban areas.

The tree has characteristic cones with hooked scales, and in this re-

Thuja plicata

×1

×2

spect differs from other thujas; compared with *T. occidentalis*, its shoots are arranged vertically.

THUJA PLICATA D. Don
Western Red Cedar **
Family *Cupressaceae*

This Thuja grows wild in the western parts of North America, from southern Alaska to California. In its original zones it flourishes in coastal areas up to a height of 1800 m in the Rocky Mountains, where it grows to 60 m tall. In Britain Western Red Cedar is valued both as an ornamental, particularly for hedging, and in forestry.

The wood is of excellent quality, yellow-brown, light and durable.

Key to **SILVER FIRS**

Leaves arranged pectinately or at least parted along shoot
– leaves slightly notched at tip
–– shoots reddish-brown, then greyish; leaves 2 cm, cones 10–15 cm:
Abies alba
–– shoots of year olive-green
––– buds resinous; leaves 2–5 cm; cones up to 10 cm long:
Abies grandis
––– buds not resinous; leaves 2–4 cm; cones 12–18 cm:
Abies nordmanniana
– leaves with blunt tip, more or less glaucous, 3–5 cm, curving upwards;
cones up to 12 cm:
Abies concolor

Leaves radially attached and arranged on branch (brush-like), so as to cover it completely
– leaves glaucous, obtuse at tip, 1–3.5 cm; cones 12–25 cm:
Abies procera
– leaves with more or less pointed tip; cones 10–16 cm
–– leaves with two white bands below, 3 cm long, sharply pointed:
Abies cephalonica
–– leaves with grey-green bands above and below, 1 cm long:
Abies pinsapo

ABIES ALBA L.
(= *A. pectinata* (Lam.) D.C.)
Common Silver Fir **
Family *Pinaceae*

height up to 45 m
crown pyramidal
trunk columnar, straight; bark greyish-white
foliage evergreen
leaves acicular, linear, flattened, 1.5–2 cm, notched at tip, grooved, with two white bands below; radially attached but twisted so that leaves spread either side of shoot
flowers unisexual; ♂ flowers catkins, oval, grouped in large clusters on lower part of branches of previous year; ♀ erect, 8–18 cm, violet, then

Abies alba
Abies cephalonica
Abies nordmanniana

axis or rachis of cone

scale of cone from above and below

×1

Abies alba

green, towards apex of tree; flowering period May–June
fruits cylindrical, erect cones, resinous, 10–20 cm, which flake off, releasing seeds and scales at maturity

The Silver Fir is widely distributed in the mountain zones of southern Europe, growing at an altitude of between 800 and 1800 m, mingled with beech and Norway Spruce and, more rarely, forming woods on its own. It prefers a climate with minimal temperature variations and high humidity, and fresh, deep soil. It likes shade and seldom grows up to the tree-line. In Britain it is naturalized in the west, particularly in parts of Cornwall and west Scotland.

The wood is light, white, without resin and highly resistant; of medium quality, it is used in much the same way as that of the Norway Spruce, mainly in the paper industry, in carpentry and joinery and, among other uses, for the production of rough wooden tiles.

Turpentine, used in medicine and veterinary practice, is obtained from the distillation of the leaves.

ABIES NEBRODENSIS (Lojac.) Mattei
Sicilian Fir
Family *Pinaceae*

This species, very similar to the Silver Fir except for the size of the needles (1–1.3 cm) and the shiny cream-white shoots, is native to the mountains of Sicily. From Roman times to the present day the distribution area of this beautiful tree has become increasingly smaller, for reasons of pasturage, fires and poor seed ger-

Abies alba   *Abies grandis*

Abies concolor

Abies pinsapo

Abies procera

Abies
procera

×⅓

Abies
alba

Abies
nordmanniana

Abies
concolor

Abies
cephalonica

×⅓

×⅓

×⅓

×⅓

mination. Today, to avoid extinction, surviving specimens are protected and new ones transplanted and grown in nurseries. It is rarely seen outside major arboreta.

ABIES NORDMANNIANA Spach
Caucasian Fir **
Family *Pinaceae*

Abies nordmanniana was dedicated to the Finnish botanist A. von Nordmann, who taught at Odessa and discovered it in the Caucasus in 1836.

The species grows wild in the eastern part of the Black Sea basin, from the Crimea to the Caucasus; in the first half of the 19th century it was introduced to central Europe and used as an ornamental tree, because of its graceful outline; branches grow from the base of the trunk, even in the older specimens. On the continent it is also used in sylviculture in zones with a harsh climate where late frosts

may occur, since, unlike the Silver Fir, seasonal regrowth is delayed.

The quality and uses of the wood are the same as for the Silver Fir.

ABIES GRANDIS Lindl.
Grand Fir **
Family *Pinaceae*

This conifer has reached heights of up to 60 m in Britain but is actually native to the western regions of North America, from Alaska to California. Brought to Europe around 1830, it has been used as an ornamental tree and for reafforestation, particularly in northern Europe. Grand Fir is occasionally used as an ornamental in Britain, and to a small extent in forestry.

The soft, light wood is used for carpentry and joinery work, and also for outdoor purposes because it resists atmospheric pollution. It is also used in the paper industry.

ABIES CONCOLOR (Gord.) Hoppes
Colorado White Fir **
Family *Pinaceae*

The specific name *concolor* is derived from the glaucous colour of the needles on both sides. Originating in western North America, the Colorado White Fir was introduced to Europe around the middle of the 19th century. It is now widely distributed throughout the United Kingdom as an ornamental species by reason of its elegant habit and dense blue-grey needles. In its zones of origin it is important for wood production, used for construction work and in the paper industry. In Europe it has only limited value in sylviculture.

ABIES PINSAPO Boiss.
Spanish Fir **
Family *Pinaceae*

height up to 30 m
crown pyramidal, fairly dense
trunk straight, regularly branched; bark dark grey to black
foliage evergreen
leaves acicular, stiff, 10–15 mm, with blunt or pointed (but not sharp) tip; upper and lower surfaces with two grey-green bands; radial, brush-like attachment
flowers unisexual; ♂ flowers oval, red to brown; ♀ flowers borne on apical part of tree; flowering period May–June
fruits long, erect cones up to 15 cm, bracts included

The Spanish Fir, similar in habit to the Silver Fir, comes originally from the southern Sierras of the Iberian peninsula, around Ronda, where it grows wild on calcareous terrain. It has become widely diffused in Britain and Europe as an ornamental park species by reason of its habit and foliage, made up of stiff needles, densely clustered in radial fashion, like little round brushes.
     Variety: *glauca*, with pale grey-green needles.

ABIES PROCERA Rehder
(= *A. nobilis* (Dougl.) Lindl.)
Noble Fir **
Family *Pinaceae*

This American conifer comes from regions extending from Washington to California, where it is an important forest species. Imported into Europe around 1830, it has been used for reafforestation in central-northern areas, though mainly grown as an ornamental. In Britain it reaches its best development as a tree in the north and west, although found in all parts. It produces characteristic cones, up to 25 cm long, heavy and often bent downwards, and not erect as in related species.
     The tree grows quite slowly but produces wood of excellent quality, notable for its lightness and strength. The green branches retain their needles for some time after being cut and are suitable for decorative purposes.

ABIES CEPHALONICA London
Grecian Fir **
Family *Pinaceae*

This fir grows wild in the mountains of Greece and the Ionian Islands, in similar conditions to those of the Silver Fir in its native areas, although it tolerates warmer and drier climates. It forms mixed woods with chestnuts and oaks, but sometimes grows on its own, between 700 and 1700 m on calcareous terrain. Used for reafforestation in south-western Europe, it has yielded good results in arid and calcareous zones as an alternative to the Austrian or Corsican Pine. The wood has uses similar to those of the Silver Fir.

ABIES BALSAMEA Miller
Balsam Fir
Family *Pinaceae*

The specific name of this fir, *balsamea*, is derived from the fact that it is highly aromatic and produces resin. The species grows to 20–25 m, has pointed leaves and small cones (up to 10 cm), flaking off at maturity. It grows wild in North America, from Labrador to Virginia, and has been melted in benzole and xylene for industrial purposes; the wood is used in much the same way as that of the Silver Fir.

Key to **SPRUCES**

Leaves acicular, tetragonal in cross-section
– needle attachment radial, mainly turned upwards
–– needles 0.6–0.8 cm, blunt, shiny: ***Picea orientalis***
–– needles longer, 1 cm, pointed
––– shoots dull, brown; needles uniformly green, stiff and pointed; cones 10–15 cm: ***Picea abies***
––– shoots white, shiny; needles stiff, pointed and soft, 1.2 cm, curving upwards, grey or grey-green; cones 5 cm: ***Picea glauca***
– needle attachment completely radial; needles blue-grey, large, stiff and sharp; cones 6–10 cm: ***Picea pungens***

Leaves acicular, more or less flattened
– needles flexible and blunt (sometimes variously pointed), up to 1.8 cm long, with two white bands below; cones up to 6 cm: ***Picea omorika***
– needles stiff and sharp, slender, up to 3 cm long, dark green above, two blue-grey bands below; cones up to 8 cm long: ***Picea sitchensis***

---

widely used in continental Europe since the end of the 17th century as an ornamental tree. It is rarely seen in Britain, except as a dwarf cultivar.
The resin, called Canada balsam, is

PICEA ABIES (L.) Karsten
(= *P. excelsa* (Lam.) Link)
Norway Spruce **
Family *Pinaceae*

height 30–50 m

Picea abies

♂

♀

detail
of needle
attachment

×1

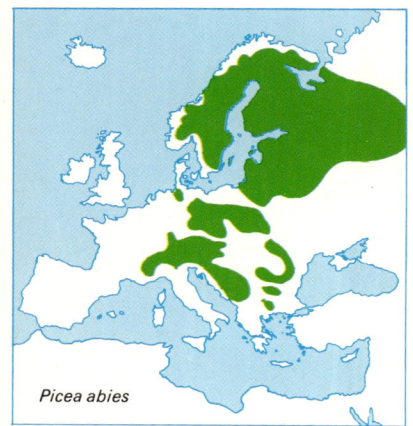

Picea abies

crown pyramidal
trunk straight, columnar, up to 2 m ∅;
bark reddish-brown-greyish, flaking
off in slabs
foliage evergreen
leaves acicular, pointed, usually
tetragonal in cross-section (sometimes appressed on shoots), 1–2.5 cm
long; radial attachment
flowers unisexual; ♂ flowers oval,
1 cm, first crimson, then yellow, at
apex of branch of previous year; ♀
flowers cones, first erect, small and
red, then pendent, green and resinous; they mature the first year in the
autumn; flowering period May–June
fruits brown cones 10–15 cm long
and 3–4 cm ∅, drooping, dropping off
when mature, after dissemination

The name of the genus derives from
the Greek *pix*, resin, which the tree
produces abundantly. The Norway
Spruce originates and grows wild
over a vast area which extends from
the Pyrenees to northern and eastern
Europe; it flourishes in mountainous
and continental environments, forming woods on its own or in conjunc-
tion with beech and Silver Fir at lower
altitudes, and with larch higher up. It
has a preference for deep, not too
dry, acidic soils, and can withstand
low temperatures.
  The Norway Spruce is one of the
most important European forest
trees and is used everywhere for timber production on a mass scale. The
yellowish-white wood is soft and
resinous, and has innumerable applications in carpentry, joinery, packaging and papermaking. The resin is
used industrially in varnishes and
ointments, and for the extraction of
turpentine used in poultices and mas-
sage preparations. Tannin, used for
industrial tanning purposes, is extracted from the bark.
  The wood of the variety *fissilis*, of
particularly high quality, is used for
making musical instruments.
  The Norway Spruce is the common
Christmas tree and is found throughout Britain as an ornamental, and on
a significant forestry scale.

PICEA GLAUCA Voss
(= *P. canadensis* B.S. & P.)
White Spruce
Family *Pinaceae*

This tree grows in North America and
is extremely important for its timber.
It has been grown in Europe since the
beginning of the 18th century and is
widely used for ornament, mainly for
its leaf colour, though it has not

Picea abies   *Picea sitchensis*   *Picea pungens*

Picea omorika

proved especially useful in sylviculture. It is uncommon in the U.K.

The wood is similar to that of the Norway Spruce, with the same uses.

PICEA ORIENTALIS (L.) Link
Oriental Spruce **
Family *Pinaceae*

Picea orientalis has a distribution which covers the regions of the Caucasus and south-western Asia, where it grows to more than 30 m in height. It has been utilized occasionally as a forest species, but more commonly for ornamental purposes in gardens and parks where it is far superior to Norway Spruce, particularly in the cultivar 'Aurea' which has golden green leaves during June.

PICEA PUNGENS Engelm.
Colorado Spruce **
Family *Pinaceae*

The Colorado Spruce grows wild in the Rocky Mountains of North America, from where it was imported into Europe around 1860. It has a wide distribution as an ornamental, chiefly in the variety *glauca*, which is popular because of the coloration of its curved, sharp leaves. A tree with high resistance to climatic rigours, it also adapts well to wet terrain with stagnant water. It produces good-quality timber and is used on a limited scale in Germany as a forest species.

Variety: *glauca*, much more widespread than the species itself.

PICEA OMORIKA (Pančič) Purkyne
Serbian Spruce **
Family *Pinaceae*

This tree grows in a restricted area of Serbia, a republic of Yugoslavia, at heights of between 600 and 1400 m. It forms single-species forests on calcareous soil. It has been brought to central and western Europe both as a forest tree and as an ornamental species by reason of its decorative, distinctively slender, pointed shape.

Picea sitchensis
Picea pungens
×½
×½
×½
×½
Picea abies
Picea omorika

PICEA SITCHENSIS (Bong.) Carr.
Sitka Spruce **
Family *Pinaceae*

Like many other conifers, this is also a North American species, widespread along the north-western coasts, on the borders of Canada and the United States. It is extensively planted in upland Britain and Denmark as a forest tree, accounting for half of new forest planting in Britain. It has but little ornamental appeal.

A tree of rapid growth, it can reach a considerable height, up to 60 m in Britain, increasing by more than a metre a year; it does not tolerate late frosts.

The foliage is blue-green; it is distinguished from other *Picea* species by its slender, very stiff, pointed, flattened needles.

The wood is light, homogeneous and strong, used for oars and in carpentry, and at one time for making aeroplane propellers.

PSEUDOTSUGA MENZIESII (Mirb.) Franco
(= *P. douglasii* Carr.)
Douglas Fir **
Family *Pinaceae*

height up to 60 m
crown pyramidal, slender
trunk straight, columnar; pubescent shoots; bark dark brown with thin cracks, grey-green in young trees
foliage evergreen
leaves acicular, 2–3 cm, soft, sharp to blunt, with two whitish bands below; radial attachment
flowers unisexual; ♂ lower part of shoots of previous year and near apex; colour violet to yellow; ♀ attached laterally, purple to green; flowering period May
fruits tapering cones, 7 × 2.5 cm, drooping when mature, brown; char-

acteristic 3-pointed bracts project about 0.5 cm from between the scales; seeds winged, wing measurement 1 cm

The Douglas Fir occupies a vast area of North America, from British Columbia to California, in mountainous regions, where it may easily grow to 80 m, constituting the principal forest species in western America. Brought to Europe around 1830, after Sitka Spruce it is undoubtedly the most important exotic conifer in European sylviculture, being found in Britain, Holland, Germany and France.

Two varieties of the species are *glauca* and *menziesii*; the former, however, is extremely susceptible to the attacks of the parasitical fungus *Rhabdocline pseudotsugae*, which limits its use in sylviculture; the latter withstands parasites well and nowadays is the only variety used for such purposes.

The Douglas Fir has shown itself capable of rapid growth and of producing large quantities of timber, in Europe as well as North America, adapting to virtually any terrain, provided it is not too firm; best results are nevertheless obtained in optimal conditions, on fresh, fertile, deep soil. It is associated with an oceanic climate and is very susceptible to late frosts.

The timber produced in Europe, less valued than in America, is mainly used in the paper industry.

Variety: *pendula*, with long, drooping twigs, ornamental.

ovuliferous scale
with 2 winged seeds

×1

Pseudotsuga menziesii

Key to **HEMLOCKS**

Cones 1.5–2 cm, short stalks; needles of 1–1.5 cm, more or less all of same length: **Tsuga canadensis**

Cones 2–2.5 cm, sessile; needles of two sizes, the smaller 0.6 cm, in double rows above twig, the larger beneath the former, up to 2 cm long, spreading either side of shoot: **Tsuga heterophylla**

Tsuga canadensis

♂

detail
of needle
attachment

×1

×2

TSUGA CANADENSIS (L.) Carr.
Eastern Hemlock **
Family *Pinaceae*

height up to 30 m
crown irregularly pyramidal
trunk erect, linear, often bifurcate;
bark grey-brown with large, but shallow, smooth grooves; hairy, pendent twigs
foliage evergreen
leaves acicular, linear, lanceolate, 1–1.5 cm, with prominent stalk and blunt tip, undersurface with two whitish bands; secondary attachment spreading, with one line of leaves above, flat along the twig
flowers unisexual; ♂ flowers globose, 3 mm ∅, yellowish, attached along branches; ♀ flowers ovoid, 6 mm, light green, attached terminally; flowering period May
fruits pendent cones, oval, up to 2 cm, short-stalked, dark brown

The genus *Tsuga* comprises 10 species distributed throughout the Far East and North America. Also known as the Canadian Hemlock, it is original to North America. In Europe it has been used exclusively for ornamental purposes since the mid-18th century

but is less often planted in Britain than Western Hemlock due to its slow growth; it holds no interest for sylviculture.

The timber is used in America by the paper industry and in joinery because it can be easily varnished or dyed and polished; the bark, too, contains plenty of tannin, used in the leather industry.

TSUGA HETEROPHYLLA (Raf.) Sarg.
Western Hemlock **
Family *Pinaceae*

This hemlock, too, is a North American species, growing along the west coast and reaching a height of 60 m. In Britain it has small forestry use but is also planted as an ornamental tree, because of its very graceful outline, in parks and gardens. In its original regions it is an important timber-

Tsuga heterophylla

♂

×1

detail
of needle
attachment

×2

producing species, forming luxuriant forests, thanks to high rainfall and a mild climate, with other conifers such as *Picea sitchensis*, *Thuja plicata* and *Abies grandis*.

Key to **PINES**

Leaves in bundles or fascicles of 2 on short shoot
– needles 3–5 cm long
– – needles often more than 1 mm thick, stiff
– – – cones pedunculate: ***Pinus sylvestris***
– – – cones sessile: ***Pinus uncinata***
– – needles often less than 1 mm thick, supple; crown umbrella-like and
trunk sinuous, more or less inclined: ***Pinus halepensis***
– needles 6–18 cm long
– – tree with pyramidal crown
– – – shoots rough and almost spinous due to leaf scars, orange-red;
needles 6–18 cm; conical cones light brown, smooth, almost sessile,
with unhooked scales: ***Pinus nigra***
– – – shoots smooth, light grey for first 3 years; needles 7 (9) cm; cone
blue-black, then brown, 7 cm, with scales hooked towards base:
                                                        Pinus leucodermis
– – tree with umbrella-like crown and vertical trunk
– – – cones oblong, 10–20 cm; seeds winged: ***Pinus pinaster***
– – – cones ovoid, about 12 × 10 cm; seeds not winged, edible:
                                                            Pinus pinea

Leaves in bundles or fascicles of 3–5 on short shoots
– needles in bundles of 5
– – needles 7–8 cm; cone oval, violet, then reddish-brown, 8 × 6 cm;
seeds edible: ***Pinus cembra***
– – needles longer; cones elongated and curved, 10–30 cm
– – – cones 10–15 cm
– – – – needles 8–10 cm; tip of cone scales curving inwards: ***Pinus peuce***
– – – – needles 5–15 cm, tip of cone scales curving outwards:
                                                          Pinus strobus
– – – cones 20–30 cm; needles 18–20 cm, supple, drooping:
                                                       Pinus wallichiana
– needles in bundles of 3
– – needles 10–15 cm, soft and supple; cones oval, 12 cm: ***Pinus radiata***
– – needles long, 15–23 cm; cones 9 cm: ***Pinus ponderosa***

PINUS SYLVESTRIS L.
Scots Pine **
Family *Pinaceae*

height 20–40 m
crown pyramidal, elongated, sparse
trunk erect, sinuous, with branches curving upwards; bark rusty, in scaly plates, deeply fissured, brick red towards top
foliage evergreen
leaves acicular, in bundles of 2, 3–5 (7) cm, curved, twisted, blue-green
flowers unisexual; ♂ flowers in axillary, oval, yellow or pink catkins, clustered in large numbers at base of new shoots; ♀ flowers at apex of new shoots, pink or purple, 0.5 cm; flowering period April–June
fruits cones which mature in second year, green and oval, 3–7 cm, when immature, brown and woody at maturity, with blunt projections (umbos) sprouting from scales; seeds winged, wing measurement 1.5–2 cm

Pinus sylvestris

♂

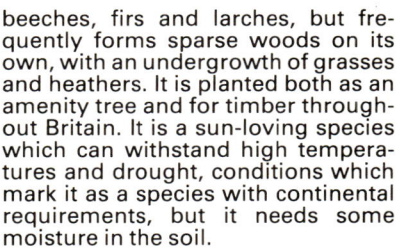

Scots Pine covers a vast area from the northern Apennines to northern Europe and eastwards to north-east Asia. There are isolated nuclei in Scotland, the Iberian peninsula, central France, the Balkans and Asia Minor. In the more northerly regions the tree is found on the plains, farther south it grows in mountainous zones, from 500 to 1800 m, sometimes reaching the tree-line. It mingles with beeches, firs and larches, but frequently forms sparse woods on its own, with an undergrowth of grasses and heathers. It is planted both as an amenity tree and for timber throughout Britain. It is a sun-loving species which can withstand high temperatures and drought, conditions which mark it as a species with continental requirements, but it needs some moisture in the soil.

This frugal tree will root in almost any subsoil, even on gravel or peat. It grows rapidly and may even reach a height of 40 m. Height, habit and characteristics of wood depend on the zone and on the climatic conditions under which the tree grows.

The wood of the Scots Pine, from the northerly or mountainous zones of Europe, is of good quality and much in demand. The sapwood is whitish, the heartwood deep red; it is strong and easy to work. It has numerous uses, for carpentry, joinery and in the paper industry.

The buds are used in medicine for their balsamic properties and turpentine is extracted from the resin; at one time the needles were soaked, the fibres removed, and used as vegetable horse-hair for padding.

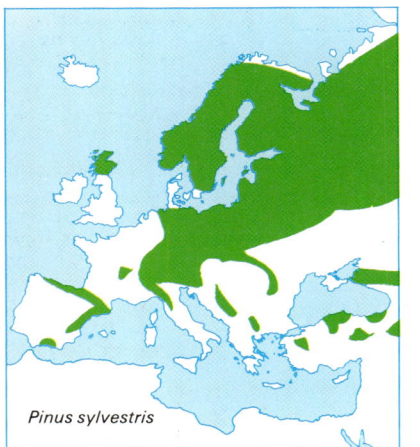

Pinus sylvestris

PINUS UNCINATA Mill. ex Mirb.
(= *Pinus mugo* var. *rostrata* Hoopes)
Mountain Pine
Family *Pinaceae*

height 15–20 m
crown pyramidal, narrow
trunk straight, with ascending basal
branches; bark reddish-grey
foliage evergreen
leaves acicular in bundles of 2, 6 cm,
stiff and spiralled
flowers similar to *P. sylvestris*
fruits asymmetrical cones, 6 cm, with
hooked pyramidal scales curving towards apex; seeds with wings of 1 cm

a *Pinus uncinata*

b *Pinus mugo* var. *rostrata*

The Mountain Pine constitutes part of
the *Pinus mugo* group, but unlike the
latter, which has a prostrate, shrubby
habit, develops like a tree with an
undivided trunk, growing to as much
as 20 m in height. It ranges from the
Pyrenees to the Central Alps, where it
flourishes for preference on cal-
careous-dolomitic terrain; in the mar-
ginal zones of its range it exhibits
forms that link it to related species,
Pinus mugo and *Pinus pumilio*. At
altitude it grows at between 1200 and
2500 m, forming extensive forests, as
in the Swiss National Park. It is rare in
Britain.
    The wood is valuable, heavy and

has many applications. It is used, like
other forms of *P. mugo*, for the extraction of an oil, used for its balsamic
properties in treating diseases of the
respiratory tract.

PINUS HALEPENSIS Miller
Aleppo Pine
Family *Pinaceae*

height 15–20 m
crown broadly pyramidal
trunk twisted and often inclined,
branchy; bark grey to reddish-brown,
deeply fissured
foliage evergreen
leaves acicular, in pairs, 6–15 cm,
linear, width often under 1 mm, light
green
flowers see *P. sylvestris*
fruits cones either single or in pairs,
ovate-conical, 5–10 cm, on peduncle
of 1–2 cm, with non-projecting
umbo; seeds winged, 1.5–2 cm

This pine, widely distributed by man
beyond its original area, now grows
in the zones around the Mediterranean, from the Iberian peninsula to
North Africa and Asia Minor. In Britain it is rarely seen outside collections. It is an undemanding species,
tolerating drought, high temperatures and bright sunlight, all characteristic of the Mediterranean climate.
It grows along the coasts, reaching
altitudes up to 600 m in Europe and
up to 2000 m in North Africa (Algeria).
    The Aleppo Pine is adapted to va-
rious types of terrain, calcareous or
very poor, where it behaves like a
pioneer species thanks to its frugal-
ity, growing rapidly and fruiting
early, the latter occurring after eight

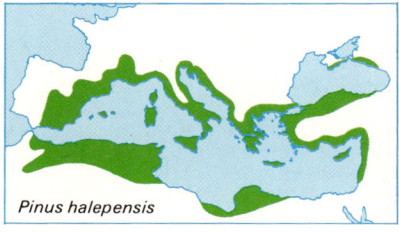

Pinus halepensis

Pinus halepensis

In medicine it is used for inhalations, for fumigation and as an antidote to phosphorus poisoning. Colophony is a solid residue left over after the distillation of the raw turpentine; it has various industrial applications for preparing varnishes, glues, adhesives, sealing-wax, candles, etc., and for the preparation of plasters and poultices. The removal of the resin causes the tree to contract, and this affects both the wood and the fruit.

The bark is used for the extraction of tannin as a dyestuff for rigging and fishing nets.

PINUS BRUTIA Tenore
(= *P. parolinii* Vis.)
Calabrian Pine
Family *Pinaceae*

The species bears a strong similarity to the Aleppo Pine, both in appearance and size; the Calabrian Pine originates in the eastern Mediterranean basin, from the regions of Syria and Anatolia to Greece. The specific name derives from *Brutium*, the Latin name for Calabria, where, although present at the beginning of the 19th century, it does not appear to be wild but introduced in ancient times. It is very rare in Britain.

It is a sun-loving tree, rugged and frugal, fairly resistant to cold, drought and wind, suitable for the reafforestation of rocky, barren soil of almost any kind.

PINUS LEUCODERMIS Antoine
Bosnian Pine
Family *Pinaceae*

The specific name of this pine is derived from the greyish-white colour of the bark of the twigs. Its range includes the Balkans and southern Italy, growing in mountain zones at altitudes of between 800 and 1600 m, sometimes higher. The Bosnian Pine is undemanding but prefers calcareous soil and dry, rocky areas. It is suitable for reafforestation projects

years. It prevents soil erosion by surface water and wind, at the same time improving the terrain by giving it organic sustenance.

The wood, of mediocre quality, with whitish sapwood and brown heartwood, has limited uses, for packaging, as fuel and in the paper industry.

Like many other pines, it is valued for its resin, and is one of the major producers, both in quantity and quality. The resin is extracted by cutting into the trunk when it has attained a diameter of at least 25 cm, and placing a receptacle at the base of the incision for collecting the exuded material. The resin or turpentine, variable in colour, is at first clear, but becomes clouded when exposed to the air. It is used directly to produce varnishes or ointments for medicinal purposes. The turpentine is then distilled to obtain oil of turpentine and rosin (or colophony). The former is a clear, colourless liquid, with an agreeable smell, used in industry as a solvent for varnishes, as colouring for oils, resins and rubber, and for the preparation of synthetic camphor for removing stains.

Pinus leucodermis

around the Mediterranean, but because it is found in zones quite widely

upright habit at lower levels, ramified from the base, and often prostrate or shrubby at higher ones. The young cones are very attractive in July, when they are a rich cobalt blue.

It is found in major collections throughout Britain and deserves wider planting.

PINUS NIGRA Arnold
(= *P. austriaca* Host)
Austrian or Corsican Pine **
Family *Pinaceae*

height 20–40 m
crown pyramidal, dense
trunk erect, sometimes sinuous, with horizontal branches; bark grey-black with deep fissures
foliage evergreen
leaves acicular, in pairs, linear, 8–16 cm, pointed and sharp, dark green
flowers see *P. sylvestris*
fruits oval cones 6 × 4 cm, with scales barely projecting; the cones may be single or in clusters of 2–4 and are sessile; seeds with wings of 2–2.5 cm.

The distribution area of this pine lies

at altitude as a preparatory species for other trees; it is robust, with an separated from one another, it exhibits a number of varieties which are sometimes regarded as subspecies and sometimes as actual species, with intermediate forms that are not easy to classify. These geographical races have differing biological characteristics, such as a varying growth rate, and ecological features, such as the tendency to associate with one another and with other species, and a preference for one type of subsoil rather than another. There is also some morphological diversity, mainly with regard to height, habit and consistency and colour of leaves.

The subspecies *nigra*, the so-called Austrian Pine, is found in Austria, north-eastern and central Italy, Yugoslavia and Greece. It is a rugged tree, adaptable to poor or calcareous, shallow soil, suitable for planting either as a colonizing species or as preparation for other less adaptable trees. It can withstand dryness in the subsoil but needs a fair amount of rain in the summer.

A sun-loving pine, it tolerates continental climate, requiring hot summers. It grows at between 500 m (or

Pinus nigra

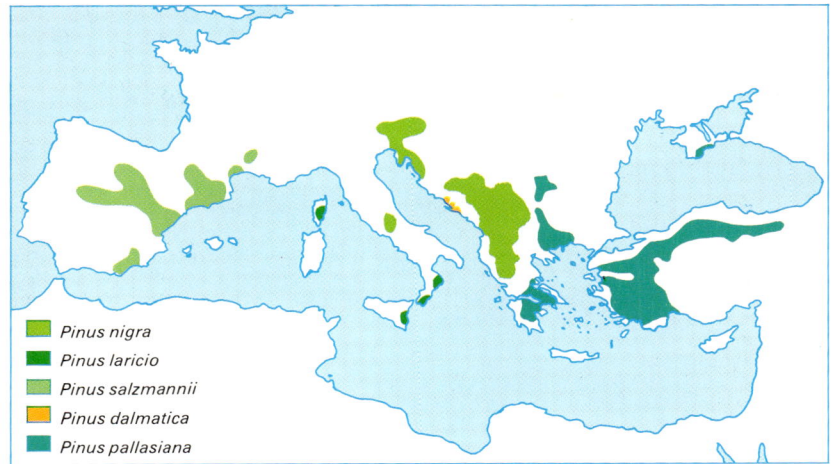

Pinus nigra
Pinus laricio
Pinus salzmannii
Pinus dalmatica
Pinus pallasiana

less) and 1550 m, either on its own or mixed with oaks, chestnuts and beeches. The wood, not greatly valued, is used in similar ways to Scots Pine.

In southern Europe it is even more susceptible than Scots Pine and other Mediterranean pines to heavy attack by the larvae of a moth, *Thaumetopoea pityocampa*, known as the processionary caterpillar, which causes decay and sometimes large-scale leaf loss. The round, white nests of these caterpillars are clearly visible. Made of silky threads, they are woven in the treetop by the larvae, which spend the day in them. Furnished with stinging hairs, the larvae venture from the nests on to the twigs to consume the leaves; when mature they descend to the ground in long processions in order to pupate. The adults, nocturnal by habit, are not very conspicuous; the females lay their eggs around the leaves and are short-lived.

Where the pines grow wild, biological control by means of numerous natural hyper-parasites keeps such attacks at bay; the situation is different in the case of artificial plantings, where the fight against this moth is particularly difficult.

Geographical subspecies of PINUS NIGRA

ssp. *nigra*: Austrian Pine (see under description of *Pinus nigra*). Found in Austria, north-eastern and central Italy, Yugoslavia and Greece.

ssp. *laricio* (Poir.) Maire (*P. nigra* var. *maritima* (Ait.) Melville): Corsican Pine. Height up to 35 m; principal axis of trunk straight up to top; leaves grey-green, often twisted, 12–18 cm. Found on mountains in Calabria, Sicily (Etna) and Corsica. In Britain Corsican Pine is a major forestry tree particularly in East Anglia and the south.

ssp. *salzmannii* (Dunal) Franco: Pyrenean Pine. Height up to 20 m; leaves blunt, 8–16 cm. Found in France (Cevennes), the Pyrenees and central-western Spain.

ssp. *dalmatica* (Vis.) Franco: Dalmatian Pine. Height 10–20 m; leaves short, straight and pointed, 4–5 cm. Found in coastal regions and on islands off Yugoslavia.

ssp. *pallasiana* (Lamb.) Holmboe: Crimean Pine. Height up to 40 m;

trunk divided about one-third of way up into 5–8 vertical branches; hard, fairly stiff leaves, 12–18 cm. Found in the Balkans, southern Carpathia, Crimea and Asia Minor.

PINUS PINASTER Aiton
(= *P. maritime* Miller)
Maritime Pine **
Family *Pinaceae*

height 5–30 m
crown oval, spreading, umbrella-like
trunk erect, with branches ascending from base almost to the top; bark rusty, deeply fissured
foliage evergreen
leaves acicular, in pairs, linear, 10–12 cm, stiff and sharp
flowers see *P. sylvestris*
fruits cones obovate-conical, often asymmetrical, 10–20 cm, light brown, shiny; keeled scales with prominent mucronate protuberance (umbo); cones in groups of 2–4; seeds with wings of 3 cm

The Maritime Pine has a range extending over the western Mediterranean basin, where it grows wild and is used along the coasts for ornamental purposes. Principally

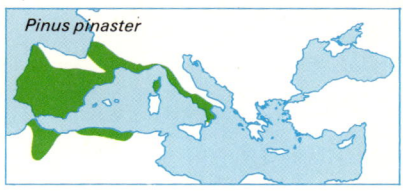

Pinus pinaster

grown in southern England it can be found as an occasional tree as far north as Edinburgh. It is associated with an oceanic climate and is particular as to humidity and light. It prefers acidic subsoils but is markedly adaptable and grows on very poor soil, including sand and moorland; it withstands sea winds and is used for fixing mobile terrain. It grows on heights facing the sea up to an altitude of 1500 m.

This pine is one of the best producers of resin; its wood is hard, heavy and strong, with uses similar to that of the Stone Pine.

PINUS PINEA L.
Stone Pine
Family *Pinaceae*

height 25–30 m

Pinus pinaster

Pinus pinea

×⅓   ×⅓

scale   seed

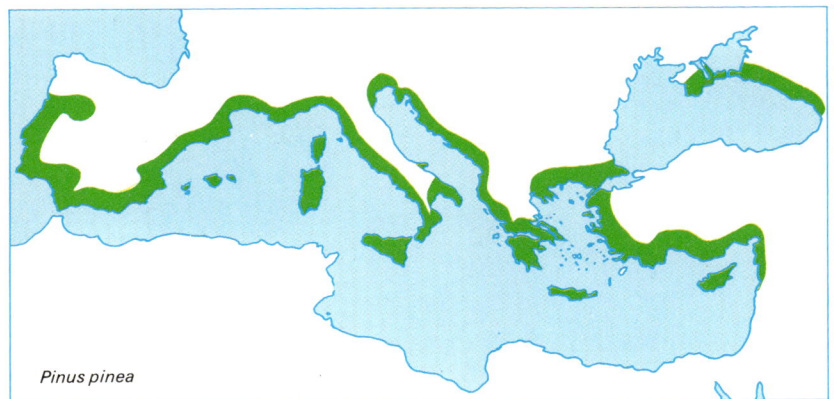

Pinus pinea

crown umbrella-like
trunk erect, branched only in upper third; bark furrowed, with grey-green plates
foliage evergreen
leaves acicular, in pairs, 10–12 cm, pointed but not sharp
flowers see *P. sylvestris*
fruits oval, subspherical cones, up to 14 × 12 cm, the scales having a pyramidal projection; cones single or in pairs; seeds enclosed in a black shell, wingless

The original home of the Stone Pine is uncertain; it probably comes from the eastern Mediterranean regions, from Asia Minor to Crete, and was subsequently introduced to the entire northern Mediterranean zone. Today it forms large forests in Italy, Spain and Anatolia, where it is cultivated for its edible seeds. Occasionally seen as an amenity tree in England, seeds were first introduced as a delicacy by the Romans.

The Stone Pine is a typically Mediterranean species, sun-loving and heat-demanding. It can tolerate some aridity and is adaptable to very diverse types of terrain, preferring loose, fresh, sandy soil, thrusting its highly developed root system deep underground. It grows along coasts and, where conditions permit, up to altitudes of 500–1000 m, mingling with other species such as Maritime Pine, Aleppo Pine, Cypress, English Oak and Holm Oak.

The large cones, which mature in three years, opening at the start of the fourth, contain two large seeds in the axil of each scale, covered with blackish dust; inside the woody shell is the ivory-white kernel, rich in oily substances. The mature cones, collected in the winter, are heaped up in the open or in stores, until the summer. The cones open by exposure to the sun, liberating the seeds, which are packed and sold either with or without their shells. These seeds are used for confectionery and in the pharmaceutical trade for oil extraction.

The wood, not of great value, is used for joinery, rafters, etc. The bark furnishes tannins and dyes; the tree also produces good-quality resin, which is extracted.

PINUS CEMBRA L.
Arolla Pine
Family *Pinaceae*

height up to 20 (25) m
crown ovate, rounded at top, dense
trunk robust, stout and often twisted at top in old specimens; branches twisted and curved upwards; bark grey-brown
foliage evergreen

×1

Pinus cembra

leaves acicular, in bundles of 5 (4–6), 7–8 cm, dark green
flowers see *P. sylvestris*
fruits oval cones with not very woody scales, dark blue to reddish-brown, 8 × 6 cm; wingless seeds, usually remaining inside cone

The Arolla Pine grows wild in Europe, in the Alps and the Carpathians; it is found in the central-western sector of the Alps, but not in the east. It makes an attractive small ornamental in Britain but is not common.

A long-lived tree, it may live to 500 years. Adaptable to a continental climate, it grows in the high mountains between 1600 and 2400 m, withstanding strong winds and harsh temperatures. In order to develop it requires average temperatures of 8°–10°C (46°–50°F) for only three months a year. Although it prefers fresh, deep soil for optimal growth, it does well, too, in stony ground, provided it is sufficiently wet, thanks to its sturdy, deep root system.

The tree forms unmixed forests at high altitudes, though sparsely grouped, as in alpine pastures; lower down it mingles with larch and Norway Spruce. Isolated specimens are oval in shape, well balanced and branched from the base.

The present area of diffusion in the Alps is more restricted than formerly and the trend continues because of such factors as overgrazing and indiscriminate felling.

The pine cones produce edible seeds which occur abundantly every 4–8 years.

The timber is highly valued and much sought after, having white sapwood and pale brown heartwood, with dark knots. It is not attacked by woodworm and does not splinter. The wood gives out a characteristic aroma of balsam which lasts some time. Very soft and light, with knots that do not become detached, it is particularly useful for carving.

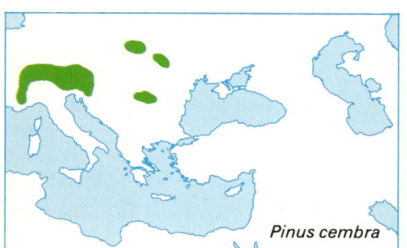

Pinus cembra

PINUS PEUCE Griseb.
Macedonian Pine
Family *Pinaceae*

This handsome tree grows wild in a restricted area between southern Yugoslavia, Albania and Bulgaria, where it was discovered in the mid-19th century. It is occasionally seen in Britain and makes an interesting ornamental species, which when mature reaches a height of 20–25 m, with a bright, pale green crown. It looks much like the Weymouth Pine, but grows more slowly.

PINUS STROBUS L.
Weymouth Pine **
Family *Pinaceae*

The Weymouth Pine originated in North America, and is found there in the areas between south-eastern Canada and north-eastern United States; it was introduced to Europe at the beginning of the 18th century as a fast-growing species, especially in central Europe, where it has become naturalized and is now wild. It is found throughout Britain.

As regards site, it is undemanding

Pinus strobus

and quite frugal, adapting to very poor soil, particularly moraine, peat and heathland, but it reacts adversely to extreme dryness. It has proved highly susceptible to attack by blister-rust (*Cronartium ribicola*) which has conditioned its forest use since the end of the 19th century.

The Weymouth Pine has yellowish-white wood, very soft and light, which after seasoning neither contracts nor becomes deformed; it is used mainly for fixtures, flooring, matches and in the paper industry.

PINUS WALLICHIANA Jackson
(= *P. excelsa* Wallich) (= *P. griffithii* McClelland)
Blue Pine **
Family *Pinaceae*

This five-leaved pine originated in the Himalayan region and grows wild in Afghanistan, northern India, Nepal and Bhutan. It was introduced to Europe around the middle of the 19th century, finding wide use as an ornamental species in parks and gardens by reason of its elegant shape, its blue-green colour and distinctive leaves, flexible and pendent, and much longer than those of other soft (five-needled) pines; the cones, similar to those of the Weymouth Pine, may be up to 30 cm long. It is additionally used in sylviculture as a swift-growing species, reaching as much as 30 m in height. It is the commonest five-needled pine in cultivation in Britain.

PINUS RADIATA D. Don
(= *P. insignis* Dougl.)
Monterey Pine **
Family *Pinaceae*

The Monterey Pine comes originally from California, from a restricted area round Monterey Bay. It was introduced to Europe about 1830 as a forest species with very rapid growth. Today it is most abundant in England, Ireland, France, Spain and, above all,

Pinus radiata

Pinus ponderosa

Portugal, where it is perfectly acclimatized, growing wild, thanks to the mild climate and generally favourable conditions.

The leaves are in groups of 3, usually not more than 14 cm long, flexible, pale green; the cones are asymmetrical, the scales have a hemispherical umbo and a deciduous tooth. The tree prefers warm surroundings with dry conditions in summer and high atmospheric humidity.

It is associated with alluvial, loose, permeable soil. In favourable conditions it effectively resists parasites. The wood is low in resin, and thus widely used in the paper industry.

PINUS PONDEROSA Dougl.
Western Yellow Pine
Family *Pinaceae*

Pinus ponderosa comes originally from the western parts of North America, where it is widespread; towards the middle of the 19th century it was brought to Europe as a forest species, but is more commonly used as an ornamental because of its dense crown and elegant lines. Occasionally planted throughout Britain.

The tree may grow to a height of 40 m, with a regular crown that is almost pyramidal, stiff leaves of about 20 cm and oval cones of 20 cm, which drop off, leaving the base attached to the branch.

LARIX DECIDUA Miller
European Larch **
Family *Pinaceae*

height up to 40 m
crown slender, pyramidal
trunk straight, with curving horizontal branches; shoots yellowish; bark yellow-brown to grey, with deeply fissured plates

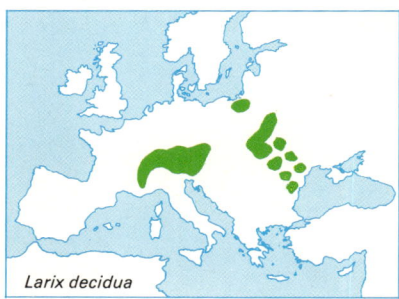

Larix decidua

Key to **LARCHES**

Not more than 40 leaves per short shoot; shoots of the year with yellowish bark; oval cones, 5 × 3 cm: ***Larix decidua***

More than 40 leaves per short shoot; shoots of the year with purple-red bark; spherical cones, 3 × 3 cm, with curving scales: ***Larix kaempferi***

foliage deciduous
leaves acicular, 2–3 cm, in clusters of 20–40 on short shoots of 2-year+ branches, solitary on current year shoots; autumnal colour golden-yellow
flowers unisexual; ♂ flowers oval, on lower part of branches; ♀ flowers at tip of short shoots, surrounded by leaves, purple then green; flowering period April–May
fruits cones oval, not woody, brown, 3 × 5 cm, persisting on branch until seeds are completely disseminated, then falling; seeds winged, wing 1 cm

Planted throughout Europe and very common in Britain as a native tree, Larch grows at altitudes of between 800 and 2500 m, but these extremes may vary according to climatic condi-tions in the zones concerned. It is a sun-loving species which forms pure, sparse woods with a luxuriant grassy undergrowth; but it is more frequent-ly found in association with beech, Norway Spruce, Scots Pine, Moun-tain Pine and Arolla Pine, depending on locality. It adapts to virtually any terrain, provided it is well drained, even colonizing stubble and waste-land. It can grow at high altitudes, withstanding frosts and high winds, preferring zones with a markedly continental climate.

The wood of the Larch is of excel-lent quality, much valued, deep red in colour; strong and aromatic, it is used for joinery, barrels, trellises, fastenings and as fuel. In water it be-comes highly waterproof and is used for piles.

Larix decidua

The resin, called Venetian turpentine, is used industrially for varnishes and to treat chills, thanks to its balsamic properties. The bark is used for the extraction of tannin and for carvings.

European Larch is very decorative in spring and autumn, being frequently used as an ornamental in mountainous surroundings.

Varieties: *pendula*, with pendent branches; *fastigiata*, with a neat conical shape.

Larix kaempferi

LARIX KAEMPFERI (Lamb.) Carrière
(= *L. leptolepis* (Siebold & Zucc.) Endl.)
Japanese Larch
Family *Pinaceae*

This species, originally from central Japan, was brought to Europe around the middle of the 19th century and is widely used as an ornamental, prized for its decorative appearance and timber, giving good results, particularly in Britain.

Compared with its European counterpart, the Japanese Larch shows certain striking differences in habit, such as very rapid growth and a lesser preference for light; it needs high humidity, indicating that it is oceanic by inclination. It is indifferent to subsoil and can tolerate urban pollution.

It produces timber in abundance, very rapidly, but the quality is inferior to that of the European Larch.

Key to **CEDARS**

Leaves up to 5 cm long; cones of 8–12 cm with rounded tips; crown pyramidal with trunk often bifurcate in adult specimens; apex pendulous: **Cedrus deodara**

Leaves up to 3 cm long; cones with flattened tip, hollowed
– cones of 8 cm; crown pyramidal with upright apex and stiff branches turned upwards: **Cedrus atlantica**
– cones of 8–12 cm; crown umbrella-like in mature specimens, flat and with horizontal branches with upright tip: **Cedrus libani**

CEDRUS ATLANTICA (Endl.) Carr.
Atlas Cedar **
Family *Pinaceae*

height up to 40 m
crown broad, pyramidal

trunk branched from base, with ascendent branches; apex upright; bark grey-black, grooved
foliage evergreen
leaves acicular, 2 cm, in bundles of more than 40 per short shoot, dark

green or, in *glauca* variety, blue-green

flowers unisexual; ♂ flowers with upright or curved spikes, 4–5 cm, yellowish; ♀ flowers cylindrical, green, 1 cm

fruits cones erect, ovoid, brown and resinous, 8 × 5 cm, truncate and hollow at tip, breaking up at maturity; seeds with broad wing of 2 cm

This majestic tree grows wild in the mountainous regions of North Africa, from Morocco to Algeria, between 1200 and 2500 m. In Britain and Europe it has been widely used since the 19th century as an ornamental species and, on a smaller scale, for

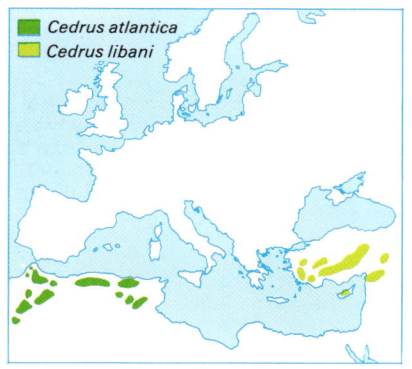

■ *Cedrus atlantica*
■ *Cedrus libani*

Cedrus atlantica

timber. The Atlas Cedar flourishes on a range of soil types, preferring siliceous soil. A sun-loving species, it needs a little humidity and cannot stand prolonged frosts.

The brown wood is highly scented and tough, resistant to atmospheric pollution.

Variety: *glauca*, much used as an ornamental for the grey-green colour of the leaves.

seed

×1

Cedrus deodara

CEDRUS DEODARA G. Don
Deodar or Himalayan Cedar**
Family *Pinaceae*

The widest-ranging ornamental cedar, it was introduced early in the 19th century from its native region, bounded by western Nepal, Baluchistan and Afghanistan. Its local name means tree of the gods. In this area it grows at 1000 to 2800 m in altitude; it needs a little atmospheric humidity, but is indifferent to the nature of the soil, provided it is fresh and deep. The wood is less valued than that of the Atlas Cedar. Like Atlas Cedar it is found in Britain as an ornamental in both town and country.

CEDRUS LIBANI Richard
Cedar of Lebanon **
Family *Pinaceae*

This cedar came originally from the mountainous areas of Asia Minor, in particular the Lebanon and Taurus ranges in Turkey. It has been known in Europe since the 17th century but is less appreciated than other cedars as an ornamental tree, because of its slow growth and less graceful appearance. The wood has been prized since antiquity for its excellent quality. In its countries of origin the tree now covers a much more limited area than was once the case and is therefore protected. In Britain this tree has recently been planted less often than the other two cedars, but the majestic cedar trees at many stately homes are of this type.

SEQUOIA SEMPERVIRENS (Lamb.) Endl.
Coast Redwood **
Family *Taxodiaceae*

height in Europe 40 m
crown narrowly pyramidal
trunk straight, columnar; bark reddish, furrowed
foliage evergreen
leaves acicular, flat and linear, 1.5–2 cm, pointed but not sharp, two

Sequoia sempervirens

white bands below; pectinate on lateral shoots, radial on main shoots
flowers unisexual; ♂ flowers ovate, 2 mm long, terminal and on lateral shoots, yellowish; ♀ flowers terminal, green
fruits ovoid cones of 2 cm, woody, formed of 12–20 scales; persistent

The generic name is derived from 'Sequoiah', the name of a Cherokee Indian chief. The original range of this conifer extends for some 1000 kilometres along the Pacific coast of North America. It grows on mountain slopes at altitudes of up to 1700 m and in natural woods exceeds 100 m in height, being the tallest living tree at 112 m. Together with other conifers and many broadleaved species, the Coast Redwood forms imposing and unusual mixed woodlands.

Brought to Europe in the 19th century, it has been much appreciated as an ornamental species, being planted in areas with a maritime climate and thriving in Britain. It prefers deep, fertile soil, and is fairly demanding.

The wood, as its name suggests, is red, and can be put to numerous uses, mainly in constructional work and joinery since it is tough and easy to work.

Sequoiadendron giganteum

×½

SEQUOIADENDRON GIGANTEUM
(Lindley) Bucholz
(= *Sequoia gigantea* (Lindl.) Decne.)
Wellingtonia **
Family *Taxodiaceae*

height up to 40 m in Europe
crown narrowly pyramidal
trunk very broad at base, then straight and tapering; bark very thick, spongy, light reddish-brown
foliage evergreen
leaves acicular, 5–7 m, with a stiff, divergent tip; spiral attachment, in three series
flowers unisexual; ♂ flowers small and numerous on edges of shoots; ♀ flowers oval, 2 cm, on main branches; flowering period April
fruits oval cones of 5 × 8 cm, pendent, green to brown, maturing in second year

The original distribution area of this gigantic tree extends over the eastern slopes of the Sierra Nevada in California, at altitudes between 1500 and 2400 m. The biggest specimens there are over 90 m tall, with a diameter of more than 9 m. This redwood, in fact, has the largest diameter of all conifers (among broadleaved trees the record is held by the baobab). This is partly due to the extreme longevity of the tree – apparently more than 2000 years. In Europe it was introduced as an ornamental in 1854 and many specimens are already 50 m tall. It is remarkably rugged and adapts to almost any subsoil, being resistant to cold. It is found throughout Britain. The reddish wood is easy to work but brittle, and makes good fuel.

CRYPTOMERIA JAPONICA (L.f.) Don
Japanese Cedar **
Family *Taxodiaceae*

height 40 m
crown narrowly pyramidal, rounded apex, sparse
trunk broad at base, then straight, knotted; bark reddish-brown to orange, flaking in long strips
foliage evergreen
leaves acicular, up to 1.5 cm long, pointed and curved inwards; spiral arrangement
flowers unisexual; ♂ flowers oval, 3 mm, along apical shoots; ♀ flowers spherical and terminal, green; flowering period March
fruits round cones, 2 cm ∅, on upward turned shoots, with 5–6 spiny extensions on each scale, green to brown

Cryptomeria japonica

This conifer grows wild in Japan, where it is used for timber, known under the name of *sugi*. Present in Europe since the middle of the 19th century, it has acquired considerable importance as an ornamental tree and is found throughout Britain. Fairly rugged, it prefers a temperate, humid climate and fertile, deep soil.

The light, durable wood is not much used outside Japan.
Cultivars: 'Compacta', with dense branches; 'Elegans', usually columnar in appearance, with reddish-brown bark and juvenile foliage.

TAXODIUM DISTICHUM (L.) Rich.
Swamp Cypress **
Family *Taxodiaceae*

height 30 m
crown pyramidal to rounded apex, loose
trunk straight to top; in swampy zones it produces pneumatophores (aerial roots) near base, emerging from the ground; secondary branches, complete with autumn leaves, deciduous; bark reddish-brown, fibrous
foliage deciduous
leaves acicular, flat, linear, 10 mm, pointed; arrangement alternate on main branches, pectinate on side shoots; autumnal colour red to brown
flowers unisexual; ♂ flowers catkins of 8 cm, in groups of 3–4 at tip of branches; ♀ flowers in small catkins

Taxodium distichum

of 0.2 cm at base of ♂, green; flowering period March–April
fruits spherical cones, up to 3 cm ⌀, with a few spiny bracts, green to reddish-brown

The generic name *Taxodium* refers to its resemblance, in appearance, to a Yew. The Swamp Cypress is one of the few conifers with deciduous foliage, and it comes from the swampy zones of the south-eastern United States and the Gulf of Mexico. In Europe it has been used since the 17th century as an ornamental and to plant heavily flooded areas, where it grows by means of aerial roots (pneumatophores), which emerge as blunt, conical projections around the trunk. These structures provide the underground parts of the tree with a sufficient supply of oxygen, which is lacking in the asphyxiated swampy soil. In Britain it is commonest in the south of England. It is very long-lived, reaching an age of up to 1000 years.

The timber has certain uses, particularly in the tree's native region, but in Europe it is mainly of ornamental interest.

*Metasequoia
glyptostroboides*

METASEQUOIA
GLYPTOSTROBOIDES Hu & Cheng
Dawn Redwood
Family *Taxodiaceae*

height 30 m
crown narrowly pyramidal, loose
trunk straight, with branches from base; bark grey-brown, flaking in long fibres
foliage deciduous
leaves acicular, flat and linear, up to 4 cm, pointed; arrangement in oppo-site pairs, pectinate; autumnal colour yellow-pink to red
flowers unisexual; ♂ flowers long, loose catkins, seldom visible; ♀ flowers short catkins of 0.6 cm, opposite on terminal shoots; flowering period April, as leaves appear
fruits oval to spherical cones, 2 cm ⌀, green, with long peduncles, non-spinous scales

The Dawn Redwood was discovered in the Sichuan and Hubei provinces of China during the Second World War. It was brought to Europe in 1948 as an ornamental and is found throughout the British Isles. Its foliage is deciduous and of great scientific interest, in that prior to its rediscovery the genus was known only through fossil remains.

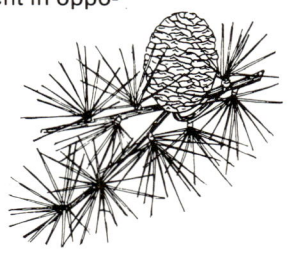

ANGIOSPERMS
Dicotyledons

Key to **WILLOWS**

Leaves oval-elliptic or obovate

– leaves hairy, especially on lower surface; dentate margins, crenate or entire: ***Salix caprea***
– leaves glabrous; central veining yellow; margins serrulate:
                                                                          Salix pentandra

Leaves lanceolate

– 'weeping' willows
–– brown shoots: ***Salix babylonica***
–– yellow-green shoots: ***Salix* 'Chrysocoma'**
– non-'weeping' willows
–– leaves hairy
––– leaves smooth, with white silky hairs: ***Salix alba***
––– leaves narrow and long, with revolute margins, white-tomentose below
–––– margins finely toothed, shoots reddish-brown: ***Salix elaeagnos***
–––– margins smooth, shoots yellow: ***Salix viminalis***
–– leaves glabrous, serrate
––– shoots glaucous bloomed: ***Salix daphnoides***
––– shoots not glaucous bloomed
–––– leaves with persistent stipules; twigs difficult to snap:
                                                                          Salix triandra
–––– leaves with deciduous stipules; twigs easily snapped: ***Salix fragilis***

SALIX CAPREA L.
Pussy Willow or Goat Willow *
Family *Salicaceae*

height up to 10 m, often shrubby
crown dense, globose
trunk sinuous, with ascendent branches, shiny, red-brown; bark grey, fissured
foliage deciduous
leaves simple, oval-elliptic or obovate, 5–10 cm, petiolate and with two pointed, toothed stipules; margins crenate or entire; lower surface tomentose; alternate arrangement
flowers dioecious; ♂ flowers ovoid catkins of 4 cm, thickly covered with

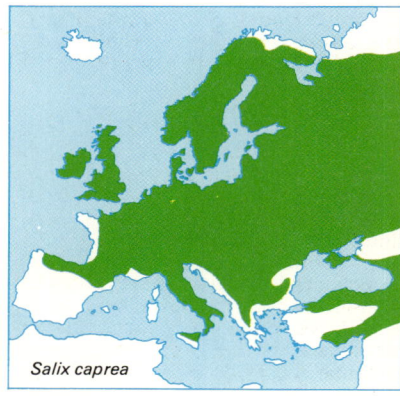
Salix caprea

Salix caprea

glucoside with properties similar to quinine used as a pain reliever and in general to dispel fevers.

SALIX PENTANDRA L.
Bay Willow *
Family *Salicaceae*

height 10 (15) m
crown domed, dense
trunk more or less upright, broadly branched from base; bark grey-brown, furrowed
foliage deciduous
leaves simple, oval-elliptic, 5–10 cm, acuminate, glabrous and shiny, sticky when young; petiolate; alternate arrangement
flowers dioecious; ♂ flowers catkins of 3–5 cm, with 5 stamens and yellow anthers; ♀ flowers similar to ♂ but more graceful; flowering period late May–June, at same time as leaves appear
fruits globose capsules in spikes

silvery hairs prior to flowering; stamens with yellow anthers; ♀ flowers larger than ♂; flowering period March–April
fruits derived from ♀ catkins, formed of large numbers of hairy capsules which then shed fluffy seeds

The Pussy Willow has a distribution area that covers the whole of Europe, except for the extreme southern and northern parts of the continent and is common throughout Britain. It is short-lived – about 50 years – and is used for colonizing slopes with shifting soil because of its adaptability to dry, stony terrain of any kind. It extends from lowlands to an altitude of 1700 m.

Like all willows, the wood is soft, light and compact; yellowish-white in colour, it splits easily but is elastic and can be compressed. It is used for sports equipment, crates, boxes, shavings, racks, fences and partitions. It yields excellent-quality charcoal. Tannin, used for tanning hides, is extracted from the bark, and reddish-violet dyes from the roots.

Willows have long been recognized as important medicinal plants, because the bark contains salicin, a

A European species, with a distribution like that of the Pussy Willow, the Bay Willow is more often found in upland plateaux, at altitudes from 600 to 2000 m. In Britain it is only found as a rare ornamental in the

flower ♂   seed

×1

×3

Salix pentandra

♂   ♀

south but from North Wales to Scotland it is a native tree. It is often planted in loose terrain because, like all willows, it roots and propagates very rapidly and reliably, with a deep, tenacious root system. Indeed, the roots spread so freely that they may cause damage to nearby cement structures such as foundations, canals and walls.

SALIX BABYLONICA L.
Chinese Weeping Willow
Family *Salicaceae*

height 10 m
crown hemispherical, 'weeping'
trunk sinuous, often folded, with branches curving down towards base; shoots reddish-brown; bark reddish-brown, furrowed
foliage deciduous
leaves simple, lanceolate-acuminate, 10–15 cm, finely serrate; alternate or sparse arrangement
flowers dioecious; ♂ flowers catkins of 4 cm, usually curved; ♀ flowers 2 cm; flowering period April–May
fruits capsules in spikes

The Chinese Weeping Willow is distributed over the central Asian re-

gions and was introduced from there into Europe in the 18th century. It has been used as an ornamental species because of its decorative, branch-drooping appearance; it likes light, deep, well-watered soil.

In Britain it is rarely planted nowadays, having been replaced by *Salix* 'Chrysocoma', similar in appearance and more rugged.

SALIX 'CHRYSOCOMA'
Weeping Willow **
Family *Salicaceae*

The familiar Weeping Willow is similar to preceding species and commonly known by the same name; it differs in having slightly smaller leaves but more especially by its shoots, which are yellow-green and not reddish-brown. It is a hybrid between *Salix babylonica* and *Salix alba*.

SALIX ALBA L.
White Willow *
Family *Salicaceae*

height 15 (25) m
crown irregularly divided, broad at top
trunk straight, branches curving upwards and outwards; bark dark grey, grooved and reticulated
foliage deciduous
leaves simple, lanceolate-acuminate, 5–10 cm, serrate and glandular; sparse silky hairs, especially below; alternate or sparse arrangement
flowers dioecious; ♂ flowers catkins of 4–6 cm, with 2 stamens; ♀ flowers similar; flowering period March–April, at same time as leaves
fruits ♀ catkins produce fruits in the form of glabrous capsules, which yield cottony seeds when opened

The White Willow is found throughout central-southern Europe, forming mixed woodlands with other water-loving species, along streams and rivers on fertile, deep soil which is

Salix 'Chrysocoma'

Salix babylonica

Salix alba

flower ♂

×2

×2

flower ♀

periodically submerged; it grows from the plains to an altitude of 1000 m. This tree is native to southern Britain and often planted both for timber and amenity. It is cultivated for its osiers, used for basket-making and wickerwork. The wood is used for crates and boxes and paper pulp. Because of its lightness, the wood is suitable for small carved and sculpted articles. The charcoal, of good quality, is used for the production of drawing crayons.

Today the variety *Salix* 'Chrysocoma' is widely grown because of its 'weeping' habit. Like other willows, this tree can withstand winds and atmospheric pollution.

SALIX ELAEAGNOS Scop.
Hoary Willow **
Family *Salicaceae*

height 5 (10) m
crown irregularly domed
trunk divided and branched; shoots pubescent; bark grey
foliage deciduous
leaves simple, linear-lanceolate, 5–15 cm, revolute at margin which is finely serrate; lower surface white,

woolly; central vein reddish; alternate arrangement
flowers dioecious; ♂ flowers catkins of 6 cm, erect, 2 stamens; ♀ flowers similar; flowering period March–April, before leaves
fruits glabrous capsules in spikes

The Hoary Willow has a range extending from the Iberian peninsula across central Europe to the Ukraine. It is particularly suitable for the colonization of calcareous and alluvial terrain exposed to watercourses, from lowlands to an altitude of 1500 m. It is occasionally planted as an ornamental in Britain.

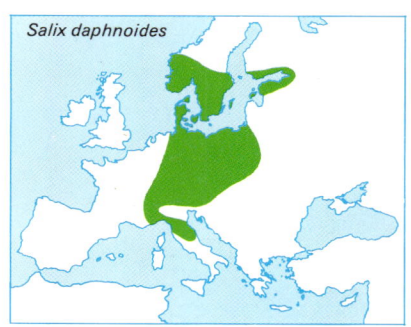

Salix daphnoides

Salix daphnoides

Salix triandra

flower ♂

×3

SALIX DAPHNOIDES Vill.
Violet Willow **
Family *Salicaceae*

height 10 (20) m
crown broad at top, open
trunk erect, branched from base; shoots glaucous bloomed, downy; bark grey, smooth
foliage deciduous
leaves simple, lanceolate-acuminate, 5–10 cm, toothed at margins, petiolate; alternate arrangement
flowers dioecious; ♂ flowers catkins of 2–6 cm, almost sessile, cylindrical, 2 stamens; ♀ flowers similar, looser; flowering period March–April
fruits glabrous capsules, sessile, in spikes

The Violet Willow is distributed over central-northern Europe, growing on the banks of streams, on loose, mainly calcareous terrain, and fairly dry subsoils, to an altitude of 1800 m. It is planted as an amenity tree.

SALIX TRIANDRA L.
Almond Willow
Family *Salicaceae*

height 5 (10) m, often shrubby
crown irregularly domed
trunk divided, branched; furrowed twigs; bark grey, smooth, flaking off in large plates
foliage deciduous
leaves simple, elliptic-lanceolate, 5–10 cm or more, serrate; leaf stipules present; alternate arrangement
flowers dioecious; ♂ catkins pedunculate, 5 cm, 3 stamens with yellow anthers; ♀ flowers similar; flowering period March–May, at same time as leaves
fruits glabrous capsules, scarcely pedunculate, in spikes

The Almond Willow's area of diffusion covers the European continent, except for the extreme northern parts, and it is only found locally in certain Mediterranean regions. It is probably native to Britain but as the tree furnishes excellent-quality osiers for wickerwork its true distribution has been lost by planting; those willows that are pollarded produce annual branches which, when cut in spring or winter, are used for making wicker baskets and chairs.

SALIX FRAGILIS L.
Crack Willow *
Family *Salicaceae*

Salix fragilis

height 15 (25) m
crown pyramidal
trunk straight, with thin, ascendent branches; twigs fragile at base; bark grey, opaque, reticulated
foliage deciduous
leaves simple, lanceolate, 10–15 cm, shiny and glabrous, with two glands at top of petiole; alternate or sparse arrangement
flowers dioecious; ♂ flowers catkins of 2–5 cm, 2 stamens with yellow anthers; ♀ flowers catkins of 7–10 cm; flowering period February–April, at same time as leaves
fruits globose, pedunculate capsules, in racemes; seeds 7 mm

This tree owes its specific name to the extreme fragility of the branches, which break off cleanly at the base. The Crack Willow's distribution area covers the whole of Europe, except for the extreme north and it is common in Britain. It grows on banks, gravel beds and along streams and rivers in hilly regions. When pollarded, it produces osiers for wickerwork.

Key to **POPLARS**

Leaves palmate-lobate:	***Populus alba***
Leaves round or triangular, not lobate	
– leaves round, crenate	
–– leaves glabrous:	***Populus tremula***
–– leaves hairy below	
––– white hairs:	***Populus alba***
––– grey hairs:	***Populus canescens***
– leaves rhomboid, triangular	
–– leaves with two glands at base:	***Populus × euroamericana***
–– leaves without glands at base:	***Populus nigra***

POPULUS ALBA L.
White Poplar **
Family *Salicaceae*

height 30 m
crown broadly domed
trunk erect, sinuous, horizontal branches; twigs with white tomentum; bark grey-white, smooth, then rougher, black

foliage deciduous
leaves simple, of two types: small, round-ovate, 5 cm, wavy margins; larger, palmate, with 5 more or less dentate lobes, 6–10 cm; leaves white, tomentose below; alternate arrangement
flowers dioecious; ♂ flowers cylindrical catkins of 5–8 cm; ♀ flowers catkins of 3–7 cm, grey-pink; flower-

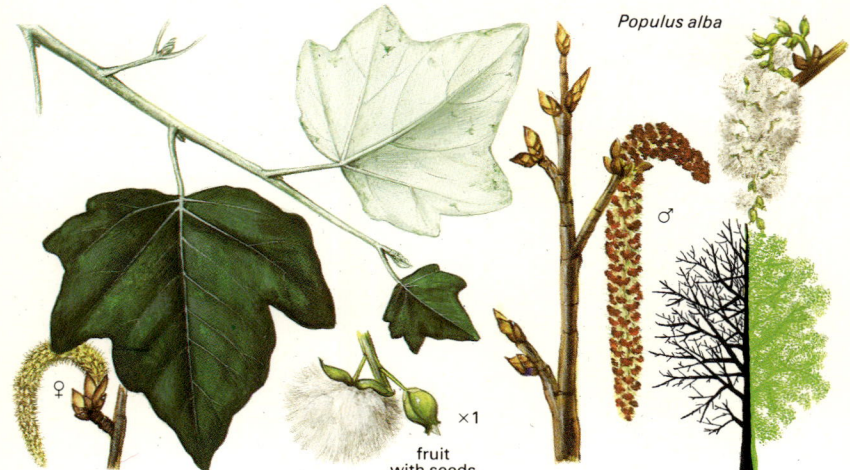

Populus alba

♂

♀

×1

fruit
with seeds

ing period February–March, before leaves
fruits glabrous capsules, in catkins; cottony seeds

The White Poplar is a species with a vast range, covering central-southern Europe, western Asia and North Africa. It grows sporadically or in small groups on river banks, up to an altitude of 1000 m. It was probably an early introduction to the U.K. where it is used as an ornamental.

It is a sun-loving, fast-growing species, associated with fertile, well-aired and sufficiently wet terrain; it will not tolerate soil that is compact or under water for long periods.

This tree is frequently planted in parks and along roads because of its decorative appearance. The soft, whitish wood is of mediocre quality and of limited use, mainly for packing cases, matches and paper pulp.

POPULUS CANESCENS (Ait.) Smith
(= *P. alba x tremula* Asch.)
Grey Poplar **
Family *Salicaceae*

height 20 (30) m
crown pyramidal or expanded at top
trunk erect, sinuous; twigs with grey tomentum; bark dark grey, smooth at top, with dark grooves lower down
foliage deciduous
leaves simple, round-rhomboid, 6–8 cm, with blunt teeth, grey-white below, pedunculate; alternate arrangement
flowers dioecious; ♀ flowers rare; ♂ flowers catkins of 5–10 cm, from grey to purple when flowering; ♀ flowers catkins which lengthen to about 12 cm; flowering period February–March
fruits glabrous or slightly hairy capsules.

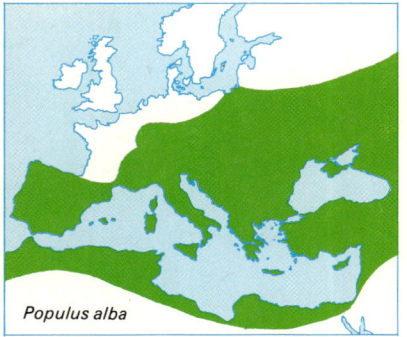

Populus alba

b *Populus canescens*

a *Populus* x *euroamericana*

Populus tremula

This tree is a hybrid of *Populus tremula* and *Populus alba*; it is frequently found in the same areas where these two species are widespread, having the same environmental requirements. The quality of the wood and its uses are similar to those of other poplars. It is planted as an ornamental in Britain.

Europe and Asia and is found in all parts of Great Britain. In the southerly regions of its range it is found sporadically or in small groups in mountainous zones, up to an altitude of 1800 m; in northerly regions, however, it is a constituent species of lowland woods.

POPULUS TREMULA L.
Aspen *
Family *Salicaceae*

height 20 (30) m
crown pyramidal, elongated, sparse
trunk erect, sinuous; suckering; bark grey-green, smooth
foliage deciduous
leaves simple, round to oval, 3–7 cm, with blunt toothed margins; long petiole (5 cm), flattened; alternate arrangement; autumn colour yellow
flowers dioecious; ♂ flowers catkins of 10 cm, grey-brown, falling after flowering; ♀ flowers reddish hairy catkins; flowering period March–May
fruits glabrous capsules with cottony seeds form from ♀ inflorescences

The Aspen grows over much of

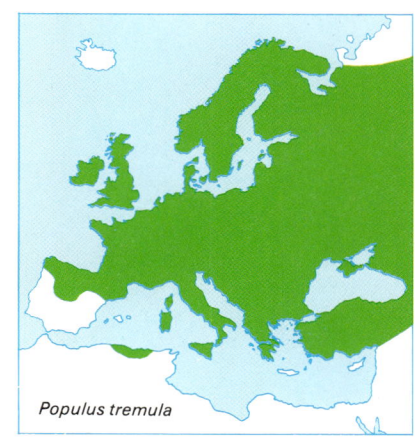

Populus tremula

The specific name *tremula* is derived from the extreme sensitivity of the leaves to the slightest breath of wind; in fact, the long compressed petiole supports the blade in elastic fashion, so that the latter quivers and rustles in characteristic manner.

A sun-loving species, extremely adaptable, and indifferent to the type of terrain, the Aspen is suitable for planting in clearings and on loose wasteland.

The wood, pale in colour, soft and light in texture, has few uses, like the White Poplar.

POPULUS NIGRA L.
Black Poplar **
cv *italica*
Lombardy Poplar
Family *Salicaceae*

height 30 (40) m
crown in Black Poplar oval, spreading, irregular; in Lombardy Poplar pyramidal or columnar
trunk erect, knotty and ridged, heavily branched and divided from base; bark brown, ridged
foliage deciduous

leaves simple, triangular-rhomboid, oval, 5–8 cm, long petiole, serrate-dentate margins; colour during foliation brown-green, shiny; alternate arrangement
flowers dioecious; ♂ flowers catkins of 5 (9) cm, reddish; ♀ flowers thin catkins, up to 12 cm long, yellow-green; flowering period March–April
fruits glabrous, ovoid capsules with feathery seeds develop from ♀ inflorescences

The Black Poplar extends over all southern Europe to western Asia and North Africa; it is also widely cultivated in Britain and elsewhere in Europe. This species is frequently found on the banks of streams and rivers, forming woods with willows and alders on permeable, deep and periodically flooded ground. It is particular as to light and temperature; and it may live to 300 years of age.

The wood, of modest quality, is used in much the same way as that of other poplars, for charcoal, in industry and medicine – for its absorbent properties (as decolorants, purifiers). The buds and bark have medicinal applications, containing properties which help to soothe fevers.

fruiting catkin

aphid gall

♂

Populus nigra

Among the insects which infest this and other poplars is the aphid *Pemphigus spirothecae* which causes the conspicuous corkscrew galls that form on the leaf petioles.

The Lombardy Poplar probably originated in western Asia and is a form of *Populus nigra*; it is found almost exclusively as a male plant. The tree is widely used for planting in rows, along roads and river banks; it is brittle and liable to damage by strong winds.

POPULUS X EUROAMERICANA
(Dode) Guiner
(= *P. canadensis* L.)
Hybrid Black Poplar
Hybrids between ♀ *P. nigra* x ♂ *P.* 'Serotina', *P. angulata*, *P. deltoides*
Family *Salicaceae*

height 25–30 m
crown elongated, ovate, sparse
trunk erect, branched; bark brown with long deep furrows
foliage deciduous
leaves simple, triangular, oval, 10–14 cm, often broader than long, serrate-dentate, with two glands at base; leaf colour at foliation redbrown; alternate arrangement
flowers dioecious; there are varieties that have only ♂ or ♀ clones; in other respects, as for preceding species

Populus deltoides Marshall
Eastern Cottonwood

Very similar, cultivated, with leaves of 10–18 cm.

The Hybrid Black Poplar, widely cultivated in Britain and other temperate regions of the world for its timber and rapid growth rate, is the result of crossing between the Eastern Cottonwood (*Populus deltoides*) and the European Black Poplar (*p. nigra*). Apart from *P. deltoides*, other poplars can be used to obtain hybrids, such as *P.* 'Serotina' and *P. angulata*,

males of these being crossed with females of *P. nigra*.

The wood is particularly rich in cellulose and one of its most important uses is in the paper industry.

Enemies of this poplar include many animal parasites, especially insects. One of the most dangerous is *Anaera carcharias* L., a long-horned beetle of the Cerambycidae, which does considerable damage, boring tunnels into the trunks, particularly of young poplars, weakening the trees and bringing them down.

The Eastern Cottonwood is widely distributed in North America. Since 1700 it has been used to create hybrid forms for timber production, particularly wood pulp.

JUGLANS REGIA L.
Common Walnut **
Family *Juglandaceae*

height 15 (30) m
crown spreading, domed
trunk erect, branched; shoots green, glabrous; bark grey-pink, initially smooth, then rough
foliage deciduous
leaves compound, pinnate, 20–25 cm long, usually comprising 7 oval-elliptic leaflets with smooth margins; apical leaflet larger and petiolate; alternate arrangement
flowers unisexual; ♂ flowers pendulous catkins of 5–10 cm, axillary, on twigs of previous year; ♀ flowers at axil of terminal leaves of new twigs, with 2–5 green flowers, each 1 cm, which have a bifid yellow stamen; flowering period May–June
fruits round drupes, 4–5 cm ∅, glabrous and smooth, green; edible seeds

The name *juglans* is derived from the Latin *Jovi glans*, Jove's gland. It is not known for certain where the Walnut originated, probably western Asia; in ancient times it was widely distributed over central and southern Europe, being cultivated for its fruit. It

Juglans regia

fruit
(drupe)

endocarp
with seed

×½

is found throughout the British Isles, though uncommon in Scotland. It grows sporadically in small groups, in glades, in exposed places in woods, and on hills and mountains up to an altitude of 1000 m. It likes fresh, loose, dry soil and is averse both to heat and extreme cold.

In Europe the Walnut has long been highly prized for its timber and its fruit. The wood, dark brown, heavy and durable, with beautiful veining, is used for expensive furniture. The stumps, with black marbling, are used for veneers and coverings.

The fruits are green drupes, whose outer part (the husk) is fleshy, rich in tannin, and used in tanning leather. The inner part, the nut proper, is woody and contains the edible seed (kernel) which is aromatic and tasty. The seed is 50% oil, being used for food and in industry for varnishes, colorants and perfumes. It contains important amounts of proteins (11%) and vitamins. The leaves are used in pharmacy for skin ailments. A brown, highly resistant dye, also used for staining the wood, is extracted from the husk.

JUGLANS NIGRA L.
Black Walnut **
Family *Juglandaceae*

height 30 m
crown domed
trunk straight and sturdy; bark brown-black

×⅓

endocarp
with seed

fruit
(drupe)

♂

Juglans nigra

foliage deciduous
leaves compound, pinnate, 30–60 cm, with 15–23 oval, lanceolate leaflets with serrate margins, sometimes without the apical leaflet; alternate arrangement
flowers unisexual, similar to *J. regia*; flowering period May–June
fruits drupes single or in pairs, green, 4–5 cm ⌀, rough and wrinkled, with husk more than 1 cm thick

This handsome tree comes from eastern North America. It was brought to Europe around 1630 and planted in the central and eastern parts of the continent for its valuable, fast-growing timber. The Black Walnut is also much used for ornament in parks and along roads, thriving throughout the British Isles.
 Juglans nigra is a fairly rugged tree, at its best in deep, fertile, well drained soil, with a continental climate. The wood is similar to that of the Common Walnut.

CARYA OVATA (Mill.) K. Koch
(= *C. alba* Nutt.)
Shagbark Hickory
Family *Juglandaceae*

height 20 m
crown broadly domed, sparse
trunk erect, divided, widely branched; bark pale grey, which flakes off in 50-cm strips
foliage deciduous
leaves compound, pinnate, 40–60 cm, composed of 5 (7) leaflets, the apical one with a petiole; serrate margins; autumnal colour golden-yellow; alternate arrangement
flowers unisexual; ♂ flowers catkins of 10–15 cm, pendulous, grouped in threes; ♀ flowers in groups of 2–3, sessile on terminal twigs; flowering period June
fruits ovate drupes of 4 cm ⌀, in groups of 2–3, with furrowed surface

The Shagbark Hickory comes from the north-eastern part of the United States; it was introduced to Europe around 1630 and is used both as an

endocarp with seed

×⅓

Carya ovata

ornamental tree and a forest species. It is uncommon in Britain.
 It is a rugged species, adaptable to all climates. The heavy, compact wood is used for making furniture and sports equipment, and for fuel. Oil is extracted from the edible fruits. The Bitter-nut (*Carya cordiformis* (Wangenh.) K. Koch) is a related species, the leaves comprising 9 leaflets and the fruits having a bitter seed.

Carya cordiformis

PTEROCARYA FRAXINIFOLIA
(Lamb.) Spach
Caucasian Wing-nut **
Family *Juglandaceae*

height 20 m
crown domed
trunk often divided from base into several sinuous, curving boles; bark grey, reticulated
foliage deciduous
leaves compound, pinnate, 30–50 cm, with 11–21 lanceolate-serrate leaflets; autumn colour yellow; alternate arrangement
flowers unisexual; ♂ flowers catkins of 5–10 cm; ♀ flowers catkins of 10–15 cm, with flowers of 3 mm; flowering period May
fruits derived from ♀ catkins, 25–30 cm, with numerous small winged nuts, 2 cm

The Caucasian Wing-nut was spread by man throughout Europe in the 18th century, from its native area in western Asia. It is cultivated as an ornamental tree for its decorative shape, and as a forest species for its light timber, used for furniture and boxes. It adapts well to wet and periodically flooded soil. In Britain its principal use is as an ornamental tree.

fruits

♀

♂

Pterocarya fraxinifolia

BETULA PENDULA Roth.
(= *B. alba* L., pro parte max.; *verrucosa* Ehrh.) *B.*
Silver Birch *
Family *Betulaceae*

height 20 (30) m
crown elongated, pyramidal, sparse
trunk erect, branched, with drooping, glabrous twigs; bark white, smooth, soft, flaking in long, very narrow, translucent strips
foliage deciduous
leaves simple, ovate-rhomboid, 4–8 mm, pointed and double toothed; autumn colour golden-yellow; alternate arrangement
flowers unisexual; ♂ flowers catkins of 3–6 cm, sessile and pendulous; ♀ flowers pedunculate and pendulous, 3 × 1 cm; flowering period April–May
fruits derived from ♀ catkins, in form of cone with membranous scales, containing glabrous, two-winged achenes

The generic name is derived from the Celtic *betu* (birch). The Silver Birch has a European distribution ranging north to latitude 65° and south to Sicily, and is frequent in Britain both as a native tree and as an ornamental specimen. It is a sun-loving species which grows sporadically or in small clumps in the sparse woodlands of hills and mountains, in association with broadleaved and coniferous trees. It does well in dry, bare soil, preferably acidic, well aired and with plenty of available water. It is highly resistant to frost.

Man has long used the various parts of the Silver Birch for many purposes. The wood is white, flexible and strong; it is used for specialized articles, such as helms, wheels and parts of barrels, and also for small domestic articles like cutlery and toys. It serves as fuel and produces good-quality charcoal, is used industrially for making inks and in medicine for intestinal disorders.

The bark is vaulable for the tanning industry, leaving a very delicate aroma on the hides. Its silvery colour is

×2

fruit
(winged achene)

Betula pendula

fruiting catkin

due to the presence of betulin; birch oil (oil of wintergreen), which contains antiseptic principles, is likewise distilled from the bark and used particularly for skin ailments. The leaves yield a yellow dye and are also used for preparing an infusion with diuretic properties. In spring, after fermentation of the sap, alcoholic drinks or vinegar are obtained. The young, flexible branches are used for wickerwork.

The Silver Birch is widely planted

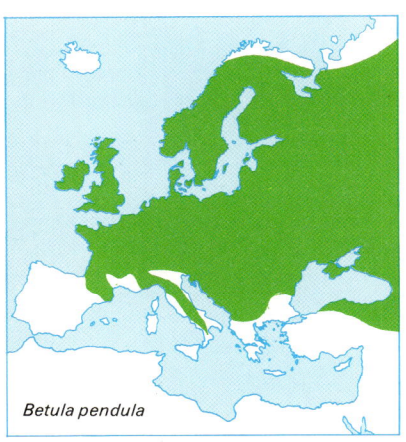

Betula pendula

for ornament because of its elegant habit and the decorative colour of the bark and leaves. In sylviculture it often serves as a species for consolidating loose, bare slopes, spreading rapidly as a result of abundant seed production and low demand for nutrients.

BETULA PUBESCENS Ehrh.
(= *B. alba* L.; pro parte min.; *B. tomentosa* Reitter & Abel)
Downy or Brown Birch *
Family *Betulaceae*

height 10–20 m
crown oval, elongated
trunk erect, with branches straight up to top; non-drooping, hairy shoots; bark grey, with broad black furrows low down
foliage deciduous
leaves simple, ovate-rhomboid, 3–5 cm, with almost equal teeth; alternate arrangement
flowers similar to *B. pendula*, except that the ♀ flowers are erect
fruits similar to *B. pendula*, except that the achene has hairs at the tip

The Downy Birch is found throughout northern and central Europe; in the

Betula pubescens

♂

×2

fruiting catkin

fruit
(winged achene)

leaves simple, obovate, 4–10 cm, cuneate base, blunt or notched apex; margins doubly and irregularly toothed; alternate arrangement
flowers unisexual; ♂ flowers cylindrical catkins of 5–10 cm, in groups of 3–5, terminal, dark brown, becoming yellow-brown; ♀ oval, 5–6 mm, pedunculate, in groups of 3–5; flowering period February–April
fruits oval, dark brown cones derive from ♀ inflorescences, 1–1.5 cm, with woody scales containing narrow-winged achenes

The generic name may derive from the Celtic, meaning 'near the banks'.

The Common Alder has a range covering Britain and almost the whole of Europe, except for the extreme north; it is native on lowland plains and in mountains up to an altitude of 1200 m. It frequents river banks, growing on clayey, sandy and poor soils, which it colonizes by means of nodules on the roots, which harbour bacteria producing atmospheric nitrogen. It also grows in places that are frequently flooded or

south it occurs only in the mountainous regions of Spain, Italy and Yugoslavia. Its requirements are similar to those of the Silver Birch. However, it tends to prefer more acidic and wetter soils than the preceding species, though both will tolerate cold climates.

ALNUS GLUTINOSA (L.) Gaertn.
Common Alder *
Family *Betulaceae*

height 20 m, often shrubby
crown ovate pyramidal, sparse
trunk erect, often divided from base; bark from dark brown to black, with sinuous fissures
foliage deciduous

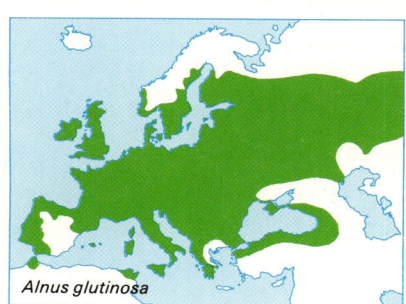

Alnus glutinosa

Key to ALDERS

Leaves with blunt or notched apex: ***Alnus glutinosa***

Leaves with pointed apex

– margin dentate, base cuneate: ***Alnus incana***
– margin crenate, base cordate: ***Alnus cordata***

Alnus glutinosa

♀

♂

fruit
×2

fruiting catkin

×1

♀

×3

inflorescence

swampy, forming pure or mixed woods with poplars, willows and other moisture-loving trees, serving as a soil-improving species. Like all alders, it is short-lived.

It is used for making poles and as fuel. The freshly cut wood is white and, as it dries, turns reddish-brown. In contact with water it becomes very hard, and for this reason it is suitable for piles and other structures liable to be submerged; exposed to the air, however, it shows little durability. It is used in joinery as it dyes well, mainly for carving and lathe-work (fixtures and toys). The bark produces a grey colorant and tannin.

ALNUS INCANA (L.) Moench
Grey Alder *
Family *Betulaceae*

height 10 (20) m, often shrubby
crown oval pyramidal
trunk erect, irregularly branched; with suckers; bark pale grey, smooth
foliage deciduous
leaves simple, oval-elliptic, 4–10 cm, pointed and downy grey below, with dentate margins, petiolate; alternate arrangement
flowers unisexual; ♂ flowers catkins of 8 cm, brown, in groups of 3–4, produced before foliation; ♀ flowers in groups of 3–8, oval, pedunculate catkins; flowering period February–April
fruits oval cones derived from ♀ inflorescences, 1 cm, with woody scales containing narrow-winged achenes

Alnus incana

♀

♂

fruiting catkins of previous year

×1

fruit

fruiting catkins of current year

The Grey Alder is distributed through central-eastern Europe, ranging north to Scandinavia and occurring locally farther south in mountainous zones, at altitudes of up to 1600 m. It grows along river banks, and will flourish on virtually any terrain so long as it is sufficiently loose and drained, though it shows a preference for calcareous subsoils. In Britain it is planted principally in site reclamation. Characteristics and uses of the wood are similar to those of the Common Alder. The species is used for reafforestation of wasteland, preventing soil erosion.

ALNUS CORDATA (Loisel.) Desf.
Italian Alder **
Family *Betulaceae*

height 10–15 (25) m
crown pyramidal, elongated
trunk straight; bark grey-brown, fissured here and there
foliage deciduous
leaves simple, oval, cordate, 5–8 cm, pointed, base truncate or cordate, margins crenate-dentate; alternate arrangement
flowers unisexual; ♂ flowers cylindrical catkins of 10 cm, pendulous when in flower, in groups of 3–5 (not expanded during winter, 3 cm); ♀ flowers ovoid, erect, 2 cm, positioned above the ♂, single or in pairs, with long peduncle; flowering period February–March

fruiting catkins of current year

♀

fruiting catkins of previous year

×1
fruit

Alnus cordata

fruits oval cones derived from ♀ inflorescences, 3 cm, brown and with woody scales which contain black, narrow-winged achenes

The distribution area of the Italian Alder is restricted to Italy and includes the Apennines and the islands, where it grows between 900 and 1300 m. Despite its southern origin it thrives throughout Britain as an ornamental species. Unlike other alders, it tolerates fairly dry soil; it is undemanding, prefers acidic terrain but adapts to almost any subsoil, improving it by the nitrogen-fixing bacteria in its roots, its abundant litter and consolidating action. The light, compact wood is used for packing cases and plywood. Sometimes it is planted for ornament, especially along avenues.

CORYLUS AVELLANA L.
Common Hazel *
Family *Corylaceae*

height 5–7 m, often shrubby
crown domed, irregular
trunk erect, branched from base; bark from reddish-brown to grey-brown, smooth

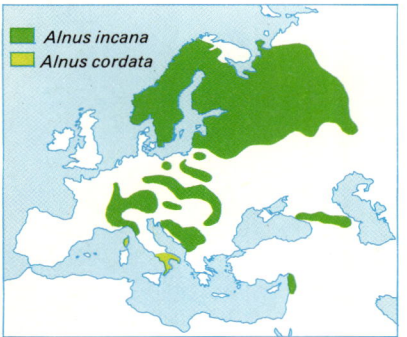

Alnus incana
Alnus cordata

♀

♂

Corylus avellana

bracts
surrounding fruit

Corylus colurna

♂

bracts
surrounding
fruit

foliage deciduous
leaves simple, obovate, 7–12 cm, mucronate, sharply toothed; alternate arrangement
flowers unisexual; ♂ flowers catkins of 6–8 cm, pendulous, forming in autumn; ♀ flowers similar to buds, from which sprout the red, bifid stigmas; 2 flowers; flowering period January–March
fruits nuts, about 2 cm, enclosed in a toothed leafy bract

Corylus colurna L.
Turkish Hazel **

Similar to *C. avellana*, but taller, up to 20 m; trunk straight, bark rough, greyish. Nuts covered by bracts which are much longer than the fruits and with glandular hairs.

The generic name is derived from the Greek *koris* (helmet), from the shape of the membranous involucre covering the fruit.
The Hazel is a common tree virtually throughout Europe including Britain, from the Mediterranean region northwards; it is found up to altitudes of 1200 m. It grows in mixed broad-leaved woods; it is also suitable for colonizing bare, crumbly terrain.

Very frugal, it adapts to different types of subsoil, though showing a preference for chalky, fertile, deep terrain. It is cultivated for fruit in many regions; the nuts have edible seeds, rich in oil, which is used for foodstuffs and in industry for colouring and perfumery.
The whitish wood, of mediocre quality, is used chiefly for poles, barrels, sticks, and as fuel and charcoal. The branches and thinner boles are used for mats, supports for climbing plants and baskets; the leaves serve as fodder for sheep. It is a tree that flowers very early, much favoured by pollen-collecting bees.

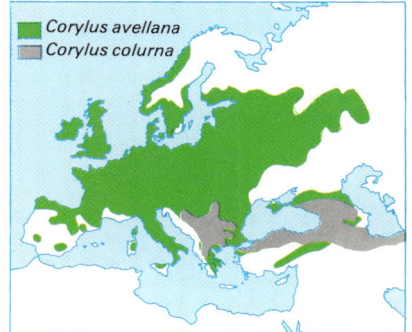

Corylus avellana
Corylus colurna

A number of varieties are cultivated for fruit and ornamental purposes; among the latter are 'Pendula', weeping, 'Contorta', of twisting habit, and 'Fusco-rubra', with purple leaves.

The Turkish Hazel originated in an area embracing south-eastern Europe, Asia Minor and the Caucasus. On the continent it is widely used for fruit and as an ornamental, but only for the latter purpose in Britain.

CARPINUS BETULUS L.
Hornbeam *
Family *Corylaceae*

Carpinus betulus

♀

♂

fruit   ×⅔

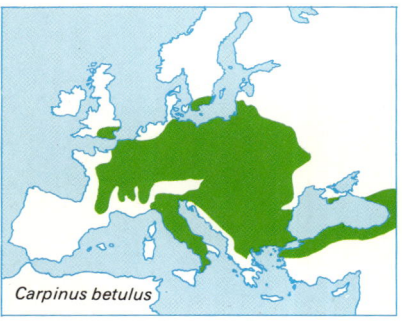

Carpinus betulus

height 20 m
crown irregularly oval
trunk straight, fissured and sinuous; bark silver-grey, smooth
foliage deciduous
leaves simple, oval, acuminate, 5–10 cm, double toothed; alternate arrangement
flowers unisexual; ♂ flowers cylindrical catkins of 5–10 cm, pendulous; ♀ flowers erect, shorter catkins; flowering period February–April
fruits pedunculate, pendent, 6–15 cm, formed of achenes covered by a trilobed bract of 3 cm

Carpinus orientalis Mill.
(= *C. duinensis* Scop.)
Eastern Hornbeam

Smaller than *C. betulus*, often shrubby; leaves only 2–5 cm; fruits covered by bracts similar to the leaves, small and roughly toothed.

At one time the wood of the Hornbeam was used to make yokes, hence the generic name, from the Celtic *car* (wood) and *pin* (head). The tree grows over a very wide area, from north-east England across central Europe to the Caucasus, in all temperate regions, up to an altitude of 1200 m. The Hornbeam adapts to almost any terrain, preferring siliceous, wet and fertile subsoils; it forms part of deciduous woodlands in bright, well exposed places, and is sometimes found on its own. Although it buds freely, it is a slow grower and is used principally as a forest species, less often for ornament or for hedging, although it tolerates pruning.

The wood is used chiefly as fuel and produces excellent-quality charcoal. The straight trunks are used for poles, handles and small utensils requiring a tough wood.

The Eastern Hornbeam (*Carpinus orientalis*) grows in south-eastern Europe, from Italy to Asia Minor, and is found in altitudes up to about 1000 m, in broadleaved woods. In comparison with the Hornbeam, it

×1
fruit

Carpinus orientalis

Ostrya carpinifolia

fruit   ×²/₃

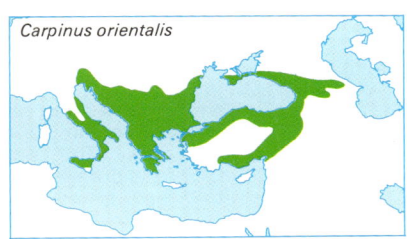

Carpinus orientalis

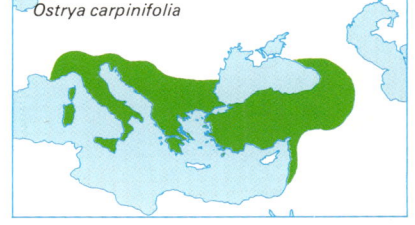

Ostrya carpinifolia

needs more sun and is frequently present on calcareous subsoil and in dry environments.

The wood is principally used as fuel and, more rarely, for small domestic objects.

OSTRYA CARPINIFOLIA Scop.
Hop Hornbeam
Family *Corylaceae*

height 10–15 (20) m
crown conical, oval, more often irregular
trunk straight, cylindrical; bark dark brown to grey, in small scales
foliage deciduous
leaves simple, oval, acuminate, 5–10 cm, doubly toothed at margins; alternate arrangement, in pairs
flowers unisexual; ♂ flowers cylin-

drical catkins of 8–10 cm, pendent and in groups of 2–3; ♀ flowers catkins of 3 cm; flowering period April–May
fruits of 6 cm, formed of achenes enclosed by white bracts, similar to fruits of hop

The generic name is derived from the Greek *ostreion* (shell), in that the bracts enclosing the fruit are swollen and dilated like the valves of a shell.

The Hop Hornbeam grows in central-southern Europe, from France to Asia Minor and the Caucasus; it is rarely seen in Britain. It is found, together with other broadleaved species, in sunny woods from foothills to mountains, to a height of 1200 m. A frugal tree, it is suitable for colonizing wasteland and inaccessible terrain, growing in calcareous and dry subsoil as well as surface soil; it has a marked improving effect on the soil, seeding itself freely in its native region and producing abundant pollen.

The timber is used for firewood and produces charcoal of good quality; the wood is mediocre, reddish, hard and tough, in its uses no different from that of other hornbeams. The young branches are used as osiers for wickerwork, and the leaves provide fodder for cattle.

FAGUS SYLVATICA L.
Beech *
Family *Fagaceae*

height 30 m
crown broadly domed, dense
trunk straight and branched; bark grey and smooth
foliage deciduous
leaves simple, elliptic-oval, 5–10 cm, hairy at margins, with a short petiole; autumnal colour yellow, reddish-brown; alternate arrangement
flowers unisexual; ♂ flowers axillary catkins, with peduncle of 5 cm, pendulous, hairy, bell-shaped perianth; ♀ flowers single or in pairs, pedunculate, enclosed in a spinous but not sharp involucre; flowering period April–May
fruits two beechnuts of 1.5–2 cm, long and pointed, enclosed in a four-valved involucre

The generic name is from the Greek *fagein* (to eat), referring to the nuts, which can be used as fodder for pigs.

The Beech has a vast distribution over western, central and southern Europe, extending from England and Spain to the Black Sea, from Norway to Sicily; on the continent it is the most important consituent of broad-leaved woods on upland plains. It is planted throughout Britain, being especially characteristic of the woodlands of the Cotswolds and Chilterns. It is found in pure stands or mixed with firs, pines, yews, ash, wych elm, maples, rowans, gean and hornbeams, up to altitudes of 1400 to 1800 m. In north-western Europe it grows in lowland woods.

This species likes an oceanic, temperate climate, with average annual temperatures of 6° to 10°C (39°–50°F) and minimum rainfall of 700 to 1000 mm (27½–39 in) a year. It is not too particular about soil as long as it is well aerated and drained, and

Fagus sylvatica

♀

×2

♂

×½

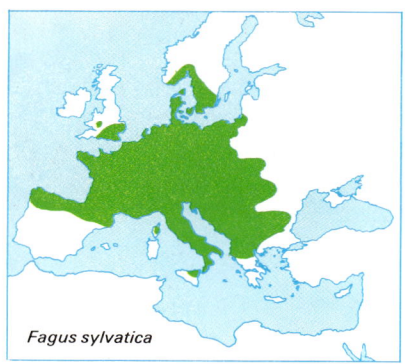
Fagus sylvatica

genus *Nothofagus*, with evergreen or deciduous species, is widespread. It was introduced to Europe as an ornamental tree in the 19th century, one of several species being *Nothofagus antarctica* (Forst.) Oerst. The genus is commonly known as Southern Beech. It is a rugged deciduous tree, up to 20 m tall, but usually with the bole subdivided from the base.

CASTANEA SATIVA Miller
Sweet Chestnut **
Family *Fagaceae*

height 20 m
crown long and broad, domed at top; young trees have a pyramidal crown
trunk erect, straight and branched at top; bark dark grey, spirally fissured; young trees are reddish-brown and smooth
foliage deciduous
leaves simple, linear-lanceolate, 10–20 cm, rounded at base, with serrate, mucronate margins; alternate arrangement
flowers unisexual; ♂ flowers bunches of long catkins, 10–20 cm, stiff, axillary, creamy white; ♀ flowers single or in groups of 2–3 at base of ♂ inflorescences, covered by a spinous cupule; flowering period June
fruits chestnuts covered by cupule of 5–6 cm ∅, with sharp spines.

The Sweet or Spanish Chestnut is native to south-eastern Europe and Asia Minor. It has been widely cultivated, however, and nowadays grows in regions far beyond its original areas, including Britain, where it is used both in forestry and as an amenity tree. In hilly and submontane plains it grows to an altitude of 900 m, while in southern parts of Europe it is found even higher (in Sicily at 1400 m).

It forms mixed and pure stands, and likes acidic soils and a moderate climate with an average annual temperature of 8°C (46°F) and between 600 mm and 1500 mm of rainfall a year. The tree grows rapidly and

tolerates both acidic and chalky soils; it is susceptible to late frosts and high winds.

Although principally found growing wild in forests, it is sometimes cultivated as an ornamental species in parks because of the beautiful colour of its trunk and leaves in all seasons – even as leaf litter beneath the trees in winter.

The Beech is mainly valued for its wood; pinkish-white, fairly hard and compact, it is used for joinery, lathework, panelling, plywood, barrels, flooring, furniture and handles for implements. It is also an excellent fuel. The beechnuts or beechmast are used as fodder for pigs and form part of the rights of pannage; they also yield oil. At one time they were roasted as a coffee substitute. The fresh leaves can be used as fodder for animals. The bark contains tannin, while the distilled wood furnishes creosote, from which guaiacol is extracted and used in medicine as an excellent balsam and antiseptic for the respiratory tract.

The following varieties are noteworthy as ornamentals: var. *purpurea*, with red leaves; var. *laciniata* or *heterophylla*, with deeply lobate and sometimes coloured leaves; 'Roseo-marginata', with leaves blotched purple, yellow and white; and var. *pendula*, of weeping habit.

In the southern hemisphere (from South America to Australia), the

Castanea sativa

is very long-lived, yielding abundant pollen.

The Sweet Chestnut is important both for its timber and fruit, although chestnuts are not as popular now as they once were; they may be eaten fresh or dried, roasted, candied for confectionery (glacé fruits) or in the form of purée. They are also used as fodder for animals.

The tree is planted in coppices and small woods and yields timber of varying dimensions for different uses. The wood is brown, flexible, resistant, averagely hard but not always of good quality because of its tendency to split, which makes it suitable for the manufacture of pales for fencing; it is also used for boxes, crates, poles, rafters, planks, barrels, simple furniture and firewood. The bark is rich in tannin. The flowers attract bees, resulting in an aromatic, much valued honey. The leaves have pharmaceutical applications, being used with sedative effect on the breathing system. The leaf-mould of the Sweet Chestnut is used in floriculture.

The tree is nowadays threatened by two parasitic fungi; the phycomycete *Phytophtora cambivora* attacks the tissues of the trunk, and the ascomycete *Endothia parasitica*, which has become wide-spread in recent years, causes canker of the bark.

In order to overcome the problems posed by parasites, two oriental species have been introduced, the Japanese Sweet Chestnut (*Castanea crenata* Sieb. & Zucc.), and Chinese Sweet Chestnut (*Castanea mollissima* B.L.). They have shown themselves to be more demanding than the European species, being averse to cold climates and late frosts, and not tolerating dry conditions.

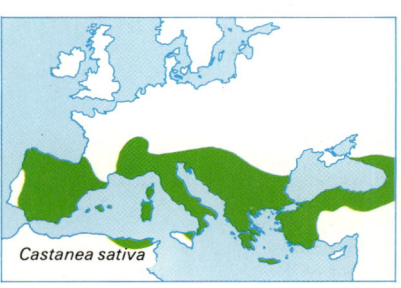

Castanea sativa

Key to **OAKS**

Leaves obovate (broadest in upper third); tree with deciduous leaves
– leaves with pointed lobes
–– lobes only mucronate; scales of cupule curled: **Quercus cerris**
–– lobes with long teeth, acuminate but not sharp; scales of cupule appressed
––– lobes cut up to halfway to midrib; leaves more than 10 (15–20) cm: **Quercus rubra**
––– lobes cut more than halfway to midrib; leaves up to 15 cm: **Quercus palustris**
– leaves with blunt lobes
–– leaves lobate more than halfway to midrib
––– leaves glabrous; petiole less than 5 mm long: **Quercus frainetto**
––– leaves more or less tomentose
–––– petiole of 5 mm: **Quercus pubescens**
–––– petiole of 10–20 mm; underside of leaves white, tomentose: **Quercus pyrenaica**
–– leaves lobate up to one-third way to midrib
––– leaf base with two auricles: **Quercus robur**
––– leaf base cuneate
–––– petiole grooved; underside of leaves more or less glabrous: **Quercus petraea**
–––– petiole not grooved; underside of leaves more or less pubescent: **Quercus pubescens**

Leaves oval-elliptic, margins smooth or wavy with sharp teeth; trees for the most part evergreen
– leaves greyish-white below, woolly; margins smooth or crinkled
–– central vein straight: **Quercus ilex**
–– central vein sinuous
––– bark with large corky ridges: **Quercus suber**
––– bark not markedly corky: **Quercus crenata**
– leaves pale green below
–– margins crinkled, with long, pointed mucros; scales of cupule appressed: **Quercus coccifera**
–– margins dentate or slightly lobate-dentate; scales of cupule curly
––– teeth numerous (more than 7): **Quercus trojana**
––– teeth pronounced, almost lobes, at most 6: **Quercus macrolepis**

QUERCUS CERRIS L.
Turkey Oak
Family *Fagaceae*

height 35 m
crown pyramidal to domed
trunk erect, sinuous; shoots hairy; buds with fibrous scales; bark dark brown, rough, fissured
foliage deciduous
leaves simple, variable, about 10 cm long, either slightly dentate or deeply lobed; lobes mucronate at apex; hairy petiole; alternate arrangement
flowers unisexual; ♂ flowers catkins of 5 cm, in axillary bunches; ♀ flowers single and sessile; flowering period June
fruits ovoid acorns of 2.5 cm, sessile; cup with long, fibrous, curved scales

The Turkey Oak is a relatively long-

Quercus cerris

♀

♂

lived tree, attaining 200 years and more. An ornamental tree in Britain, it is found wild in southern Europe, in lowland plains and foothills; it adapts to all subsoils including clay, provided they are sufficiently deep, but not those that are markedly calcareous. Sensitive to late frost and prolonged cold, it is averagely demanding as regards light and temperature.

Growth is fairly slow, while pollen production is prolific. The wood has similar uses to that of other oaks; the somewhat bitter acorns are not to the taste of most animals.

The bark is valued for its high tannin content. Used in tanning hides, the tannins, which coagulate albu-

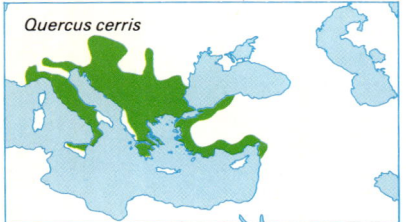

Quercus cerris

men and gelatine, act as both softening and anti-rotting agents.

Turkey Oak and English Oak are both hosts to an insect which seriously affects acorn growth, but more so in the case of the latter where the formation of knopper galls – hexagonal pyramidal woody growths on the acorn – usually prove fatal.

QUERCUS RUBRA L.
(= *Q. borealis* Michx.)
Red Oak **
Family *Fagaceae*

height 25 m
crown pyramidal to domed
trunk sturdy, often bifurcate; shoots glabrous, red; bark light grey, smooth, fissured and reticulated
foliage deciduous
leaves simple, obovate, 12–22 cm, with deep lobes cutting up to halfway to midrib; lobes dentate-mucronate; autumnal colour, red in young trees, also yellow-brown in adult specimens; alternate arrangement
flowers unisexual, like those of other oaks; flowering period May
fruits oval acorns of 2–3 cm, flat or slightly incurved cup, peduncle 1 cm

Quercus palustris Münchh.
Pin Oak **

Similar to *Q. rubra*, but with smaller leaves (8–15 cm) and with relatively shallow lobes; acorns 1–1.5 cm, round, in thin cup.

These two American oaks are both frequently planted as ornamental trees in Britain. The Red Oak comes originally from eastern North America, in the area lying between latitudes 35° and 47°N. Introduced to Europe at the end of the 17th century, it has been widely planted as an ornamental tree for its decorative crown and habit. It is less sensitive to light than European oaks, allergic to calcareous soils and does best in fertile, impermeable ground. Recently it has found a use in sylviculture, espe-

Quercus rubra

cially in France, Holland, Belgium and Denmark, giving satisfactory results as to timber yield and resistance to the fungus *Microsphaera quercina*.

The wood is not as valuable as that of European oaks, but is durable and easy to work, being used chiefly for floors, windows and poles, and as fuel.

The Pin Oak grows wild in the eastern United States, and was subsequently imported to Europe for ornament, because of its decorative slender branches and deep red autumnal leaves.

QUERCUS PUBESCENS Willd.

(= *Q. lanuginosa* Thuile)
White or Downy Oak
Family *Fagaceae*

height 20 m
crown domed, hemispherical in adult specimens
trunk sinuous, erect; shoots hairy; bark dark grey, fissured into small rough plates
foliage deciduous; the dry leaves persist on the tree during winter
leaves simple, obovate-lobate, 5–10 cm, more or less pubescent, especially in young trees; base cuneate; petiole short (1 cm), hairy; alternate arrangement
flowers unisexual; ♂ flowers loose catkins of 4–6 cm; ♀ flowers single or in groups of 2–4, sessile or with short peduncle; flowering period April–May
fruits long, oval acorns, 2 cm, half covered by cup

Quercus pubescens

Quercus palustris

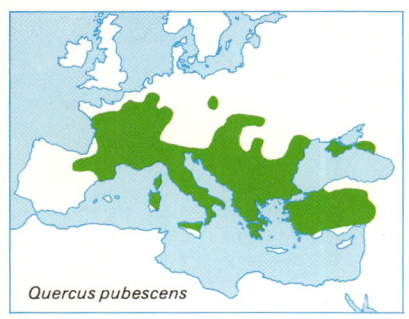

Quercus pubescens

Quercus frainetto

The huge distribution area of the White or Downy Oak extends over central, southern and eastern Europe, from the Pyrenees to Asia Minor but is rarely planted in Britain. It is common on hills and the lower slopes of mountains, where it forms pure or mixed stands with Turkey Oak, Eastern Hornbeam, Manna Ash and Field Maple. Extremely frugal, it adapts to calcareous, clayey, arid and rocky terrain and is suitable for colonizing wasteland. Sun-loving, sensitive to frost, it is one of the most drought-resistant of all oaks.

The Downy Oak produces stout timber, similar to that of the English Oak, but more irregular and less easy to work; it is used mainly for railway sleepers, for charcoal and as fuel. It has very limited importance as an ornamental tree.

Roasted, the sweet acorns of this and other oaks can be used as a coffee substitute.

QUERCUS FRAINETTO Ten.
Hungarian Oak **
Family *Fagaceae*

The distribution area of the Hungarian Oak covers southern Italy and the Balkans, where it forms pure stands or mixed woodlands, together with Holm Oak, Downy Oak and Turkey Oak. Less common than formerly, mainly due to felling and fire devastation, it is comparatively unde-

manding as to site, though preferring acidic soils; like other oaks, it thrives in average conditions of light, temperature and humidity. It is a majestic tree and planted as an amenity tree in Britain. The growth rate is slow, though pollen production is high. The wood has similar characteristics and uses to the Downy Oak.

QUERCUS PYRENAICA Willd.
(= *Q. toza* Bast.)
Pyrenean Oak
Family *Fagaceae*

The Pyrenean Oak is restricted to the Iberian peninsula and Atlantic coast of France; it is rarely found in Britain as an ornamental. Similar to the Downy Oak, its shoots are thickly covered with yellow down; the leaves and buds are also hairy.

This oak, notable for its late leafing, has fairly large leaves (20 cm). 'Pendula' is planted for ornamental purposes. The very hard, mediocre-quality wood, is used principally as fuel.

QUERCUS ROBUR L.
(= *Q. pedunculata* Ehrh.)
English or Pedunculate Oak *
Family *Fagaceae*

height 20 m; occasionally specimens may grow to over 40 m
crown irregularly oval, domed, very full
trunk stout and branched; shoots glabrous; bark grey, ridged, with short, narrow plates
foliage deciduous
leaves simple, obovate-lobate, about 10 cm, with wavy surfaces; base with two auricles; very short petiole (0.5–1 cm), glabrous; alternate arrangement
flowers unisexual; ♂ flowers loose catkins of 2–4 cm, pendulous; yellow stamens; ♀ flowers single or in groups of 2–5 on a long peduncle (2–5 cm) (= *Quercus pedunculata*); single flowers round, brown, with red stigma; flowering period April–May
fruits long oval acorns of 1.5–4 cm; cup with appressed scales and tomentose, a quarter or half covering the acorn

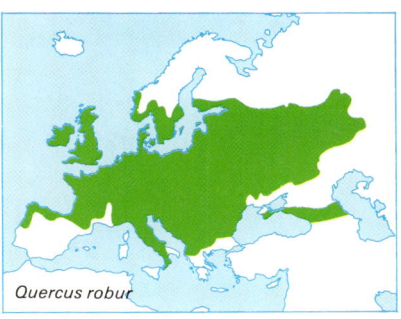

Quercus robur

English Oak is a very long-lived species: it can reach an age of more than 500 years. It is distributed over the whole of Britain and continental Europe, from southern Scandinavia to the Mediterranean, growing at altitudes up to 1000 m. Its preferences are for soils that are fresh, deep and fertile. Fairly tolerant of winter frosts, it thrives in high summer temperatures – conditions that favour its diffusion in continental Europe. It is at the northern limit of its range in Britain. It craves light, especially in its early years of growth.

The most valued product of the English Oak is its hard, light brown wood, used for expensive furniture and barrels, for producing quality charcoal and as fuel. The bark contains an average of 15% tannin, used for tanning hides, while the acorns make excellent fodder for pigs. It is rarely used for ornamental purposes, because of its slow growth rate.

Quercus robur

QUERCUS PETRAEA (Mattuschka) Liebl.
(= *Q. sessiliflora* Salisb.)
Sessile or Durmast Oak *
Family *Fagaceae*

height 30 (40) m
crown domed
trunk erect, slender; shoots glabrous; bark grey, ridged and fissured
foliage deciduous

Quercus petraea

leaves simple, obovate-lobate, 8–12 cm, with 1–2 (3) cm petiole; alternate arrangement
flowers unisexual; ♂ flowers pendulous catkins of 5–8 cm, set apart, with yellow stamens; ♀ flowers single or in groups of 2–6, axillary, sessile on shoots (= *Q. sessiliflora*); single flowers round, with red stigma; flowering period April–May
fruits oval acorns of 1.5–3 cm in groups of 2–6, sessile or slightly pedunculate; cup with compressed scales covers one-third of acorn

The Sessile or Durmast Oak is native to Britain and central-southern Europe, widespread on hilly and upland plains in proximity to chestnuts, hornbeams and beech, up to altitudes of 1300 m. It replaces the Downy Oak in cooler, wetter zones; like the English Oak, it can tolerate cold better than other oaks and is thus to be found in central European regions with a continental climate. Although it can adapt to dry, arid terrain, it prefers cool, deep soils.

It is sometimes used in parks and gardens for its decorative appearance. The highly valued wood, similar to that of the English Oak, has the same uses.

Many insects, particularly gall wasps of the hymenopterous family Cynipidae, infest oaks; in laying their eggs these wasps cause galls to develop on the tree – the galls contain large amounts of tannin, which can be extracted and used. A far more sinister enemy of oaks is the fungus oidium (*Microsphaera quercina*) which causes considerable damage, leading to early leaf drop.

QUERCUS ILEX L.
Holm Oak **
Family *Fagaceae*

height 20 m, often shrubby
crown domed, dense
trunk erect and sturdy, divided or branched from base; shoots pubescent; bark brownish-black or black, almost smooth, then cracked into small square plates
foliage evergreen
leaves simple, leathery, oval-elliptic, 3–7 cm, pointed; shiny above and grey, tomentose below; margins smooth or wavy; petiole pubescent, 1–2 cm; alternate arrangement

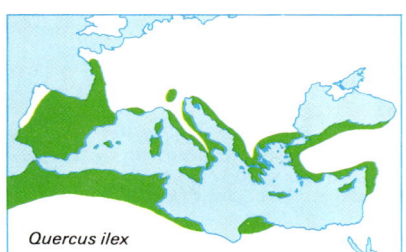

Quercus ilex

flowers unisexual; like those of other oaks

fruits ovoid acorns of 2–3 cm, one-third or one-half covered by pale, short-scaled cup

The Holm Oak abounds in the Mediterranean regions, being found, when conditions are suitable, in the lowland evergreen maquis, and on higher plains dominated by chestnuts, up to altitudes of 700–1000 m. Whereas at one time it formed pure or mixed thickets with Pine, Cork Oak, Strawberry Tree, White Heath, Phillyrea, Sweet Bay, Downy Oak, Manna Ash and Elm, the ecological scene has been subject to change due to grazing and fires. Groves of Holm Oak are still one of the most characteristic features of the Mediterranean landscape.

The Holm Oak is an adaptable species in terms of soil, on which it has an improving action. It tolerates extremely dry conditions, and is not too particular about light and temperature. Its growth is slow; it is very long-lived – even reaching 1000 years. It is particularly suited to a maritime environment and in England is found principally on the south coast. As an ornamental, it has little to commend it.

The dark red wood, very hard and heavy, is difficult to season and work; it makes good fuel and high-quality charcoal.

QUERCUS SUBER L.
Cork Oak
Family *Fagaceae*

height 10 m
crown domed
trunk sinuous, divided and bifurcate; branches twisted; shoots pubescent, yellow; bark corky, yellow-brown, with deep fissures; when stripped, red
foliage evergreen
leaves simple, oval and pointed, 3–7 cm, leathery, margins often revolute, with mucronate teeth; lower side grey, tomentose; small petiole

Quercus ilex

Quercus suber

of 1 cm; alternate arrangement
flowers unisexual; like those of other
oaks; flowering period May
fruits oval acorns of 1.5–3 cm; folded
cup with tomentose grey scales

Quercus crenata Lam.
(= *Quercus* x *hispanica* Lam.; *Q.
pseudosuber* Santi)
Lucombe Oak

Hybrid of *Q. carris* and *Q. suber*; similar to the latter, but with not very
corky bark; leaves persistent during
winter and falling in February; acorns
of 3–4 cm, with cup covering up to
one-half of acorn and with scales
similar to those of Turkey Oak.

The Cork Oak may live for about 300
years, but less if the tree is exploited
for its cork. It grows wild in a restricted area of the central-western
Mediterranean, and is also cultivated
in Portugal, Spain, Algeria, Morocco
and Sardinia. It forms part of the
Mediterranean maquis landscape, in
wetter areas, with an average annual
temperature of over 10°C (50°F) and
with a fair amount of summer rainfall
(700–800 mm – 27½–21½ in). Overall
it prefers a more oceanic climate than
the Holm Oak, growing in acidic subsoils with a reasonable amount of
available water. In cultivation it is
rarely seen in Britain outside the
south-west.

Both in its natural surroundings
and in artificial plantations, the Cork
Oak is exploited for its eponymous
content; this practice, often carried
out in a haphazard way, combined
with overgrazing and fires, has
threatened the equilibrium and vital-
ity of the trees in many areas. Trees
are ready for stripping at the age of
25–30 years, when they attain a cir-
cumference of about half a metre,
and the process is repeated every ten
years until the tree is 150 years old.
The cork layer is stripped during
spring and summer, and the operation has to be expertly carried out to
avoid lesions to the deeper layers of
the bole.

The first stripping produces a
rough, porous cork of little value except for secondary uses; after some
ten years the tree will produce a cork
of better quality and greater industrial value, which will be used mainly
for stoppers, panels and coverings.
The layer underlying the bark can
also be used for its high tannin content, but when this is peeled off the
tree soon dies.

The Lucombe Oak is a natural hybrid of the Turkey Oak and Cork Oak,
mixing in the wild with the latter species. The bark contains little cork, is
hard and of no commercial value. In
Britain it is grown purely as an
ornamental.

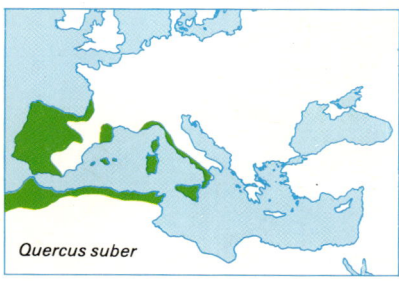

Quercus suber

QUERCUS TROJANA Webb

(= *Q. macedonica* D.C., *Q. aegilops* Griesb.)
Macedonian Oak
Family *Fagaceae*

height 10 m
crown broadly domed
trunk erect, branched, divided from base; bark dark brown, fissured
foliage deciduous at end of winter (February)
leaves simple, oval, elongated, 4–9 cm; margins serrate with mucronate teeth; base round or slightly heart-shaped; alternate arrangement
flowers unisexual; ♂ flowers catkins, pendulous; ♀ flowers axillary and sessile on shoots; flowering period April
fruits round or ovoid acorns of 2.5–3.5 cm, with cup enclosing more than half of it; scales elongated, curving towards peduncle.

This oak, at one time certainly more widespread, now has a very restricted distribution area, with two regions where it still grows naturally: in south-eastern Italy and in the central Balkan peninsula, bordering Macedonia and Bulgaria.

It grows on submontane plains, at an altitude between 200 m and 400 m, on calcareous soils, in mixed stands with other oaks such as the Downy Oak, Valonia Oak, Kermes Oak and often the Holm Oak. It is a semi-evergreen species, losing its leaves only at the time when the new ones sprout, and it is suited to the Mediterranean climate, hot with some rainfall. The large acorns mature after two years.

QUERCUS MACROLEPIS Kotschy

Valonia Oak
Family *Fagaceae*

The Valonia Oak has a restricted distribution in the south-eastern Mediterranean, from Italy to Asia Minor, where it is found growing sporadically in dry scrubland, on calcareous soil, often in association with Kermes Oak, Macedonian Oak, Holm Oak and Downy Oak. In Britain it is rarely seen except in arboreta. The wood is of similar quality to that of

Quercus trojana

Quercus macrolepis

other oaks and is put to the same uses; the woody cupules are used in tanning and for making inks and dyes.

QUERCUS COCCIFERA L.
Kermes Oak
Family *Fagaceae*

This oak is usually found in shrub form, its branches twisted and foliage dense. It comes from south-eastern Europe, primarily from the driest zones of the Mediterranean maquis and is rarely seen in Britain. Sun-loving, extremely frugal, it grows on calcareous, rocky, degraded terrain and may be regarded as one of the best soil-improving species. It produces an abundance of pollen and, because of the sharply pointed leaf margins, is seldom browsed by livestock.

The oak is host to a scale insect, *Chermes vermilio*; in ancient times a

Quercus coccifera

bright red substance was extracted from the dried, powdered bodies of the adult females and used as a dye.

Key to **ELMS**

Fruits with long peduncle and hairy margins; petiole not covered by the asymmetrical lobe of the leaf base: ***Ulmus laevis***

Fruits with short peduncle or sessile, glabrous; petiole covered by the asymmetrical lobe of the leaf base
– leaf rough on top; seed at the centre of the wings: ***Ulmus glabra***
– leaf shiny and glabrous on top; seed towards apex of wings: ***Ulmus minor***

ULMUS GLABRA Huds.
(= *U. montana* With.)
Wych Elm *
Family *Ulmaceae*

height 15 (40) m
crown broadly, irregularly domed
trunk erect, divided into several main boles; branches large and rigid; bark light grey, at first smooth, later with dark ridges and cracks

foliage deciduous
leaves simple, oval-elliptic, 8–16 cm, asymmetrical base with lobe completely covering the very short petiole (3–5 mm); rough on top; alternate arrangement
flowers in axillary clusters, sessile with small red perianth; 5–6 stamens with red anthers; flowering period March–April
fruits glabrous samaras of 1.5–2 cm, with seed at centre

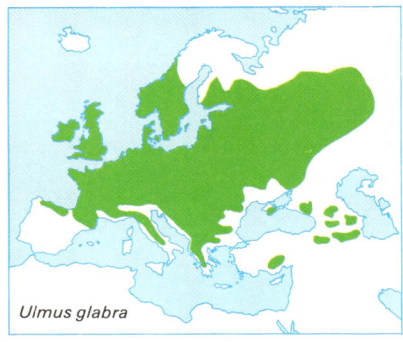

Ulmus glabra

The Wych Elm has a European distribution, including Scandinavia and the British Isles, growing up to 1500 m. It is a constituent of deciduous woodlands, preferring loose fertile soils. It is not as long-lived nor does it grow as big as the Smooth Leaved Elm; the wood is less valued, though put to similar uses.

The species is sometimes planted to line avenues in parks in mountainous regions; 'Pendula', with weeping habit, is popular.

Today European elms throughout their range are in grave danger of extinction because of Dutch Elm disease, caused by the ascomycetic fungus *Ceratocystis ulmi*, which clogs the vascular system of the tree and

prevents the passage of sap, thereby killing the tree. Carriers of the disease are beetles of the genus *Scolytus* which bore tunnels under the bark and spread the disease by moving from sick to healthy trees. It is an extremely difficult disease to fight because there are no satisfactory chemical remedies.

ULMUS MINOR Miller
(= *U. carpinifolia* Suckow; *U. campestris* Auct. non L.)
Smooth Leaved Elm
Family *Ulmaceae*

height 20–30 m
crown variable, dense and elongated, broadened at top
trunk straight and branched at top; shoots narrow and glabrous; bark grey-brown
foliage deciduous
leaves simple, obovate-elliptic, 5–10 cm, asymmetrical base with lobe covering the petiole; margins doubly dentate-serrate; apex acute or acuminate; upper surface of leaf shiny and glabrous; alternate arrangement
flowers in axillary clusters, more or less sessile with small perianth; 4–6 protruding stamens and reddish-brown anthers; flowering period March–April, before foliation
fruits samaras of 1–2 cm, with seeds directed towards apex; wings glabrous at edges

This beautiful tree is very long-lived (over 600 years), has a central and southern European distribution and does not normally grow above 800–1000 m. It was probably introduced into Britain by Celtic tribes and is found in the south and east. It prefers cool, fertile soil but will tolerate firm, heavy ground; it is highly adaptable to climatic conditions. All elms have a decorative crown, withstand pollution, and tolerate drastic pruning. They are sometimes used for training vines. The foliage provides good fodder for cattle.

The wood of the Smooth Leaved Elm, pinkish-white to brown, is fairly

Ulmus glabra

Ulmus minor

hard and heavy, very durable and not liable to split. Although difficult to season, it is easy to work, and is used for furniture and coffins. It resists damp particularly well and after immersion in water is used for farming implements and turnery. The leaves and bark have pharmaceutical uses as astringents, cicatrizers and laxatives. The new fruits, with an aromatic, pleasant taste, can be used in salads.

Ulmus laevis

ULMUS PROCERA Salisbury
English Elm
Family *Ulmaceae*

This majestic tree used to dominate the British landscape from 1700 till 1970 but has virtually disappeared as a result of Dutch Elm disease. It is probably a form of *Ulmus minor*, or a hybrid therefrom and rarely sets viable seed.

ULMUS LAEVIS Pall.
(= *U. effusa* Willd.)
European White Elm
Family *Ulmaceae*

height 10–20 m
crown irregular, full
trunk erect, more or less sinuous; shoots hairy; bark grey-brown, flaking off in small plates
foliage deciduous
leaves simple, oval, 5–15 cm, base asymmetrical, short petiole not covered by asymmetrical base lobe; margins doubly serrate; apex acute or acuminate; leaves shiny above; alternate arrangement
flowers in clusters, small, pedunculate, with 6–8 stamens; flowering period March–April
fruits oval samaras of 1–1.5 cm, with peduncle of 3–5 cm, ciliated at edge of wings

The European White Elm is rare in Britain but is native to central Europe, with various separate populations occurring from the Pyrenees to the Caucasus. It is found sporadically in moist woodlands, up to an altitude of 400–500 m, on fertile, well aerated soil. It is frequently cultivated as a shade-giving species, while the wood, more irregular and not as hard as that of other elms, has only limited uses in joinery.

ULMUS PUMILA L.
Siberian Elm
Family *Ulmaceae*

The Siberian Elm is a central Asiatic

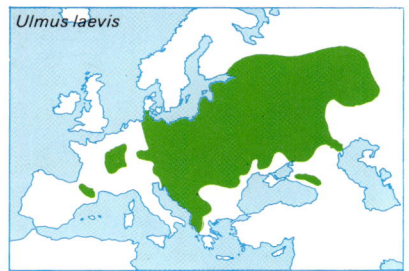
Ulmus laevis

species, also found in northern China and Siberia. It was imported into Europe in the 1930s because of its resistance to Dutch Elm disease. It can withstand summer drought and severe winter cold, adapting to virtually any terrain and growing very rapidly.

As an ornamental tree it is used along streets, to create windbreaks and in land reclamation.

Key to **NETTLE-TREES**

Leaves oval-lanceolate, acuminate, 5–15 cm; margin serrate
– leaves toothed along entire margin; bark smooth: *Celtis australis*
– leaves toothed halfway to midrib, margin entire at base; bark deeply fissured: *Celtis occidentalis*

Leaves cordate-ovate, 5–7 cm, with margin crenate teeth (not serrate):
                                             Celtis tournefortii

---

CELTIS AUSTRALIS L.
Southern Nettle-tree
Family *Ulmaceae*

height 20 m
crown domed, broad and dense
trunk straight; bark dark grey, smooth
foliage deciduous
leaves simple, oval-lanceolate, 5–15 cm, rounded or asymmetrical at base, petiole short (about 1 cm), apex acuminate and margins serrate; alternate arrangement
flowers single or in groups of 3–5, axillary, with yellow-green perianth of 2–3 mm; flowering period April–May
fruits round or oval drupes, brown or black, of about 1 cm ⌀, with long peduncle

The Southern Nettle-tree has a distribution area covering Mediterranean Europe, extending eastwards to Asia Minor. It is often cultivated as an ornamental species in central Europe but rarely in Britain. Sun-loving and extremely frugal, it grows in dry surroundings on calcareous or stony soil, its strong and well developed root system thrusting into rock fissures.

It associates with other sun-loving broadleaved species such as oaks, maples, hazels, hornbeams and manna ash, in woods up to an altitude of 800 m. It is sensitive to severe cold and late frosts; it may live for up to

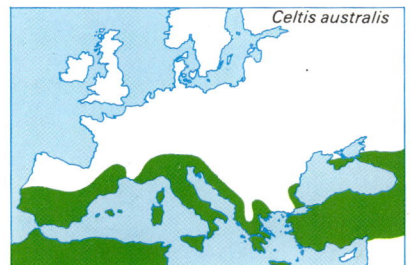
Celtis australis

Celtis australis

flower ×4

young fruit

×1

500 years. The tree is used for ornament along avenues because of the attractive habit of the branches, upright at first, then drooping; it is used in reafforestation of stony, unamenable terrain in southern Europe.

The greyish-white wood is elastic and hard, used principally for equipment and implements subject to wear and tear, such as wheels, joints, oars, whip handles and walking sticks, also for lathe-work and cabinet-making. It makes good fuel and high-quality charcoal. The edible fruits contain seeds from which a pleasant-tasting oil is extracted, while the bark produces a yellow dye.

CELTIS OCCIDENTALIS L.
Nettle-tree
Family *Ulmaceae*

This species originates in the eastern parts of the United States, where it is known as the Sugar Berry or Hackberry. Introduced to Europe around the middle of the 17th century as an ornamental tree, it is used along streets and is sometimes seen growing wild. In Britain it is uncommon.

It gives a light-coloured hard wood, used for furniture and packaging, as well as for the same purposes as *Celtis australis* from which it is distinguished by the deeply fissured bark and leaves which are narrower and not completely serrate.

CELTIS TOURNEFORTII Lam.
Hackberry
Family *Ulmaceae*

This is a species native to southeastern Europe. In the mountains of the Balkan peninsula it grows sporadically in thickets up to 800 m. It is usually of shrubby habit (sometimes a small tree) and differs from *C. occidentalis* in that it has ovate-cordate leaves with rounded teeth. In Sicily *Celtis aetnensis* Strobl. represents a local population of *C. tournefortii*. Both trees are very rarely seen in cultivation in Great Britain.

ZELKOVA CARPINIFOLIA Koch
(= *Z. crenata* Spach)
Caucasian Elm
Family *Ulmaceae*

height 25 (35) m
crown oval, domed
trunk erect, irregular in shape, ridged, often divided and much bran-

Zelkova carpinifolia

×1

♂

×1

Morus nigra

inflorescences

ched from base; bark grey, smooth, flaking away in scales.

foliage deciduous

leaves simple, elliptic, 5–9 cm, pointed, with crenate-dentate margins, subsessile; autumn colour light brown to orange; alternate arrangement

flowers unisexual; not very conspicuous, with small perianth; ♂ flowers in axillary clusters, anthers greenish-yellow; ♀ flowers solitary, axillary; flowering period April

fruits asymmetrical, ridged nuts, 5–8 mm

The original distribution area of this species covers the Caucasus from where it was introduced to Europe in the mid-18th century as an expensive and rare ornamental tree for regions with a mild climate. In Britain it is an uncommon amenity tree. The golden-brown wood is similar in quality to that of the elm and is used in cabinet-making.

MORUS NIGRA L.
Black Mulberry
Family *Moraceae*

height 10 (15) m
crown dense, rounded

trunk erect, broadly ramified; pubescent shoots; bark brown, rough, with small scales and reticulated

foliage deciduous

leaves simple, cordate, also oval-lanceolate on lateral branches, stiff and rough above; margins dentate; alternate arrangement

flowers hermaphrodite and unisexual (prevalently); ♂ flowers cylindrical catkins of 2–4 cm, with short peduncle, 4 stamens; ♀ flowers oval catkins of 1 cm or less, short peduncle; perianth of 4 parts which at maturity become fleshy; flowering period April-May

fruits fleshy, oval 2–2.5 cm; edible mulberries, purple, acid until ripe

***Morus alba* L.**
White Mulberry

Similar to *M. nigra*, but with following differences:

shoots smooth and glabrous

leaves cordate, entire and irregularly lobate, with 1–3 lobes, glabrous beneath

fruits mulberries of 1–2 cm, whitish or pink, sweet even when unripe

The Black Mulberry is thought to have come from the south-western

Morus alba

The White Mulberry arrived in Europe from China rather later than the Black Mulberry, around the 12th century. Since then it has become naturalized and extensively cultivated, the leaves being widely used as food for silkworms. Although this species is to be found in northern Europe and Great Britain, the map shows the area in which conditions are most suited to its growth.

This species requires deep, fresh, well-drained soil, with good exposure to sun. It is normally pollarded, with a short trunk bearing a number of curving branches which are periodically pruned. The yellowish-brown wood is not affected by water. Because of its hardness, it is used in joinery for articles subject to wear, for lathe-work and the manufacture of barrels.

The pinkish-white fruit is sweet, juicy and edible.

FICUS CARICA L.
Fig
Family *Moraceae*

height 5 (10) m
crown spreading and domed, sparse
trunk sinuous, widely branched; branches fragile; bark grey, smooth and soft
foliage deciduous
leaves simple, palmately-lobed, up to 20 cm and more, divided into 3–5 lobes, rough and pubescent; long, sturdy petiole; alternate arrangement
flowers produced in the cavity of a fleshy, pear-shaped receptacle (syconium), with a very narrow orifice opening to top; flowers unisexual; ♂ flowers close to aperture, ♀ flowers in lower part of cavity; the two types of flowers are not always present; flowering period June-August
fruits consisting of a fleshy receptacle of 5–7 cm, yellow-green to brown-violet, inside which are the fruits proper (achenes), incorrectly called seeds, edible

parts of Asia and was introduced into Europe in antiquity, being grown for its wood and fruit, and subsequently for rearing silkworms. It is fairly common in Britain, but nowhere frequent. A rugged, economic species, it is fairly resistant to cold; it grows on plains up to an altitude of 800 m.

The blackish fruits are sweet and edible, being used for jams and syrups; when fermented they produce an alcoholic drink. The leaves are used in pharmacy for their astringent properties; they also yield a yellow colorant mainly used for heightening the sheen on silk.

The wood is similar to that of the White Mulberry and used for the same purposes. In Japan a textile fibre is extracted from the bark.

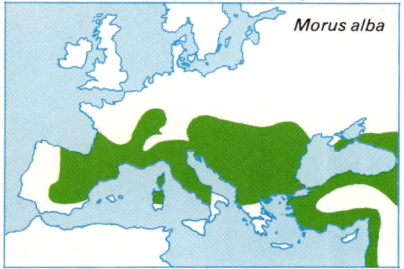

Morus alba

South-western Asia is the Fig Tree's

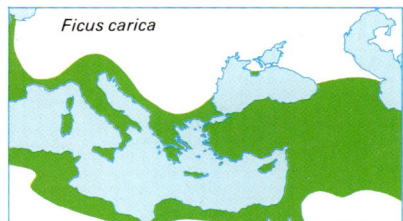

Ficus carica

main distribution area whence it came to be cultivated in all European countries around the Mediterranean. Fig trees are found in most of Britain, but only in the south, with protection, does the fruit ripen. Very frugal, in the wild it roots in difficult terrain, adapting to stony, rocky and arid soil, and may even be found in the cracks of sheltered walls. It makes a small tree, furnishing a light, ivory-white wood, which has few applications (though at one time used for rulers), and is even poor as fuel.

Ficus carica domestica is cultivated for its excellent fruit, which is very sweet and nutritious; fresh figs contain 20% sugar and dried figs 50%; they are used in popular medicine to cure skin ailments and constipation. The latex emitted by the leaf petioles is effective in healing warts.

Ficus carica

The fruits of the wild fig, known as syconia, ripen at three different times in the year. Early figs ripen in June, the so-called true figs in August–September, and the late figs develop in the autumn, becoming ripe the following spring. These appear as proper fruit (achenes) only if fertilization is effected by *Blastophaga psenes*, the fig wasp, which completes its cycle of development inside the syconia with two or three generations annually.

Within the female flowers of the late figs are small galls containing the insects' eggs. From these, in the spring, emerge the winged females which, after being fertilized by the wingless males, emerge from the ostiole (aperture) of the syconium, boring into the newly developed spring figs and laying their eggs in the female flowers. From these eggs develop the second-generation females which, when mature, will themselves emerge from the ostiole of the syconium, laden with pollen collected from the male flowers, and proceed to fertilize the true figs.

The third generation of fig wasps develops inside the figs, finds its way into the late figs and thus resumes the cycle. Fertilization of the figs is thus effected only by the winged female wasps.

The female flowers of the domestic fig are not suitable for egg-laying by *Blastophaga psenes* and are therefore unable to produce new generations of pollinating insects; since ancient times it has been the practice to hang on the branches of the domestic fig fruits of the wild caprifig, which contain pollen and insects, or alternatively to plant wild figs next to domestic ones.

FICUS ELASTICA Roxbg.
Rubber Plant
Family *Moraceae*

This tree originated in tropical Asia, where it reaches a considerable size. It was introduced to Europe as an ornamental species and is a very popular house plant. It is cultivated outdoors only in a few places around the Mediterranean. A latex exuded from the trunk provides rubber and gum for lacquer in its native regions.

MACLURA POMIFERA (Raf.) C.K. Schneider
Osage Orange
Family *Moraceae*

height 12–20 m
crown irregularly spreading
trunk sinuous, much branched; branches with strong spines of 1–2 cm; bark orange-red, deeply ridged
foliage deciduous
leaves simple, oval-acuminate, shiny above, opaque beneath; entire margins; alternate arrangement
flowers unisexual; ♂ flowers with long peduncle, in racemes of 2–3, each with 4 petals and 4 stamens; ♀ flowers in rounded clusters of 2 cm, with short peduncle, composed of 30 green flowers, 2 mm, with long styles, persisting also in fruit; flowering period May–June

Maclura pomifera

fruits rounded, 10–15 cm ∅, first green, then bright yellow, with a rough, ridged surface; not edible

The generic name commemorates the American naturalist Maclure. The tree is native to the central-western United States and was introduced to Europe around the middle of the 19th century. It is uncommon in Britain. A rugged species, it is not especially particular as to soil or climate, but it does not bear fruit in conditions of extreme cold.

The tree is principally used as an ornament because of its beautiful orange-yellow fruit (non-edible), and for hedges and as dense thicket screens.

The wood is similar to that of the mulberry; tannin is extracted from the trunk as well as an orange-yellow colorant from the roots. The leaves are used for feeding silkworms.

BROUSSONETIA PAPYRIFERA (L.) Vent.
Paper Mulberry
Family *Moraceae*

height 15 m
crown spreading at top
trunk sinuous, branched; bark pale brown, longitudinally ridged
foliage deciduous
leaves simple, oval with pointed tip, often deeply lobed; woolly-tomentose beneath; alternate arrangement
flowers dioecious; ♂ flowers cylindrical catkins of 4–7 cm, pedunculate, 4-lobed perianth, 4 stamens; ♀ flowers round, 1.2 cm ∅, perianth with 4 small teeth; flowering period May–June
fruits round (syncarp), 2 cm ∅, orange in colour

The generic name commemorates the French naturalist P. M. A. Broussonet (1761–1807).

This species ranges from China to Japan. It was introduced to Europe in

Broussonetia papyrifera

the middle of the 18th century as an ornamental tree and became naturalized. It has a broad, shade-giving crown, which makes it ideal as a tree for city streets. This tree is occasionally found in arboreta.

Fairly rugged, indifferent to subsoil, it is suitable for colonizing sterile and rough terrain; it can withstand cold and poor light. In its regions of origin the bark is pulped and used for making paper.

Cercidiphyllum japonicum

fruits

CERCIDIPHYLLUM JAPONICUM
Sieb & Zucc.
Katsura Tree **
Family *Cercidiphyllaceae*

height 15 m
crown oval, more or less spreading
trunk erect and sinuous, often divided; light brown, smooth and irregularly fissured
foliage deciduous
leaves simple, round and cordate, 8 cm, veins fanwise; margins slightly dentate-crenate; red petiole of 3 cm; spring colour red; autumn colour yellow to purple; opposite arrangement
flowers dioecious; ♂ flowers in clusters of 15–20, with stamens that protrude 0.8 cm and red anthers; ♀ flowers in erect clusters of 3–5, with stigmas protruding 0.6 cm, dark red; flowering period April, before foliation
fruits formed of green, shiny, upright pods, up to 5 cm long

The generic name underlines the similarity of this tree's leaves with those of *Cercis siliquastrum*, except the former grow in opposing pairs on the branches. The Katsura Tree was introduced to Europe after the mid-19th century from Japan, where it grows wild. In Britain it is used essentially for ornament because of its beautiful leaves, reddish when young, its elegant shape and splendid autumn coloration. It adapts to almost any terrain, but prefers acidic, fairly moist soils; it also needs sheltered sites and a mild climate.

In its native habitat its wood, which is soft and lightweight, fine-grained and easy to work, is used mainly for panelling and cabinet-making.

PHYTOLACCA DIOICA L.
Phytolacca
Family *Phytolaccaceae*

height 6 m
crown domed
trunk erect and stout, broadly branched; bark pale brown

foliage evergreen
leaves simple, ovate-lanceolate, 5–13 cm, mucronate at apex, with entire margin and petiole of 4 cm; alternate arrangement
flowers tree dioecious, inflorescence unisexual, in clusters of 12 cm; perianth with 5 free elements, green spotted with white, 5 mm; ♂ flowers with 20–25 stamens as long as the petals; ♀ flowers with 7–10 styles; flowering period July–August
fruits purple-black berries of 5–7 mm

The genus *Phytolacca* comprises plants from which is extracted a juice used for dyeing, a fact reflected in the generic name, meaning 'plant which produces juice'. The distribution of the arboreal Phytolacca extends from Peru to Brazil. Imported into southern Europe after the mid-18th century, it became naturalized in regions with a Mediterranean climate. It is, in fact, a tree for mild climates, undemanding in respect of soil, resistant to sea winds. It is not found out of doors in Britain.

LAURUS NOBILIS L.
Sweet Bay or Bay Laurel **
Family *Lauraceae*

height 6–10 m
crown pyramidal, dense
trunk erect, sinuous, broadly ramified with thin branches; bark grey-brown, dark, smooth
foliage evergreen

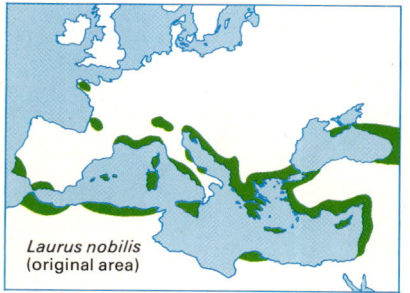

Laurus nobilis
(original area)

Laurus nobilis

leaves simple, lanceolate, 5–10 cm, shiny, dark green above, lighter beneath, leathery and aromatic; margins wavy; petiole short; alternate arrangement
flowers tree dioecious, inflorescence in axillary umbels; flowers with perianth of 4 free tepals of 3 mm ∅; stamens numerous (approximately 10); inflorescence similar, white, with some atrophied stamens; flowering period March–April
fruits black berries of 1–2 cm, pedunculate, similar to olives

The generic name is of uncertain origin; some authors suggest a derivation from the Celtic *laur*, green, others from the Latin *laudo*, because the laurel was used to make crowns and decorations on festive occasions.

As the Sweet Bay is cultivated in all countries with a Mediterranean climate, where it also grows wild, its original distribution is in doubt. Fairly rugged, it grows on deep, fertile soil, in evergreen and broadleaved woods of the Mediterranean maquis. It tolerates low temperatures, though not for long. It survives most winters in southern England, being cut to ground level in the severest.

The wood is pale greyish-brown or pinkish, hard and easy to polish, and because of its uniform quality much used for cabinet-making. The straight, sturdy trunks make excellent poles. Because it can stand pruning, the tree is used as ornament for hedges and borders.

The strongly aromatic leaves contain about 3% essential oils which are used in the preparation of food dishes, liqueurs and medicines. The fruits also contain essential oils, and a fat content (25%) which is used in perfumery and the manufacture of soap; mixed with other substances it provides an ointment used to treat gout and rheumatism. The laurel is traditionally the symbol of glory and faith, concepts still reflected in titles like 'laureate'.

MAGNOLIA GRANDIFLORA L.
Evergreen Magnolia or Bull Bay **
Family *Magnoliaceae*

height 25 m
crown pyramidal, oval
trunk erect, often branched from base; bark dark grey, smooth
foliage evergreen

leaves simple, elliptic, 10–20 cm, with short petiole, shiny dark green above, mainly brown and hairy beneath; pointed apex; leathery consistency; alternate arrangement
flowers large, white; initially tapering and conical, then opening into cup shape; 6 petals, up to 20 cm long; flowering period May–September
fruits oval, 7–10 cm long, on a short stem with traces (scars) of petals and stamens, formed of numerous orange achenes and purple-green scales

The generic name commemorates Pierre Magnol (1638–1715), director of the Botanical Gardens at Montpellier. The species originated in the Atlantic regions of the United States and the Gulf of Mexico, where it grows wild on moist plains. It was introduced to Europe at the beginning of the 18th century, and quickly became popular because of its huge, beautiful flowers and large, decorative, persistent leaves.

Bull Bay is cultivated in areas associated with mild climates, tolerating occasional cold spells if planted in sunny sites, sheltered from wind. It may be grown as a wall plant up the side of a house because of its fragrant

stamen
×1
Magnolia × soulangiana
Magnolia grandiflora

flowers, although this is rare in Britain. It prefers deep, acidic soils. The light-coloured wood is sometimes used for joinery, being durable and easy to work. The bark contains certain medicinal properties.

MAGNOLIA × SOULANGIANA Soul. Bod.
Magnolia **
Family *Magnoliaceae*

Among the deciduous-leaved magnolias is this hybrid obtained in 1820 by crossing two Chinese species: *M. liliflora* and *M. denudata*. It is widely planted as an ornament for its splendid early flowers which precede foliation; it grows to 7 m but is also known in shrub form; it has ovate-lanceolate leaves which are pale green, and flowers are abundant in April.

LIRIODENDRON TULIPIFERA L.
Tulip Tree **
Family *Magnoliaceae*

height 20–30 m
crown broadly pyramidal, rounded at top
trunk erect and regularly branched; branches sinuous; bark grey-brown, reticulated
foliage deciduous
leaves simple, with 4 lobes and squarish or notched apex, about 15 cm, with petiole; autumn colour golden-yellow; alternate arrangement
flowers large and conspicuous, terminal, 5–6 cm, many free yellow-green petals with orange spots; caducous calyx; flowering period May–July
fruits in form of cones, 5–8 cm, erect and pointed, formed of short winged achenes

The flowers, which are in the shape of lilies or tulips, give rise to both the generic and specific names. The species originated in the eastern part of North America and was introduced to

Liriodendron tulipifera

Europe around the middle of the 17th century, becoming popular as an ornamental tree because of its beautiful flowers and leaves; in central Europe it is also valued for its timber. Hardy except in the far north of Britain, it is a frequent ornamental tree.

A sun-loving species, fairly rugged and long-lived, it can stand intense cold quite well but needs deep, fertile soil. The pale yellow wood is of average quality, resistant to woodworm, and widely used, mainly for furniture, musical instruments, packing cases, and in the paper industry.

LIQUIDAMBAR STYRACIFLUA L.
Sweet Gum *
Family *Hamamelidaceae*

height 15 m
crown pyramidal, broad, dense
trunk erect, with narrow branches; bark brown, ridged
foliage deciduous
leaves simple, palmate, well spaced, 12–15 cm, divided into 5 (7) pointed, triangular lobes; serrate margins; autumn colour from yellow to purple; alternate arrangement

flowers unisexual; ♂ flowers erect, terminal, spherical, in spikes of 5–7 cm; ♀ flowers spherical, pendulous and with long peduncles
fruits round and spiny, 3 cm ∅, with 5 cm peduncle, formed of numerous beaked seed capsules which remain on winter branches

The fact that this tree produces resin explains the generic and specific names ('liquid amber', 'secreting resin').

The Sweet Gum comes originally from the Atlantic regions of North America and was imported into Europe around 1680, as an ornament and for its timber, in Britain being grown for the attractive hues of the foliage in autumn. It is long-lived, very rugged, adapting to virtually any soil, even if wet or temporarily flooded; it can stand temperatures as low as −15° to −20°C (5° to −4°F).

In its areas of origin it is important for its wood, which is similar to mahogany, heavy, uniform, easy to work and used for panelling and furniture. In Europe the species is chiefly ornamental, but recently it has also found a use in sylviculture, as a tree that grows rapidly. The resin exuded from the bark, known as American storax, has a strong scent; it is used for perfuming hides in tanneries and as an emollient in skin diseases, at one time even used as chewing gum. It is of less value than the resin produced by *Styrax officinalis*.

PLATANUS HISPANICA Menhh.
(= *P. acerifolia* (Ait.) Willd.)
London Plane **
Family *Platanaceae*

height 15–40 cm
crown broadly domed
trunk erect, with large, curving branches; bark grey-green, smooth, flaking off in thin scales revealing the very pale new bark beneath
foliage deciduous
leaves simple, palmately lobed, 10–25 cm, with 3–5 lobes, often polymorphous; alternate arrangement
flowers unisexual; ♂ flowers axillary; ♀ flowers with globose heads, terminal and with long peduncle; flowering period May
fruits spherical, 3 cm ∅, in groups of 2–4 on a long peduncle, one terminal, the other(s) axillary, formed of cylindrical achenes with a ring of hairs at the tip; the fruits, first green, then yellow-brown, persist in winter

Platanus orientalis L.
Oriental Plane

Similar to *P. hispanica*, but distinguished as to:
bark rough, flaking off in small plates on old trees
leaves deeply lobate, with 5–7 lobes
fruits joined in groups of 3–6

The generic name of the London Plane is derived from the broad shape of the leaves, i.e. Greek *platys* (broad, large).

The origin of this very widely diffused tree is unknown; it is probably a hybrid from *Platanus orientalis* and

Liquidambar styraciflua

Platanus hispanica

P. occidentalis, created in northern Europe at the end of the 17th century and subsequently finding its way all over the continent as an ornamental species. Today it is the commonest of all planes and exhibits marked variability in shape. It is much used in parks for shade and planted along roads because it can take drastic pruning.

Recently in parts of Europe it has been gravely threatened by the attacks of an insect parasite, *Corythucha ciliata*, which causes galls and early leaf fall. The wood is similar to that of *Platanus orientalis*, but of superior quality; it is used in joinery for trellises and as fuel; because it is so hard and firm it is suitable for butchers' blocks.

The young parts of the tree are covered in white fluff which may cause allergies of the human respiratory system.

The Oriental Plane originated in south-eastern Europe and western Asia; from here it has been spread through Europe and is found in the Balkans and, less commonly, in southern Italy. This tree is occasionally grown in southern Britain.

It grows well in thin, airy woods because it likes light and deep, moist soil; it is less tolerant of pollution than other planes. The pinkish-white speckled wood is similar to that of the Common Beech but is less easy to work since it splits and bends. The roots are prized for their beautiful veining; the branches contain a

Platanus orientalis

fruit   ×1

brown colouring substance suitable for dyeing textiles. The bark and leaves, with their astringent action, are applied to burns and skin inflammations. The tree is mainly important as an ornamental species in parks, though more often than not supplanted by London Plane.

American Plane (*Platanus occidentalis* L.), introduced in the early years of the 17th century from North America (where it grows in central-eastern parts), is a large tree which may reach a height of 50 m. It has 3-lobed leaves, single fruits and bark which sloughs off in small flakes. In America it may live for 500 years. Nowadays the species has practically vanished from Europe and been replaced by the London Plane.

Crataegus monogyna

PITTOSPORUM TOBIRA (Thunb.) Ait.
Pittosporum
Family *Pittosporaceae*

height up to 4 (5) m, more often shrubby
crown domed
trunk twisted, branched; shoots pubescent; bark rough and blackish
foliage evergreen
leaves simple, obovate obtuse, 10–12 cm long; arrangement sparse, almost verticillate
flowers in terminal umbels, each flower with 5 white or yellowish petals of 1 cm ⌀, scented; flowering period March–May
fruits subglobose capsules of 1 cm

The seeds of this plant are covered in a dark resinous layer, from which the generic name is derived, from the Greek *pitta* (pitch) and *sporos* (seed).
The Pittosporum comes originally from China and Japan, and was brought to Europe as an ornament in the 19th century. In places it came to spread beyond the area of cultivation and now grows wild in parts of Italy. Tolerant of all but cold climates and not too demanding as to soil, it has been widely used for hedg-

ing and for replanting sandy, coastal areas because it can withstand a salt-laden environment. It is rare in southern England.

The genus also includes *P. tenuifolium* Gaertn., a small tree with wavy-edged leaves. The cultivar 'Variegatum', with white variegated leaves, is a popular ornamental.

CRATAEGUS MONOGYNA Jacq.
Hawthorn or May *
Family *Rosaceae*

height 5 (10) m, often shrubby
crown irregularly domed, elongated
trunk sinuous, much branched; branches with spines of 2 cm; shoots reddish; bark orange-brown
foliage deciduous
leaves simple, oval, deeply lobed, 4–8 cm, mostly with 2–4 lateral lobes; margins doubly toothed; veins curving outwards
flowers numerous (15–20) in terminal, upright corymbs; calyx with 5 sepals, corolla with 5 white, concave, rounded petals; 20 stamens with pink anthers; one style and lower ovary; flowering period April–May
fruits pomes of about 1 cm, red; one seed

Crataegus laevigata (Poir.) D.C.
(= *C. oxyacantha* L.)
Midland Hawthorn

Similar to *C. monogyna*, except for leaves, which are only slightly lobate (3–5 lobes); veins curving towards tip; 2 styles and 2 seeds.

The distribution of the Hawthorn or May extends over the whole of Europe including Great Britain; it is found growing wild along roads, in hedges and woods, usually exhibiting a shrubby habit but sometimes attaining the size of a small tree. Very long-lived, it is rugged, sun-loving and adaptable to almost any climate or soil.
  The wood is yellowish-red, fine-grained, difficult to season and work; because of its size it is mainly used for small domestic articles and fuel.
  The Hawthorn has long been known for its medicinal properties; the flowers contain substances that act in a similar way to digitalin, though less powerfully; they help the circulation and may be used, with extreme caution, as anti-spasmodics and sedatives.
  The plant is much used for hedging, and a number of pink-flowered cultivars are frequent ornamentals.

Crataegus laevigata

CRATAEGUS AZAROLUS L.
Azarole
Family *Rosaceae*

Similar in appearance to the Hawthorn, this is a small tree, often a shrub, with tomentose shoots and leaves. The rhombic leaves, 3–5 cm, are slightly lobate, leathery, with sickle-shaped stipules. The flowers are 1.5–2 cm in $\varnothing$; the fruit globose, 2–2.5 cm in $\varnothing$, orange-red or yellow, with 1–3 seeds.
  Since antiquity, the Azarole has been widespread in the Mediterranean region, having come originally from Asia Minor. It is found wild or cultivated for its fine flowers and deep red pomes although it is rare in Britain. Very rugged and undemanding, it needs a sunny, protected site in order to produce an abundance of pulpy fruit.
  The tree is only moderately important for timber and fruit; the fruits or pomes are, in fact, edible but with little pulp and many seeds. They really need to be over-ripe to taste pleasant, though they can be used for jam-making. The wood makes good fuel and high-quality charcoal.

MESPILUS GERMANICA L.
(= *M. vulgaris* Rchb.)
Medlar **
Family *Rosaceae*

height 5 m, often shrubby
crown broad, hemispherical
trunk short and sinuous, branched from base; branches with straight spines; bark grey-brown, ridged, flaking off
foliage deciduous
leaves simple, elliptic-lanceolate, 8–15 cm, short petiole, margins serrate and apex pointed; underside of leaves tomentose; alternate arrangement
flowers single or in pairs, each 4–5 cm in $\varnothing$; calyces with persistent linear lobes; corolla with 5 rounded, white petals; large numbers of stamens with red anthers; 5 styles;

Mespilus germanica

flowering period May–June
fruits pomes of 3 cm (5 cm in culti-vated forms), russet in colour, de-pressed tip surrounded by 5 lobes of calyx

The generic name, from the Greek *mesos* and *pilos* (half ball), refers to the hemispherical shape of the fruit.

Despite its specific name, the Med-lar originated in Asia Minor, and arrived in Europe centures ago. Now-adays it is found, though rarely, growing wild in thickets and may flourish at heights of up to 1000 m. It is occasionally cultivated in Great Britain.

It likes sunny positions and adapts to poor, rocky subsoils. The actual fruits are not commonly known or used. They are collected when still unripe and cannot be eaten because of the hard, bitter pulp; but they be-come sweet and edible when they are over-ripe, the pulp then changing colour, consistency and taste.

The brownish wood, which is fairly hard, is used for small domestic articles and makes good-quality char-coal. The leaves and bark, which have a large tannin content, have curing and astringent properties.

ERIOBOTRYA JAPONICA (Thunb.) Lindl.
Loquat
Family *Roseaceae*

height 5–10 m
crown long and domed
trunk erect, divided and branched; branches tomentose; bark blackish, rough
foliage evergreen
leaves simple, elliptic-lanceolate, 12–25 cm, dentate-serrate, brown and tomentose beneath; alternate arrangement
flowers inflorescence in spikes, flowers 1 cm ⌀, with 5 yellow-white petals; 20 stamens; the flowers are often hidden by the hairy, pale brown calyx; flowering period October–February
fruits pomes which ripen in spring, 3 cm, yellow-orange, edible, with one seed

The generic name is derived from the Greek *erion* (wool) and *botrys* (bunch), from the woolly appearance of the spiked inflorescence.

The Loquat was imported into southern Europe as an ornamental species in the 18th century from

Eriobotrya japonica

China and Japan. It was later culti-vated for its fruit, which has a sweet-acidic pulp which does not keep well. Loquats are usually eaten raw or as jam, and can also be used for making alcoholic drinks.

The Loquat needs a temperate to warm climate in order to produce fruit satisfactorily which it rarely does in southern England; it flowers in late autumn and the fruit reacts adversely to the approaching cold season. To-day it serves mainly for ornamental purposes, being fast-growing and displaying decorative evergreen leaves.

CYDONIA OBLONGA Miller
Quince
Family *Rosaceae*

height 5 m
crown domed, dense
trunk sinuous and twisted; shoots hairy, then glabrous; bark grey-brown
foliage deciduous
leaves simple, oval-elliptic, 5–10 cm, with entire margins; underside tomentose; alternate arrangement
flowers single and terminal, 4–4.5 cm ∅, with short, tomentose peduncles;

petals pink, 15–25 stamens; 3 free styles; flowering period April–May
fruits pomes of 3–5 cm (up to 12 cm if cultivated), pubescent and velvety

The Quince probably originated in south-western Asia, being intro-duced to southern and western Europe. It cannot stand hard frost, and in order to develop properly re-quires sunny, sheltered sites and fresh soil. It is hardy in Britain, but only occasionally cultivated.

The fruits ripen in mid-October, are highly perfumed, keep for a long time and are usually made into jams and jellies. (Marmalade was original-ly made from quinces.)

Quince stock can be used for graft-ing and dwarfing the pear.

MALUS SYLVESTRIS (L.) Mill.
(= *Pyrus malus* var. *sylvestris* Auct.)
Crab Apple *
Family *Rosaceae*

height 7 (10) m
crown broad, dense
trunk erect, short, broadly ramified; branches spiny at tip; bark grey-brown, ridged
foliage deciduous

Malus sylvestris

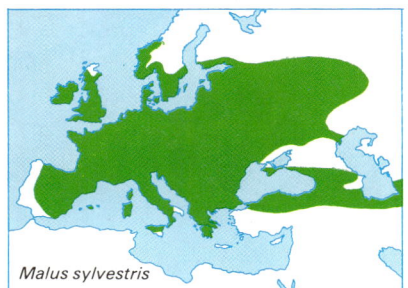

Malus sylvestris

leaves simple, oval, 4–8 cm, with rounded base and pointed tip; margins finely toothed; petiole half the length of blade; alternate arrangement
flowers inflorescence in corymb of 3–7 flowers, each flower 3–4 cm ⌀, with 5 petals pink on outside; 20–50 stamens; flowering period April–May
fruits globose pomes of 2–4 cm ⌀, green to red

The Crab Apple grows wild throughout Europe, in broadleaved woods and on plains to an altitude of 1400 m. Very rugged, indifferent to subsoil, it is mainly used as stock for cultivated varieties. The fruits, which are bitter and not very pleasant, are sometimes used for making cider and vinegar. The pinkish-red wood, very heavy and resistant, is fine-grained and difficult to work.

M. sylvestris is one of the principal species contributing to *M. pumila*, the Edible Apple, which has been cultivated since the Stone Age; innumerable varieties now exist.

Orchard apples contain 10% sugars, vitamins and mineral salts, and by reason of their excellent digestive qualities can be eaten whole, raw or cooked. They are used for making syrups, cider and jellies, and some varieties can be dried.

The apple has important medicinal properties: as an integrator of water and salts in the body, as an antitoxic, antiseptic and intestinal astringent.

PYRUS COMMUNIS L.
Wild Pear
Family *Rosaceae*

height 15 (20) m
crown elongated, spreading
trunk erect, branchy; branches spinous; bark grey-brown, finely ridged
foliage deciduous
leaves simple, orbicular-elliptic, with rounded base and pointed tip, 2–7 cm, margins finely toothed; petiole as long as blade; alternate arrangement
flowers in corymbs of 3–9 flowers, each with 5 oval, white or pinkish petals; 20–25 stamens; flowering period April–May
fruits pyriform (pear-shaped) pomes of 1–4 cm, yellow to brown

The distribution of the Wild Pear extends over the whole of Europe, except for Scandinavia and the Baltic regions; a sun-loving tree, it needs a reasonably dry environment, adapting to virtually any soil.

Its wood – red, hard and, when impregnated with iron salts, turning as black as ebony – is used mainly for carving, inlay and lathe-work; it also makes reasonable fuel. It is of little interest as a forest species because,

Pyrus communis

despite easy propagation, it is of slow growth, produces a lot of branches and therefore does not yield sufficient timber from the main trunk.

Prehistoric remains show that man has known the pear for some 35 centuries. The small wild forms, with a pleasant, astringent taste, do not keep well and are used as fodder for pigs. Orchard pears derive part of their vigour and fruit size by hybridization with several European species.

They can be eaten raw for their sweet, aromatic and pleasant flavour, as jams, juices and preserved in syrup and crystallized form. Pears contain 10% sugar and an appreciable quantity of vitamins and mineral salts; they are prescribed for some kidney ailments because of their low sodium content.

Key to **ROWANS** and **WHITEBEAMS**

Leaves pinnate
– fruits pear-shaped, green-brown; bark ridged: *Sorbus domestica*
– fruits spherical, red; bark smooth: *Sorbus aucuparia*

Leaves simple, lobate or pinnate only at base
– leaves green below, deeply lobate: *Sorbus torminalis*
– leaves grey or white below, hairy
–– leaves with margin only dentate, not lobate: *Sorbus aria*
–– leaves lobate
––– leaves without free leaflets: *Sorbus intermedia*
––– leaves with 2 pairs of leaflets free at base: *Sorbus hybrida*

SORBUS AUCUPARIA L.
Rowan or Mountain Ash *
Family *Rosaceae*

height 5–15 (20) m
crown oval, sparse

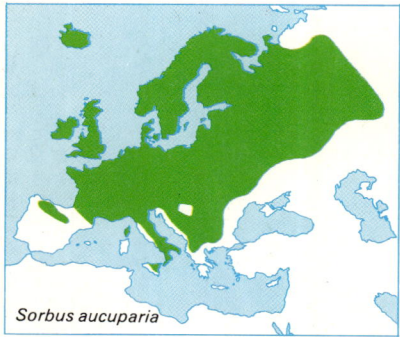
Sorbus aucuparia

trunk straight; shoots grey-purple; buds red-purple, tomentose and not sticky; bark grey to grey-brown, smooth, then ridged and dark
foliage deciduous
leaves compound, pinnate, 10–20 cm, formed of 9–19 elliptic leaflets with serrate margins, sessile; hairy beneath; autumn colour red; alternate arrangement
flowers inflorescence a corymb, 15 cm ⌀; flowers 1 cm ⌀, white; flowering period May–July
fruits subspherical pomes of about 1 cm ⌀, red, smooth; fruits derived from inflorescence, pendulous

Sorbus domestica L.
True Service Tree

Similar to *S. aucuparia* except that the green buds are glabrous and

Sorbus aucuparia

sticky; the bark is rough; the leaves and flowers are bigger; the fruits are not round but apple- or pear-shaped, 2–4 cm ⌀.

The specific name derives from the archaic word *aucupio*, meaning bird-liming, because the fruit, attractive to birds, was used in fowling.

The Rowan is found all over Great Britain and Europe, in forests, thickets, thin scrubland and sporadically up to altitudes of 2000 m. A sun-loving species, it can also flourish in shade, and is adaptable to virtually any soil; it is often cultivated in mountainous areas as an ornament, for the attractive appearance of its foliage, flowers and fruit.

The acid fruits, rich in tannin, can be used for making jams and liqueurs and, with their medicinal properties, for treating coughs and intestinal complaints. The leaves make reasonable fodder for sheep. The hard and resistant wood is used for lathe-work, for making parts for carts and sledges, as fuel and charcoal.

The Service Tree was introduced all over southern Europe from Asia Minor. It is found growing wild in cool, bright woods, on calcareous soil and is uncommon in Britain. Different varieties are cultivated, varying in the shape of fruit, similar to a pear or an apple, which cannot be eaten when picked but must be left to become over-ripe.

Sorbus domestica

Sorbus torminalis

SORBUS TORMINALIS (L.) Crantz
Wild Service Tree *
Family *Rosaceae*

height 10–15 m
crown flat-domed, dense
trunk erect, divided with angular branches; bark pale grey-brown, with many lenticels
foliage deciduous
leaves simple, oval, deeply lobate, 7–12 cm, with cordate base; 3–5 pointed lobes; margins irregularly dentate-serrate; autumn colour red; alternate arrangement
flowers inflorescence an upright corymb, 10–12 cm ∅; white corollas of 5 rounded petals; stamens with yellow anthers; flowering period May–June
fruits ovoid pomes, 1–1.5 cm, reddish-brown

The specific name *torminalis* indicates the properties of this tree in treating colic and dysentery.
    The Wild Service Tree is found in southern England and throughout Europe, except for Scandinavia, where it is replaced by *Sorbus inter-*

media. It is encountered, though rarely, in lowlands and mountains, up to an altitude of 1000 m, in woods and coppices, on sunny slopes and in calcareous soil. The wood is seldom of large dimensions, but of excellent quality, easy to work and polish, and much in demand for cabinet-making and for musical instruments.

SORBUS ARIA (L.) Crantz
Whitebeam *
Family *Rosaceae*

height 10 (20) m
crown irregularly ovate
trunk erect, sometimes divided; shoots grey, hairy; bark grey, smooth
foliage deciduous
leaves simple, oval-elliptic, 10 × 5 cm, shiny above, white, tomentose beneath; margins doubly serrate; autumn colour exceptional, the shiny brown upper surface contrasting with the clear white underside; alternate arrangement
flowers inflorescence in erect corymbs of 5–8 cm, flowers 1.5 cm ∅, white; flowering period May–June
fruits ovoid pomes of 1.5 cm, orange-red when ripe, edible

The Whitebeam is found throughout Britain and Europe, except in Scandinavia. It grows in woods on hills and mountains, and in clearings, up to an altitude of 1600 m. It likes calcareous subsoil, but is remarkably adaptable; sun-loving, it tolerates drought and low temperatures.

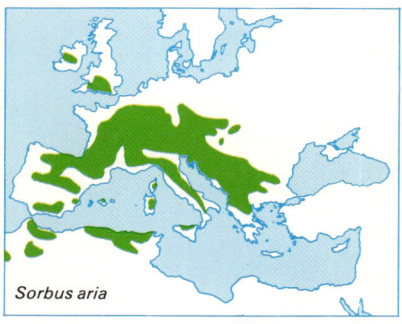

Sorbus aria

Sorbus aria

Because it rarely grows very tall, the wood has only limited uses. The fruits are edible, although somewhat insipid; the pulp is floury and in times of famine used to be eaten extensively by mountain-dwelling people.

SORBUS INTERMEDIA (Ehrh.) Pers.
(= *S. scandica* Fries)
Swedish Whitebeam **
Family *Rosaceae*

height 10 (15) m, often shrubby
crown dense, domed
trunk short and branchy; bark pinkish-grey, smooth, with transverse ridges
foliage deciduous
leaves simple, shallowly pinnately lobate, oval, 6–10 cm; underside of leaves grey, tomentose; margins serrate; petiole of 2–5 cm; alternate arrangement
flowers inflorescence in corymbs of 8–10 cm ⌀, flowers of 1.5–2 cm, with round white petals; pink anthers; flowering period May
fruits oval pomes, 1.5 cm, scarlet

Sorbus latifolia (Lam.) Pers.
Service Tree of Fontainebleau

Similar to *S. intermedia*, but with less pronounced lobes, leaves almost round; sometimes exhibits drop lobes at base; fruits yellow-brown, with large lenticels.

Sorbus hybrida L.
(= *S. fennica* (Kalm) Fries)
Bastard Service Tree

Similar to *S. intermedia*, but with two pairs of free leaflets at base; fruits with a few small lenticels.

Sorbus hybrida and *Sorbus intermedia* are species native to Denmark, Sweden, Norway and Finland, while *Sorbus latifolia* is found in Portugal, Spain, France and south-western Germany. All three are cultivated as amenity trees, particularly in streets.
The trees are unusual in producing seeds without fertilization; they do not need to be pollinated and their pollen production is correspondingly reduced; thus all specimens possess the same genetic material.
Sorbus hybrida probably originated in a cross between *Sorbus aria* and *Sorbus aucuparia* and possesses twice as many chromosomes as is normal.
Sorbus intermedia is probably related to *S. torminalis*; *Sorbus latifolia* is thought to be derived by hybridization of *S. aria* and *S. torminalis*.

PRUNUS MAHALEB L.
(= *Cerasus mahaleb* Mill.)
Saint Lucie Cherry
Family *Rosaceae*

height 5 m, often shrubby
crown domed
trunk short, very branchy, divided from base; bark violet-grey, with transverse stripes, shiny
foliage deciduous
leaves simple, oval-pointed, 4–8 cm; round or cordate at base; margins with crenate-teeth; petiole 1–2 cm, without glands; alternate arrangement

Key to **CHERRIES** and **PLUMS**

Leaves oval or rounded
– leaves of 6–9 cm; fruits hairy: **Prunus armeniaca** (cult.)
– leaves of 2–3 cm; fruits glabrous: **Prunus mahaleb**

Leaves elongate, lanceolate
– leaves evergreen (leathery and shiny)
–– shoots and petioles green: **Prunus laurocerasus**
–– shoots and petioles red: **Prunus lusitanica**
– leaves not evergreen (often thick and soft)
–– leaves oval-elongate, narrow
––– flowers single or in pairs
–––– bark reddish-brown, petals pink, leaves of 8–10 cm:
Prunus persica (cult.)
–––– bark grey-brown; petals white or slightly pink; leaves of 5–6 cm:
Prunus dulcis (cult.)
––– flowers in a cluster
–––– petals 6–9 mm: **Prunus padus**
–––– petals 2.5–4 mm: **Prunus serotina**
–– leaves elliptic-obovate
––– drupes with long peduncle
–––– leaves with two glands on petiole: **Prunus avium** (cult. and wild)
–––– leaves without glands: **Prunus cerasus** (cult. and wild)
––– drupes with short peduncle
–––– petals pink: **Prunus persica** (cult.)
–––– petals white, at most veined pink:
Prunus domestica (cult. and wild)

flowers inflorescence in corymbs, 6–10 scented flowers, each with 5 white petals; flowering period March–May **fruits** drupes of 0.6–1 cm ⌀, at first pinkish, then black and shiny when ripe, bitter

The Saint Lucie Cherry ranges over southern Europe, where it is frequently found on hillsides, in mountain woods, and on dry, calcareous, rocky slopes up to 1500 m. The tree needs plenty of light and warmth, and is not long-lived. It is occasionally grown for ornament in Britain.

The heavy, yellow-brown wood is of limited use because of its size, serving mainly for lathe-work, canes, handles, boxes and pipes, the latter retaining the pleasant aroma of the original product; the wood and bark are perfumed because they contain cumarin, used to scent tobacco. The tree is of value for planting on steep, dry slopes or as a shrub in gardens.

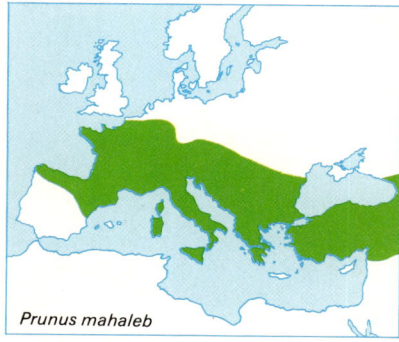

Prunus mahaleb

Prunus mahaleb

light green and opaque beneath; margins toothed; petiole short (1 cm), grooved; green; alternate arrangement
flowers inflorescence erect in raceme of 8–12 cm; flowers with short pedicels, with white corolla of 1 cm ∅; flowering period March–May
fruits black, oval drupes, of about 1 cm

Prunus lusitanica L.
Portugal Laurel **

Compared with *P. laurocerasus*, it may grow to as much as 20 m; it has oval, elongated (not obovate) leaves; and it is distinguished by its dark red shoots and petioles as well as its bigger inflorescence (10–28 cm); it flowers in June.

The Cherry Laurel arrived in Europe from its original home in south-west Asia in the 16th century.
It is a much-cultivated evergreen ornamental, which is also planted to form thick, fast-growing hedges. A rugged and adaptable species, it does not need a lot of sunlight and can tolerate cold.
The whole plant is poisonous, except for the fruit pulp, because of the presence of the glucoside prulaurasin which, in association with enzymes, releases prussic acid. The distilled leaves yield a liquid used as a cough mixture.
The Portugal Laurel, native to the Iberian peninsula and south-western France, is to be found outside this area as an ornamental garden and park species; it is, however, not so hardy as the Cherry Laurel.
Both Cherry and Portuguese Laurel are cultivated primarily for hedging in Britain and are naturalized.

PRUNUS LAUROCERASUS L.
Cherry Laurel **
Family *Rosaceae*

height 4–8 m, more often shrubby
crown oval, domed
trunk sinuous, branched from base; shoots green; bark brown-black, rough
foliage evergreen
leaves simple, obovate-lanceolate, 8–15 cm, dark green and shiny above,

Prunus laurocerasus

PRUNUS PADUS L.
(= *Padus avium* Mill.)
Bird Cherry *
Family *Rosaceae*

height 15 m

Prunus padus

crown pyramidal to domed
trunk erect, upper branches ascending; bark dark grey to reddish, fissured, cracking in horizontal bands
foliage deciduous
leaves simple, ovate-elongate, acuminate, 5–12 cm, almost truncate at base; petiole of 2 cm, reddish, with two green glands at tip; autumn colour red-yellow; alternate arrangement
flowers inflorescence in cluster of 8–15 cm, bearing numerous white flowers of 2 cm ∅; flowering period April–June

fruits spherical drupes of 8 mm ∅, black, bitter

The Bird Cherry extends over the whole of Europe, apart from the Mediterranean regions and the Balkans, to north-eastern Asia. In Great Britain its natural distribution is mainly in the north and west although cultivated throughout. Less dependent on light than other cherry species, it grows wild, though infrequently, in lowland and upland plains up to 1800 m, preferably on acid soils.

Sometimes it is cultivated for its ornamental flowers and fruit. When cut, the brownish-yellow wood emits an unpleasant smell; it is used mainly as fuel and charcoal. The fruits, when fermented, provide an alcoholic drink.

Apart from its medicinal properties, the bark also furnishes a green dye.

PRUNUS SEROTINA Ehrh.
Black Cherry **
Family *Rosaceae*

Similar to the Bird Cherry, mainly in its inflorescence, the Black Cherry flowers in June; the leaves are oval, smooth and shiny, and the lower midrib has brown hairs.

Prunus padus

The Black Cherry grows wild in New England and the eastern parts of the United States, and is widely planted in Europe as an ornament. Here, too, it sometimes grows wild, proving adaptable, rugged and easily disseminated.

The hard wood, easy to polish, and looking similar to mahogany, though lighter, is easily seasoned and used for expensive furniture.

PRUNUS AVIUM L.
(= *Cerasus avium* (L.) Moench)
Gean *
Family *Rosaceae*

height 20 m
crown pyramidal
trunk erect, sinuous; shoots glabrous; bark reddish-grey, shiny; lenticels in transverse rows; later with horizontal fissures
foliage deciduous
leaves simple, obovate-acuminate, 10–15 cm, pendulous; margins serrate; reddish petiole of 2–3.5 cm with two red glands at top; alternate arrangement
flowers in umbrella-like bunches of 5–8, with a white corolla; calyx urn-shaped; flower peduncle of 3–5 cm;

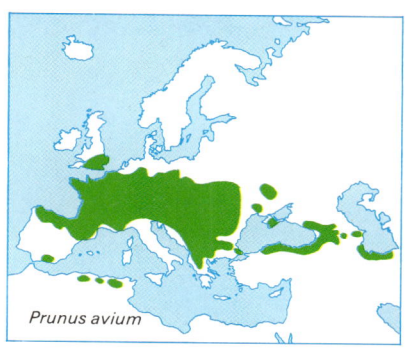

Prunus avium

flowering period April–May
fruits drupes (cherries) of 1–2 cm ⌀, red when ripe

Prunus cerasus L.
(= *Cerasus vulgaris* Mill.)
Sour Cherry **

Similar to *P. avium*, but smaller in size, leaves ovate-elliptic, 6–8 cm, petiole without glands; cherries red or reddish-black.

Gean may have originated in Asia Minor but today it grows wild throughout Europe, on hills and mountains, up to 1500 m, as shown on the map, and is usually considered native to the British Isles.

A frugal, sun-loving species, it grows in clearings and thin woodland on calcareous, dry soil; it is rugged enough to tolerate low temperatures and deserves wider diffusion both for timber and fruit.

The cherries are used for the production of liqueurs such as kirsch and cherry brandy. The light red wood (very like mahogany) darkens with age; it is much in demand for furniture, flooring, barrels and sculptures.

Bark, leaves and seeds contain amygdalin, which give them a bitter taste and releases prussic acid. The wild Gean has given rise to many cultivated varieties of fruit, which differ in shape and colour.

Prunus avium

Prunus cerasus

The Sour Cherry's area of origin is the Balkans. It is cultivated elsewhere in Europe for its fruits, known as Morello cherries, which are used to produce syrups, jams and maraschino liqueur. The wood is used for making quality pipes and holders.

The dried peduncles of the fruits can be used for medicinal purposes.

PRUNUS DOMESTICA L.
Plum **
Family *Rosaceae*

height 10 m
crown domed
trunk sinuous, erect, divided; pubescent shoots without spines in cultivated trees, with spines if wild; bark reddish-brown, opaque
foliage deciduous
leaves simple, obovate-elliptic, 5–8 cm; margins toothed; alternate arrangement
flowers in groups of 2–3; peduncles of 1–2 cm; white petals of about 1 cm; flowering period March–April
fruits drupes of 2–7 cm ⌀

The following subspecies are to be distinguished:
subsp. ***domestica***: tree without spines, with ovoid, violet, red or purple fruit; endocarp (stone) separated from mesocarp (fleshy covering of fruit)
subsp. ***insititia*** (L.) C. K. Schneider: tree with spines, fruit round, red, purple, yellow or green; endocarp not separated from mesocarp

The origin of this species is also uncertain; it probably came from regions extending from the Black Sea to central Asia, coming to Europe in ancient times, perhaps in the latter stages of the western Roman Empire. Today it is naturalized or cultivated everywhere.

An averagely hardy species, it can be harmed by wind and extreme cold, especially by late frosts when these coincide with flowering; it adapts to virtually any soil, loose, clayey or shallow, provided it is well drained.

The fruits (plums or prunes) are eaten raw, dried, candied or in jams; some varieties in particular are used for distillation (slivovitz or plum brandy), and the late-flowering varieties are best for drying. Plums contain up to 10% sugar, malic acid and citric acid as well as, albeit in small quantities, vitamins. They can be used as mild laxatives.

PRUNUS ARMENIACA L.
(= *Armeniaca vulgaris* Lam.)
Apricot
Family *Rosaceae*

height up to 5 m
leaves rounded, oval, 6–9 cm, serrate

CULTIVATED PRUNUS SPECIES

the appearance of the crown and trunk differ according to the type of cultivation; all species have deciduous foliage and alternate leaves.

flowers single or in pairs, 2–3 cm ∅, with white or pink petals; flowering period March-May, before foliation
fruits drupes (apricots) of 3–6 cm, orange-yellow, downy

The scientific name might seem to indicate that this species originated in Armenia; but almost certainly the tree comes from China and Manchuria, whence, at some unknown date, but certainly very long ago, it reached the eastern Mediterranean regions and then, under Arab influence, spread to the other parts of Europe where it is nowadays found. Hardy as a tree in southern England, it will only ripen regular crops of fruit when grown against a wall.

The Apricot is cultivated in regions with a temperate climate suitable for fruit production; the fruit is eaten raw, dried or made into jam. Apricots are very nutritious, containing 8% sugars, salts, organic acids and vitamins (especially vitamin A), which explains their overall anti-infective qualities and beneficial effect on eyesight.

PRUNUS PERSICA (L.) Batsch
(= *Amygdalus persica* L.; *Persica vulgaris* Mill.)
Peach
Family *Rosaceae*

height up to 7 m
leaves narrow and elongated, 8–10 cm, serrate
flowers solitary, occasionally in pairs, almost sessile, 2–4 cm ∅; petals deep pink, reddish-violet; flowering period April–May
fruits drupes (peaches), reddish-yellow, 4–8 cm ∅, downy

This species also originated in the Far East, and was introduced from there to western Asia – hence its specific name *persica*. It had already reached Europe by the 4th century BC.

The Peach is widely cultivated for its fruit throughout the Mediterranean basin and in other parts of the world where the climate is suitable. In Britain this usually means giving it

the protection of a wall if ripe fruit is sought. Peaches contain, in addition to a high percentage of water, 8% sugars, organic acids, salts and vitamins (especially vitamins A and C). They can be eaten fresh or used for jams, syrups and confectionery.

The many cultivated varieties are subdivided according to the ripening season and the characteristics of the fruit. Increasingly popular in recent years has been the related nectarine, differentiated by its smooth, shiny skin.

PRUNUS DULCIS (Miller) D. A. Webb
(= *P. amygdalus* Batsch; *Amygdalus communis* L.)
Almond **
Family *Rosaceae*

height 5–10 m
leaves lanceolate, 5–6 cm, serrate
flowers in pairs, almost sessile, 3–4 cm ∅; petals pink; flowering period January–March, before foliation
fruits drupes (almonds), green, 3–4 cm, downy

The Almond, probably originating in the Orient, has spread all over the Mediterranean basin, where it is frequently cultivated in association with the olive and the vine. It is one of the earliest and most reliable of spring ornamental trees and also produces good crops of almonds in England.

A very economic species, it adapts to dry, poor and stony subsoils, but cannot stand hard frost and strong winds.

The tree is grown for its seed, which is partly edible; it contains 50% fats and is also full of proteins, vitamins and mineral salts. The best known of many different varieties are the bitter almonds, with hard seeds smelling of amygdalin, which contain an oil used in perfumery and as a cough syrup; and the sweet almonds, with soft, odourless seeds, used mainly in confectionery. The wood, although easily workable and of a fine red colour, is not much used.

PRUNUS CERASIFERA Ehrh.
(= *P. myrobolana* (L.) Loisel.)
Cherry Plum or Myrobalan **
Family *Rosaceae*

height 5–8 m, often shrubby
leaves elliptic, 3–4 cm, serrate
flowers solitary, pedunculate, 2 cm
∅, white; flowering period March–
April
fruits drupes (cherry plums) of 2–
3 cm ∅, red or yellow, smooth

Cultivated or naturalized, the Cherry
Plum or Myrobalan comes originally
from the Balkans; it is valued for its
fruit, but even more as root stock for
other cultivated *Prunus* species.
There is a cultivar used for ornament
in avenues and gardens, with deep
reddish-brown leaves (anthocyanin
content) and many pink flowers; this
is *P. cerasifera* 'Pissardii'.

CERCIS SILIQUASTRUM L.
Judas Tree **
Family *Leguminosae*
Subfamily *Caesalpinioideae*

height 8 m
crown irregularly spherical, spreading

Cercis siliquastrum

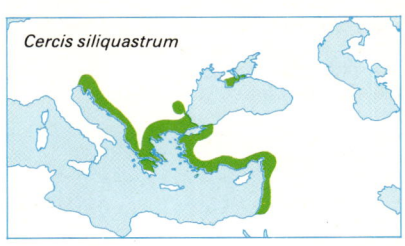

Cercis siliquastrum

trunk erect, sinuous; flexible
branches; bark blackish with brown
cracks
foliage deciduous
leaves simple, rounded and kidney-
shaped, 5–10 cm ∅, margins entire,
shiny above; petiole of 5 cm; alternate arrangement
flowers in short clusters of 3–6, also
on trunk; flowers papilionaceous
(butterfly-shaped), 2 cm, red-violet;
flowering period March–May, before
foliation
fruits legumes of 10–15 cm, flat, initially purple, then brown when ripe,
attached to tree until winter

Cercis in Greek signifies 'needle' or
'shuttle', referring to the shape of the
fruits. The common name alludes to
the legend whereby Judas Iscariot,
overcome by remorse, was said to
have hanged himself from this tree.
The distribution of the Judas Tree
covers the northern Mediterranean to
the Balkans and Asia Minor; it is cultivated for its fine flowers, and is found
in southern Britain.
    This tree prefers calcareous, as
well as dry and rocky, subsoils, not
growing at more than 300 m; it will
not tolerate prolonged frosts. It is suitable for planting along roads and as
an ornamental in parks, successfully
resisting urban pollution.
    The wood is used in cabinet-
making and lathe-work, because of
its hardness and beautiful dark-
veined red colour. At one time a
yellow dye was extracted from the
branches. The flowers are edible and
can either be preserved in vinegar or
eaten fresh in salads; the floury seeds
are likewise edible.

CERATONIA SILIQUA L.
Carob or Locust Tree
Family *Leguminosae*
Subfamily *Caesalpinioideae*

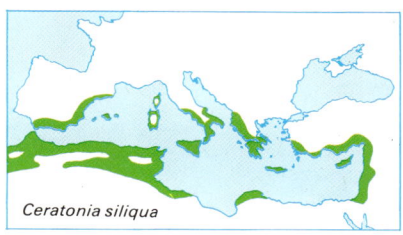
Ceratonia siliqua

height 8 m
crown spreading, domed
trunk squat and irregular, often curved and divided from base; bark light brown, ridged
foliage evergreen
leaves compound, pinnate, formed of 2–5 pairs of ovate leaflets, leathery, 5 × 3 cm; alternate arrangement
flowers hermaphrodite and also unisexual both present, in linear clusters, without corolla, with 5 stamens of 1 cm, ovary of 1 cm; flowering period May–November
fruits indehiscent, fleshy legumes, compressed, 10–20 cm, edible (carobs), brownish-violet, pendulous

The elongated shape of the pods, thick and brown, accounts for the generic name, from the Greek *keras* (horn).

The tree probably originated in Asia Minor, and then spread throughout the Mediterranean basin as a result of cultivation since antiquity. One of the earliest mentions of the Carob is by Theophrastus (3rd century BC).

The Carob is cultivated on coastal belts; it grows in poor, calcareous soil up to 600 m. It thrives on sun, tolerates heat and drought, and acts both to protect and improve barren and stony ground.

The fruits (carobs) are indehiscent, fleshy, edible legumes, used as fodder for animals. The pulp has various uses in popular medicine. The lentil-shaped seeds used to serve as units of measurement for weighing precious stones (carats); nowadays they furnish size for the textile industry and gums for the paper industry. Bark and leaves contain tannins.

The pinkish-purple wood, much veined, is used for lathe-work.

× ⅓
Ceratonia siliqua
× 1

GLEDITSIA TRIACANTHOS L.
Honey Locust **
Family *Leguminosae*
Subfamily *Caesalpinioideae*

height 10 (30) m
crown broad at base, domed
trunk straight, with characteristic ramified spines of 3–8 cm; bark brown, smooth or slightly ridged
foliage deciduous
leaves compound, in two forms, pinnate or twice-pinnate, the former 15 cm, the latter 20 cm; alternate arrangement
flowers inflorescence in cluster of 10 cm, axillary, shorter than leaves; single flowers of 0.5 cm with 3–5 similar greenish petals (non-papilionaceous corolla); long-sprouting yellow anthers; flowering period May–June
fruits legumes up to 40 cm long, very prominent, brown, smooth, curved and twisted

The generic name commemorates J. G. Gleditsch, director of the Berlin Botanical Garden in the 18th century; the specific name refers to the three-part spines which are abundant on the bole.

Gleditsia triacanthos

The Honey Locust comes originally from the central-eastern parts of the United States, and was introduced to Europe during the early years of the 18th century. In Britain it is mainly planted as an ornamental species.

The tree is not particular as to terrain, adapting even to poor, loose soils; it can also withstand harsh climatic conditions. It grows on lowland plains up to 800 m, but is used mainly as an ornamental along roadsides and as thick hedging. The pink-brown wood, although used in joinery, is difficult to work. Fermentation of the sweet pulp of the pods produces a drink similar to beer; the pods can also be used as fodder for sheep, while the seeds, roasted, make a coffee substitute.

The variety *inermis*, without spines, has shorter reddish-brown fruits.

ACACIA DEALBATA Link
Mimosa or Silver Wattle
Family *Leguminosae*
Subfamily *Mimosoideae*

height up to 10 (20) m
crown irregularly pyramidal, with pendulous branches
trunk straight; shoots green, flexible and ridged; bark grey to black, ridged
foliage evergreen
leaves compound, pinnate, up to 12 cm long; leaflets 5 × 1 mm, very numerous, grey-green; alternate arrangement
flowers inflorescences terminal or axillary, in heads of 20 or more round, yellow, fluffy flowers; flowering period February–March
fruits glaucous legumes of 6–12 cm, brown when ripe

Trees of the genus *Acacia* come from tropical and subtropical regions; the Mimosa originated in south-western Australia and came to Europe in the last decade of the 18th century. Because of its early flowering, it is popularly used for ornament and in southern Europe, where the climate permits, it has become naturalized.

Acacia dealbata ×½ ×1 ×1

Along the south coast of England it proves hardy but will not survive a very severe winter.

The Mimosa is particular as to temperature; in fact, it can only tolerate brief and irregular frosts, and may be harmed by cold winds. So it must have sites which are sheltered and sunny, preferably with acidic, well drained soils.

Other species of *Acacia* introduced to Europe include *A. decurrens*; *A. pycantha*, exploited for the tannin in its bark; *A. cyanophylla* and *A. saligna*, both with shrubby habits, used for recolonizing sandy and loose subsoils; and *A. melanoxylon*, which produces dark red or blackish wood, suitable for cabinet-making.

ALBIZZIA JULIBRISSIN (Willd.)
Pink Siris or Persian Acacia
Family *Leguminosae*
Subfamily *Mimosoideae*

height up to 10 m
crown hemispherical, umbrella-like
trunk straight, branched at human height; bark brown, ridged
foliage deciduous
leaves compound, pinnate, up to 20 cm long, with up to 40 sickle-shaped, mucronate leaflets, inserted opposite in pairs on lateral pinnae; alternate arrangement
flowers inflorescences in round heads, joined in terminal corymbs; particularly conspicuous due to violet-orange tufts of stamens on individual flowers, though with small calyx and corolla; flowering period June–August
fruits compressed legumes of 15 cm, very numerous and hanging from branches even in winter

The genus was named after the Italian naturalist F. Albizzi.

The Pink Siris grows wild throughout Asia, from Iran to Japan, in regions with a warm climate. Around 1740 Albizzi brought it from Constantinople, where it was already cultivated, to Florence, from where it spread to the rest of southern Europe as an ornamental tree treasured for its lovely pink, fluffy flowers and delicate leaves. Rarely seen in Britain.

A tree which thrives on light, somewhat dry soils; averagely hardy, it does not tolerate prolonged frosts. Because of its resistance to urban atmospheric pollution it is often

Albizzia julibrissin

Laburnum anagyroides

×2

seed

planted as an ornamental in city streets.

The variety *rosea* has smaller, bright pink flowers, and is more tolerant of cold.

LABURNUM ANAGYROIDES Med.
(= *L. vulgare* Presl; *Cytisus laburnum* L.)
Common Laburnum **
Family *Leguminosae*
Subfamily *Faboideae*

height 6 (10) m
crown narrow and irregular
trunk erect, with ascending branches; twigs grey-green, hairy; bark initially green, then light brown, smooth

foliage deciduous
leaves compound, with three elliptic leaflets of 3–8 cm, silky beneath; alternate arrangement
flowers inflorescences in bunches of 20 cm or more; papilionaceous yellow flowers of 2 cm; flowering period April–June
fruits compressed legumes, 4–8 cm, initially pubescent, then glabrous

Laburnum alpinum (Mill.) Bercht. & Presl
Scotch or Alpine Laburnum **

Similar to *L. anagyroides*, but distinguished by glabrous twigs, like the leaves and legumes; the leaves are smaller and pointed; flowering occurs about two weeks after the Common Laburnum.

The Common Laburnum is distributed over central-southern Europe, from the Balkans to eastern France. It is cultivated in Britain in parks and gardens for ornament.

Growing together with other broadleaved species on hill and mountain plains, it is chiefly found in not too crowded woods of hornbeam, chestnut and beech. It prefers calcareous soils but tolerates a degree of acidity.

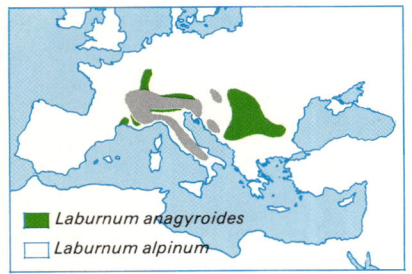

■ *Laburnum anagyroides*
□ *Laburnum alpinum*

The wood is one of the hardest known, dark brown and hence sometimes called false ebony; it is used in turnery, carving and inlay work, and in the making of musical instruments, especially the stocks of bagpipes; the straightest trunks are used for poles. All parts of the tree, but especially the seeds and bark, are poisonous, due to the presence of cytisine.

The related species *Laburnum alpinum* has the same distribution, but is found at greater heights, on upland plains, in beech and coniferous woods. It is also more resistant to cold.

ROBINIA PSEUDACACIA L.
Robinia or Black Locust **
Family *Leguminosae*
Subfamily *Faboideae*

height 25 m
crown domed, spreading
trunk erect, sometimes bifurcate; shoots very spiny; bark grey-brown, ridged and variously twisted
foliage deciduous
leaves compound, pinnate, 20–30 cm, with 13–15 elliptic leaflets of 3–4 cm, with petioles, more or less opposite; autumn colour yellow; alternate arrangement
flowers inflorescences in clusters of 10–25 cm, formed of 15–25 papilionaceous, white, scented flowers; flowering period May–June
fruits pendulous brown legumes of 5–10 cm which remain on the tree until winter

The generic name commemorates J. Robin, curator of the Botanical Garden of the king of France, who in 1601 introduced the tree to Europe.

The Robinia came originally from the Allegheny Mountains in the eastern United States; it was brought to Europe as an ornamental species and soon became naturalized in regions with a sufficiently warm climate, ranging from lowland plains to altitudes of 1200 m. In Britain it is a common ornamental tree.

Its wide diffusion is stimulated by the habit of suckering and, in suitable sites, a capacity for spontaneous dissemination; furthermore, the young shoots are protected by sharp spines. As a result the species forms dense thickets in competition with other wild trees and often gets the upper hand aided by the fact that it is a rapid grower.

Robinia pseudacacia

The wood, greenish-yellow or greenish-brown, has a fairly large grain and splits easily, but lasts well in the open; for this reason it is used for stakes and frames in viticulture, for example. It is used in joinery for its strength and suitability for the manufacture of objects subject to wear and tear; it also makes good fuel which burns even immediately after being cut.

The fibres from the wood are used for rigging and mats. Leaves and bark contain dyes, and the former are used for animal fodder. The flowers are sometimes used in the kitchen for preparing sweets and infusions; they also produce an excellent honey. The seeds are very hard and used for rosaries and necklaces.

The tree is poisonous, particularly the seeds, bark and roots; so all parts must be used cautiously.

As an ornamental species, the Robinia is noted for its extreme hardiness and resistance to urban pollution. Extremely frugal, it is indifferent to subsoil as long as it is well drained, but shows some preference for acidic soils. It likes light and helps in the consolidation and improvement of loose, crumbling soil.

AMORPHA FRUTICOSA L.
False Indigo
Family *Leguminosae*
Subfamily *Faboideae*

height up to 5–6 m, often shrubby
crown irregularly domed
trunk ramified from base, sinuous; shoots pubescent; bark grey-brown, smooth
foliage deciduous
leaves compound, pinnate, 15–20 cm, with 11–23 elliptic leaflets of 3.5 cm, with short petiole; alternate arrangement
flowers inflorescences in erect, terminal spikes of 10 cm; individual flowers with papilionaceous corolla, narrow, 1 cm, blue-purple; long, protruding stamens with yellow anthers; flowering period July

Amorpha fruticosa

fruits legumes of 1 cm, yellow-brown, glandular

The irregular flower, from the Greek *amorphos* (formless), provides the generic name. This shrub or small tree originated in the southern parts of North America and arrived in Europe around 1730, becoming widespread and naturalized along rivers and in gorges, even tolerating subsoil periodically under water. It is restricted to arboreta in the British Isles.

A fairly rugged species, it can tolerate frosts of short duration, and adapts to virtually any soil, consolidating loose terrain.

The suckers that grow abundantly from the base, once stripped of bark and made flexible, are used (in Italy especially) for wrapping and covering wine bottles, i.e. the well known Chianti flask.

SOPHORA JAPONICA L.
Pagoda Tree
Family *Leguminosae*
Subfamily *Faboideae*

height 10 (25) m
crown domed
trunk broadly ramified, with sinuous

branches, hanging in cultivated forms; bark grey-brown, with numerous parallel ridges
foliage deciduous
leaves compound, pinnate, with 7–13 oval leaflets of 3–5 cm, shiny above and pubescent below; alternate arrangement
flowers inflorescences in erect racemes of 25 cm, with numerous papilionaceous, creamy yellow flowers; flowering period August–September
fruits flat, loment-like (with spaces between seeds) legumes of about 10 cm, wrinkled and brown at maturity

The Pagoda Tree originated in China and Korea, and was introduced to Europe in the mid-18th century. It is used as an ornamental, being highly valued for its foliage, attractive flowers and graceful habit. Long-lived, it is less common in Britain than it deserves to be.

It adapts to almost any soil, dislikes stagnant water, needs a sunny site, and is intolerant of frost.

Sophora japonica

The hard, tough wood is used in cabinet-making. Buds, flowers and bark contain a yellow colorant used for dyeing; the leaves, containing rutin, can be used as a stimulant to blood circulation.

'Pendula', with weeping habit, and 'Violacea', with violet-white flowers, are both popular cultivars.

CLADRASTIS LUTEA (Michx.) K. Koch
(= *C. tinctoria* Raf.)
Yellow-wood
Family *Leguminosae*
Subfamily *Faboideae*

height 10 (20) m
crown domed
trunk erect, sinuous; bark dark grey, smooth, reticulated
foliage deciduous
leaves compound, pinnate, 20–30 cm long; 5–7 pairs of oval, elliptic leaflets, attached alternately onto the rachis; drooping leaves; autumn colour yellow; alternate arrangement
flowers inflorescences in clusters of 25–35 cm; white papilionaceous flowers of about 3 cm, scented; flowering period June
fruits legumes of about 10 cm, pointed at tip, with 4–6 seeds

The extreme fragility of the branches inspired the generic name, from the Greek *klados* (branch), and *thraustos* (fragile).

The species originated in North America, particularly the eastern regions of the United States. Introduced to Europe in the 19th century, it has been widely but sparsely planted in sunny spots and fertile soil for ornamental purposes. The yellow-coloured wood contains dyeing properties.

CITRUS LIMON (L.) Burm.
Lemon
Family *Rutaceae*

height up to 5 m
crown rounded

trunk short, branchy; shoots with spines at leaf axil; bark dark grey, smooth
foliage evergreen
leaves simple, oval-lanceolate, 5–10 cm, leathery, with serrate-crenate margins; petiole sometimes winged up to leaf base, elliptic in shape
flowers single or in racemes, corolla of 5 white petals, pink in lower part; 25–40 stamens, joined at base; flowering period April–December
fruits lemons, particular types of berry (hesperidia)

It is not known for certain when the Lemon was introduced to Europe, but it was probably around the 12th century, by the Arabs from its original areas in central Asia. Today cultivation of this species is widespread throughout the Mediterranean region and other areas with a mild climate. This and the following Citrus species must have winter protection in Britain and are therefore restricted to Botanic Gardens.
   The tree is cultivated principally for its fruit, used in the kitchen for flavouring and thirst-quenching drinks. But it also has important medicinal properties; the juice contains 5% to 9% citric acid and vita-

Citrus sinensis

mins, especially vitamin C. A special oil, used in perfumery, is extracted from the peel.

CITRUS SINENSIS (L.) Pers.
Sweet Orange
Family *Rutaceae*

This species originated in China and reached Europe around 1600, being widely cultivated in Mediterranean regions. Today the tree is mainly grown for its fruit, valued for its nutritive qualities, with a high vitamin C content.

AILANTHUS ALTISSIMA (Mill.)
Swingle
(= *A. glandulosa* Desf.)
Tree of Heaven **
Family *Simaroubaceae*

height 20 (25) m
crown irregularly domed
trunk straight, broadly ramified; bark grey-brown, smooth with white bands in young trees, brown bands in adult trees
foliage deciduous
leaves compound, pinnate, 40–90 cm long, with 6–15 pairs of oval-elliptic, pointed leaflets toothed at base; they give out an unpleasant smell; alternate arrangement
flowers inflorescences unisexual, terminal, 10–20 cm; individual flowers not conspicuous, 5–7 mm ∅, with greenish (red in bud) petals; 10 ♂ flower stamens; flowering period May–July
fruits samaras with long, lanceolate, twisted wings of 4 × 1 cm, reddish-brown, persisting on tree in winter

The Tree of Heaven, originally from northern China, was widely naturalized in central-southern Europe during the 18th century. It is a prominent amenity tree in many British towns.
   It is a strong, frugal species, adaptable to almost any soil, provided there is protection from strong

Melia azedarach

Ailanthus altissima

×1

winds, to which it is vulnerable because of its fragile branches. It is frequently found on wasteland, along rivers, on rugged terrain and in thickets, where it often plays an invasive role.

The tree multiplies rapidly by means of seeds and suckers, is fast-growing but not very long-lived.

In the 19th century the species was widely used for the experimental rearing of the saturnid moth *Philosamia cynthia*, in the hope that it would replace the silkworm, then threatened by epidemic disease. Results were not encouraging because the moth had difficulty in adapting.

The wood is soft and used mainly in the paper industry. The bark is used in medicine for its astringent properties. As an ornamental species, the tree has the disadvantage that the leaves give off a disagreeable smell.

MELIA AZEDARACH L.
Indian Bead Tree
Family *Meliaceae*

height 5–15 m
crown ovate, spreading
trunk straight; pubescent shoots; bark rough, furrowed, green-brown
foliage deciduous
leaves compound, twice-pinnate (sometimes pinnate), 50–90 cm, 5–7 leaflets to each lateral pinna, elliptic and pointed, 3–5 cm, toothed; alternate arrangement
flowers inflorescences axillary, 10–20 cm; 5-petalled violet flowers, 10 joined stamens forming a tube around the stigma; flowering period May–June
fruits spherical yellow drupes, 1 cm ∅, with a hard, ridged seed

Because of the divided leaves, the generic name is derived from the Greek *melia* (the ash); the specific name comes from the Persian word *azzadirackt* (noble tree).

This tree originated in south-east Asia and spread mainly to Australia, where it was naturalized. In southern Europe it is used occasionally for ornament. It requires a warm climate sheltered from cold and wind, preferring slightly acid soils but disliking stagnant water. It is therefore unsuited to the British climate.

In its original habitat it is valued for its light red, easily worked wood, which is suitable for joinery. Bark and roots harbour medicinal properties, while the seeds produce oil for burning in lamps. The vernacular name indicates the use to which the seeds can be put, namely as beads for necklaces and rosaries.

PISTACIA LENTISCUS L.
Mastic Tree
Family *Anacardiaceae*

height 5 m, usually shrubby
crown densely domed
trunk sinuous, ramified from base; twigs glabrous, brown; bark brown, scaly
foliage evergreen, with resinous scent
leaves compound, pinnate with 8–12 elliptic, leathery, segments, about 1 cm; smooth margins; winged petiole; alternate arrangement
flowers inflorescences in axillary raceme; flowers very small, yellow to reddish-brown
fruits ovoid drupes of 5 mm ∅, first red, then black

The Mastic Tree is a Mediterranean species at home in the maquis. It is not hardy in Britain. It enjoys sun and warmth, and can withstand extreme

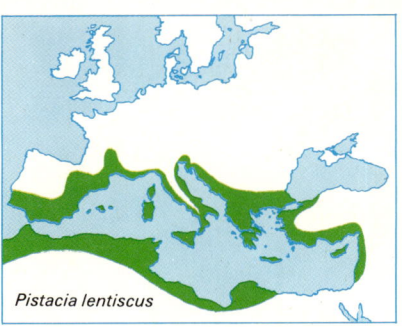
Pistacia lentiscus

drought, adapting to almost any soil, but preferring siliceous, fertile terrain, eventually attaining the dimensions of a small twisted tree or, more commonly, a shrub. It has a protective and improving action on the soil.

At one time the wood was used for producing excellent charcoal and, due to its hardness and beautiful red-veined colour, for turning small articles. An edible oil is extracted from the pressed fruits; tannin and potash are obtainable from the leaves. A resin from the trunk is used for making varnishes and for medicinal purposes.

PISTACIA TEREBINTHUS L.
Turpentine Tree or Terebinth
Family *Anacardiaceae*

height up to 5 m, more often shrubby
crown irregularly domed
trunk sinuous, divided at base; smooth green twigs; smooth greyish bark
foliage deciduous, with resinous scent
leaves compound, pinnate, 10–20 cm, formed of 5–9 elliptic, pointed leaflets; alternate arrangement
flowers inflorescences axillary; flowers small, green-brown; flowering period April–July
fruits ovoid drupes of 7 mm, red and pedunculate

This species has the same distribution as the Mastic Tree. Its roots

Pistacia lentiscus

Pistacia
terebinthus

Rhus typhina

× ⅕

probe deeper into the soil and it grows bigger. A sun-loving plant, it, too, is a feature of the Mediterranean maquis, growing in calcareous soil. Although it does not require as much warmth as the Mastic Tree and can tolerate lower temperatures better, it is not found as frequently.

The Turpentine Tree is used as rootstock for *P. vera*. The wood, with yellowish sapwood and brown heartwood, has restricted uses in cabinetmaking as it is as a rule of insufficient size.

PISTACIA VERA L.
Pistachio
Family *Anacardiaceae*

The Pistachio probably came originally from the eastern Mediterranean region, and spread in ancient times from that area as a cultivated species, but is not hardy in Britain.

It is valued for its seeds, which are used for food flavouring and confectionery, mainly caramels and ice cream. The nuts contain 50% fats and 18% sugars, plus proteins, and yield an oil which has medicinal applications for skin ailments.

RHUS TYPHINA L.
(= *R. hirta* Sudw.)
Stag's Horn Sumach **
Family *Anacardiaceae*

height 8 (12) m
crown domed
trunk straight, ramified at top; twigs hirsute; bark dark brown, rough
foliage deciduous
leaves compound, pinnate, 25–50 cm, formed of 7–31 lanceolate, sessile, serrate leaflets; petiole and rachis hairy; opposite arrangement
flowers inflorescences up to 15 cm long, erect, dense and hairy; corolla with 5 yellow-green petals; flowering period June–July
fruits in form of many hairy, purple drupes, constituting one erect pear-shaped structure

Rous was the Greek name for the Sumach (*Rhus coriaria* L.) and is preserved in the present generic name. This tree originated in the eastern parts of the United States and was introduced to Europe after the mid-17th century. It has widespread application as an ornament and has become naturalized in Britain.

It is very sturdy, grows well on

almost any soil, and can be planted in any site in temperate regions. It is much appreciated for its handsome foliage, rich autumn colour and strange, upright, purple fruits.

SCHINUS MOLLE L.
Pepper Tree
Family *Anacardiaceae*

height up to 8 m
crown domed
trunk sinuous, with drooping branches; bark grey-brown, ridged
foliage evergreen
leaves compound, pinnate, 12–20 cm, pendulous, formed of 15–25 narrowly linear, lanceolate leaflets, sickle-shaped, with toothed margins; alternate arrangement
flowers inflorescences in terminal pannicle of 3 cm; flowers small, yellow-white; flowering period June–July
fruits small, pea-size, red drupes

The similarity of this species to the Mastic Tree is revealed in its generic name from the Greek name for the Mastic Tree, *schinos*. The Pepper Tree originated in the tropical regions of Central and South America, par-

ticularly Chile and Peru; from there it was brought to the Mediterranean region in the 16th century as an ornamental species. Because of its elegant shape it is cultivated in gardens and used as a street ornamental in southern Europe, but is not tough enough for Britain.

The common name is due to the fact that the fruits contain seeds with a sharp taste, used for flavouring as a pepper substitute. The tree is rich in essential and volatile oils, and produces an aromatic resin used as a masticatory. The pollen can cause dermatitis and asthmatic reactions, on contact or when inhaled.

ACER NEGUNDO L.
Box-elder **
Family *Aceraceae*

height 10–15 m
crown irregularly domed
trunk erect, sometimes divided; pendulous twigs; bark grey-brown, grooved
foliage deciduous
leaves compound, pinnate, up to 20 cm long, with 3–7 leaflets, each oval, 5 cm, with petiole and toothed margins; terminal leaves with only 3 leaflets; opposite arrangement

Schinus molle

Acer negundo

Key to **MAPLES**

Leaves compound, pinnate, with 5–7 leaflets, but also with only 3 leaflets: **Acer negundo**

Leaves simple, palmately lobed
– lobes obtuse, without markedly pointed apices; leaves over 10 cm
–– leaves with 3 lobes: **Acer monspessulanum**
–– leaves with 5 lobes, margins entire or toothed
––– margins entire or with a few individual teeth per lobe:
Acer campestre
––– margins toothed: **Acer obtusatum**
– lobes terminal with pointed or mucronate apices
–– leaves with slightly divided lobes, not bigger than 10 cm:
Acer opulifolium
–– leaves with deeply divided lobes, up to and beyond midrib
––– lobes entire, without teeth: **Acer lobelli**
––– lobes toothed
–––– lobes divided up to midrib
––––– teeth turned towards apex: **Acer pseudoplatanus**
––––– teeth turned outwards: **Acer platanoides**
–––– lobes divided towards leaf base, usually not cordate:
Acer saccharinum

flowers dioecious; ♂ inflorescences in corymbs; ♀ in clusters; individual flowers with small perianth, yellow-green; flowering period April–May
fruits winged double samaras of 4 cm, the wings forming an acute angle.

The Box-elder comes from the eastern part of North America, and has been cultivated in Britain and Europe for ornamental purposes since 1690. It is to be found, mainly for its delicate pale foliage, in parks, along roads and in gardens. The wood, of mediocre quality, is little used, except for boxes and cases and in the paper industry. Sugar can be extracted from the sap, as with *A. saccharum*. The cultivar 'Variegatum' has speckled leaves.

ACER MONSPESSULANUM L.
Montpellier Maple
Family *Aceraceae*

height 6 (12) m
crown broadly domed

trunk twisted, much branched; bark grey to black, furrowed
foliage deciduous
leaves simple, trilobate, 4–5 cm, with petiole and entire margins; opposite arrangement

Acer monspessulanum

×2

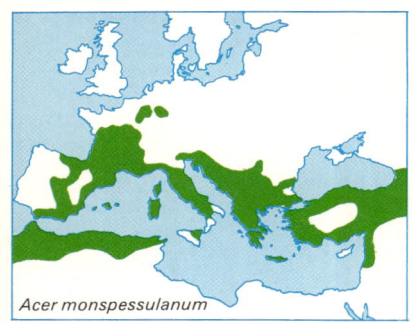

Acer monspessulanum

flowers inflorescences in corymbs, first upright, then drooping; flowers 1 cm $\oslash$ or less, with peduncles 4 cm long; petals and sepals similar, yellow; flowering period April, during or before foliation
fruits double samaras with wings more or less parallel; colour red to brown

The Montpellier Maple is distributed over large tracts of southern Europe, Asia Minor and North Africa, in warm broadleaved woodlands, up to altitudes of 500–600 m. Sun-loving, particular as to temperature, it prefers dry, even stony and calcareous soil.

A slow-growing tree, it is not used for ornamental purposes in spite of looking quite decorative; it is sometimes used for training vines and for reafforestation of stony terrain.

ACER CAMPESTRE L.
Field Maple *
Family *Aceraceae*

height 10–15 (20) m
crown domed
trunk short, divided and ramified, sometimes bending; bark brown, ridged in plates; with corky ridges on branches
foliage deciduous
leaves simple, 8–10 cm, with 5 (3) obtuse lobes and petiole; opposite arrangement; autumn colour yellow
flowers inflorescences in upright corymb of about 10 flowers, each with 5 sepals and 5 similar petals, yellow-green; flowering period April–May, during foliation
fruits double samaras of 5–6 cm, with wings perpendicular to peduncle

This tree, which is Britain's only native maple, grows wild throughout Europe, flourishing as far north as Britain and southern Sweden and is

×1

Acer campestre

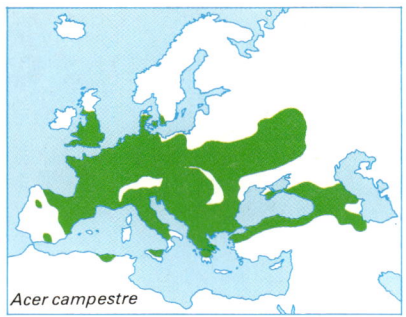

Acer campestre

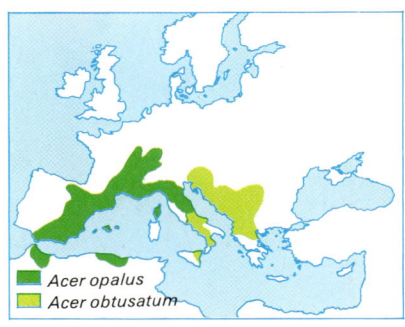

■ Acer opalus
□ Acer obtusatum

widely present elsewhere on the continent. The Field Maple grows in broadleaved woods, and on hills and mountains up to heights of 1200 m, preferring sunny sites but it is the least particular of all maples as to temperature. It grows on fresh, evenly moistured deep soil.

A slow-growing species, it is little used as an ornamental, sometimes for hedging because it can withstand browsing by animals and is unaffected by drastic pruning; it is occasionally used for training vines and in sylviculture for recovering bare ground.

The durable red wood is used for handles of implements and sometimes as fuel, the leaves as fodder for sheep and goats.

ACER OPALUS Mill.
Italian Maple
Family *Aceraceae*

height 10–20 m
crown broadly domed, dense
trunk erect, ramified from base; bark grey-brown, smooth
foliage deciduous
leaves simple, palmate, up to 10 cm long, with 3–5 not very prominent lobes; teeth of margins more or less pointed; underside glabrous; opposite arrangement
flowers inflorescences in corymbs with many yellow flowers with long, glabrous peduncles; flowering period April–May, before foliation

fruits double samaras joined at axis of inflorescence; the two wings form a right angle

Acer obtusatum W. & K.
Hungarian Maple
Family *Aceraceae*

Similar to *A. opalus*, but with obtuse teeth to margins, underside of leaves hairy-tomentose and floral peduncles pubescent; these features, but with leaves almost twice the size, distinguish *A. neapolitanum* Ten., the Neapolitan Maple.

The Italian Maple grows wild in regions of central-western Europe, up

×2

Acer opalus

Acer obtusatum

Acer pseudoplatanus

to altitudes of 1400 m. It is found sporadically, mainly in broadleaved woods in warm, sunny surroundings, on several soils, but preferably calcareous. It can withstand both cold and drought. Sometimes used ornamentally in city streets.

The pinkish-white wood, firm and easily workable, is used in turnery.

The Hungarian Maple is found in central-eastern Europe, from southern Italy to Greece, where it sometimes grows alongside oaks and chestnuts; it is widely tolerant as to soil.

This tree is slow-growing and of little interest in sylviculture. The appearance and uses of the timber are similar to those of the Italian Maple. Both species are occasionally cultivated in Britain as amenity trees.

ACER PSEUDOPLATANUS L.
Sycamore **
Family *Aceraceae*

height 25 (40) m
crown broadly and regularly domed
trunk straight, broadly ramified; twigs smooth; bark dark grey, divided in plates
foliage deciduous

leaves simple, palmately lobed, 10–15 (20) cm, with 5 acute lobes, cordate base; long, reddish petiole; opposite arrangement; autumn colour golden-yellow, or brown
flowers inflorescences in pendulous heads of 15 cm, flowers with 5 sepals and 5 similar petals, yellowish-green; flowering period April
fruits double samaras with wings forming a V; wings about 5 cm

The Sycamore ranges from the Pyrenees to the Caucasus, all through central-southern Europe. It is found, though infrequently, in mountainous regions, in woods together with beech, Silver Fir and Norway Spruce,

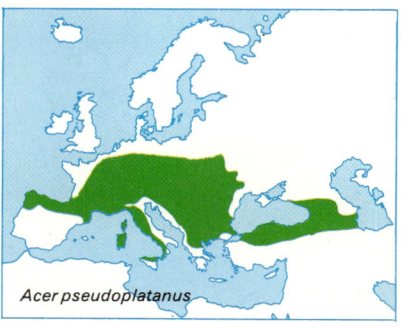

Acer pseudoplatanus

up to 1800 m. It has excellent regenerative powers, multiplying in fairly large groups as a result of large seed production. It is partial to fresh, moist soil.

Because it grows so rapidly, the Sycamore is important for sylviculture. The much valued ivory-white wood, with brown veining, is compact, homogeneous and reasonably heavy; it is used for furniture, flooring, handles (cutlery, etc.) and musical instruments; it makes an excellent fuel.

The Sycamore was probably introduced in the 16th century to Britain where it is now naturalized.

ACER PLATANOIDES L.
Norway Maple **
Family *Aceraceae*

height 20 (25) m
crown broadly ovoid, dense
trunk straight, rather short main bole; pale grey bark, smooth or ridged
foliage deciduous
leaves simple, palmate, 10–15 cm, with reddish petiole of 10 cm; 5 obtuse lobes, cordate base, long, pointed teeth to margins, turned outwards; opposite arrangement; autumn colour yellow
flowers inflorescences in upright corymbs; 5 sepals and 5 similar petals, yellow; flowering period April, before foliation

Acer platanoides

fruits double samaras with perpendicular, pedunculate wings, each 3–5 cm

The Norway Maple grows all over Europe, from the Pyrenees to the Caucasus, as far north as southern Scandinavia. It is found in hill and mountain habitats up to an altitude of 1000 m, occasionally in broadleaved woods, on deep soil, in light and sunny surroundings. Like the Sycamore, it is naturalized in Britain.

It is sometimes cultivated for ornament because of its fine decorative foliage. The timber, of less importance than that of the Sycamore, is used mainly for domestic utensils. The fresh leaves make good fodder. It can be confused with *A. saccharum*, but the leaves of the latter have shorter teeth and lobes that are narrow at the base; also, the buds of the Norway Maple are green.

ACER SACCHARINUM L.
(= *A. dasycarpum* Ehrh.)
Silver Maple **
Family *Aceraceae*

height 20 m
crown broadly domed
trunk erect, with branches curving

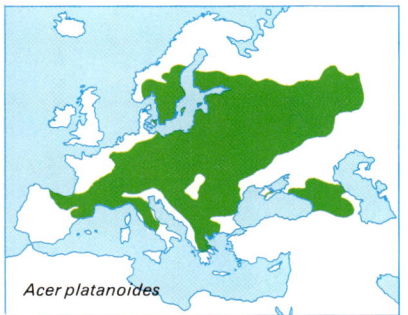

Acer platanoides

outwards; pendulous twigs; bark grey, smooth
foliage deciduous
leaves simple, deeply palmately lobed, 8–15 cm; pointed lobes doubly serrate; alternate arrangement; autumn colour yellow
flowers inflorescences with ♂ or ♀ flowers, in greenish-red umbels with flowers having a small perianth; flowering period February-March, before foliation
fruits pendulous double samaras with long peduncles and perpendicular, pedunculate wings of 3–5 cm, which separate at maturity

The Silver Maple came originally from the eastern parts of North America, and was introduced to Britain around 1730, finding great popularity as an ornamental species for parks and avenues. The deeply lobate leaves have a silver underside and in autumn turn a very decorative yellow or red.

ACER PALMATUM Thunb.
Japanese Maple **
Family *Aceraceae*

This tree, from Japan and Korea, reached Britain in the early years of

Acer palmatum

the 19th century and has achieved wide popularity as an ornamental species. It has delicate, decorative foliage and the leaves, with their narrow, pointed lobes, turn a splendid scarlet colour in autumn.

ACER SACCHARUM Marsh
Sugar Maple
Family *Aceraceae*

The Sugar Maple comes from eastern North America, and was long used by the Indians for the extraction of sugar. This operation is done in March: holes are bored into the trunk to obtain the sap which contains from 1% to 4% saccharose. This is concentrated by boiling to produce maple syrup. The leaves are similar to those of the Norway Maple, with which confusion is possible, but have shorter teeth and lobes narrow at the base; the buds are brown, whereas those of the Norway Maple are green. It is occasionally found in Britain as an ornamental tree.

AESCULUS HIPPOCASTANUM L.
Horse Chestnut
Family *Hippocastanaceae*

height 15–30 m
crown elongated, very fully and densely domed
trunk sturdy, erect, broadly ramified; branches curved towards top; bark dark grey-brown, rough, in small plates
foliage deciduous
leaves compound, palmate, with 5–7 sessile, obovate, mucronate leaflets, with doubly serrate margins, over 20 cm long; petiole likewise 20 cm long; opposite arrangement; autumn colour yellow
flowers inflorescences in erect, terminal racemes, 20–30 cm; flowers with 5 white petals, spotted pink or yellow at base; 7 prominent stamens, turned upwards, with orange anthers; flowering period May
fruits oval, green, with blunt spines,

Aesculus × carnea

Aesculus hippocastanum

3–5 cm ∅, containing one or more seeds similar to chestnuts.

The Horse Chestnut is a species native to eastern Europe, found in the mountain woodlands of the Balkans. Introduced to central Europe around the middle of the 16th century by the Italian Mattioli, it became widely used as an ornamental shade-giving species; it is naturalized in parts of Britain. Rugged and frugal, it adapts to the most diverse soils and uncongenial conditions.

The bark supplies yellow and black dyeing principles for textiles. The wood splits easily as it is soft and is mainly used for cases and boxes.

A flour extracted from the fruits has various applications in perfumery; it contains a bitter property which prevents its use for human consumption, but not as animal fodder. The fruits also serve as food for deer in captivity and for horses and cattle, in moderation, however, in the case of the latter animals, as it can have toxic effects.

Extracts of the Horse Chestnut are used in pharmacy in treating circulatory problems, while the leaves and flowers are effective against rheumatism and gout.

A similar species is Pink Horse Chestnut (*Aesculus × carnea*), a hybrid of Horse Chestnut crossed with a species from the south-eastern regions of the United States, used as an ornamental on account of its beautiful pink flowers.

KOELREUTERIA PANICULATA
Laxm.
Pride of India or Golden Rain Tree **
Family *Sapindaceae*

height 15 m
crown elongated, domed
trunk erect with curved, ascending branches; bark brown, rough
foliage deciduous
leaves compound, pinnate, 30 cm, formed of 7–15 oval, dentate, serrate leaflets; alternate arrangement
flowers inflorescences in erect, loose, terminal racemes; individual yellow flowers of 1 cm; flowering period August
fruits conical, 3-valved capsule of 4 cm, membranous, brown

Koelreuteria paniculata

The generic name commemorates J. G. Koelreute, an 18th-century historian and naturalist from Karlsbad. The tree's original distribution covered eastern Asia, China, Korea and Japan. It became popular in Europe as an ornamental tree after 1760, chiefly in the southern parts of the continent, notable in July for its crown and conspicuous panicles of yellow flowers. It is uncommon in Britain.

This species is indifferent to soil but particular about temperature, as it cannot withstand prolonged cold, preferring sites in full sunlight. On the other hand it can endure long periods of drought.

ILEX AQUIFOLIUM L.
Holly *
Family *Aquilifoliaceae*

height 8 m, often shrubby
crown pyramidal, sparse
trunk straight, branches perpendicular; twigs green, smooth; bark grey, smooth
foliage evergreen
leaves simple, oval with smooth or undulate margins, 4–9 cm (spiny leaves low down, smooth farther up), shiny and leathery

flowers unisexual in axillary bundles; ♂ flowers with white, pink-edged corolla, 4–8mm ∅, 4 stamens; ♀ flowers with white corolla; flowering period April–May
fruits round berry of 1 cm ∅, coral-red, shiny

The young leaves of the Holm Oak (*Quercus ilex*), wavy and spinous, resemble those of the Holly, and it is for this reason that the word *ilex* is used for the scientific terminology of the latter species.

The tree grows wild in Great Britain and central-western Europe, with a

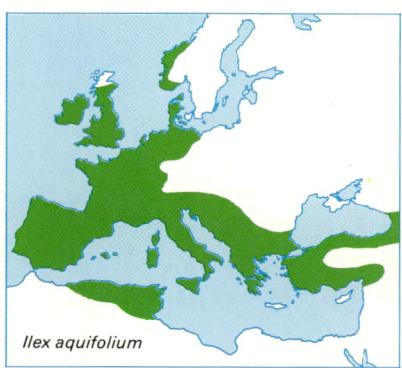

Ilex aquifolium

range that embraces the Atlantic and Mediterranean regions as far as Asia Minor. It prefers maritime climates, with few extremes of temperature, plenty of rain and an average amount of drought in summer. Nowadays it is found only sporadically, because it is so much sought after, in moist broad-leaved woods in upland areas with acid soils.

It is widely planted as an ornamental species for its splendid deep green foliage, in decorative contrast to the red berries, and because of its resistance to urban atmospheric pollution. It is particularly appreciated as an evergreen in northern Europe, its range extending to Scandinavia.

The Holly has unisexual flowers, caused by the abortion of the stamens and the pistil respectively in flowers that were originally hermaphroditic; so plants usually have either male flowers or female flowers.

The Holly grows very slowly and produces hard, compact, light grey wood which turns brown with age. It has staining properties and is used for cabinet-making, sculpture, walking sticks and handles. Leaves and bark contain the glucocide ilicin, effective in the treatment of rheumatism and fevers; the berries, however, are better left alone as they can result in severe poisoning. The bark furnishes a sticky extract used in some countries for liming birds.

There are a number of selected varieties, cultivated for their characteristic features, notably the leaves, which may, for example, be speckled, large or small.

STAPHYLEA PINNATA L.
Bladder-nut
Family *Staphyleaceae*

height 5 m, often shrubby
crown irregularly pyramidal, sparse
trunk erect or slightly curved, branches bending slightly upwards; bark dark grey

Staphylea pinnata

× ½

foliage deciduous
leaves compound, pinnate, 10–20 cm; 5–7 sessile, elliptic leaflets, with toothed margins; opposite arrangement
flowers inflorescences in clusters, long-stalked and pendulous; flowers 1.5 cm ∅, with 5 white petals; flowering period April–May
fruits translucent, vesicular capsule, 3–4 cm, green, formed of 2–3 lobes containing 1–2 spherical, pea-like, very hard seeds

The generic name, from the Greek *staphyle* (bunch), is derived from the hanging inflorescences.

This species originated in central-southern Europe, its range extending from the Iberian peninsula to Asia

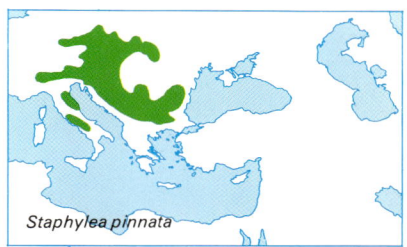

Staphylea pinnata

Minor. It grows, infrequently, in warm, hilly broadleaved woodlands and is occasionally cultivated in Britain.

As it is a small tree, the timber is used mainly as fuel. The very hard seeds, brown with grey markings, are used for bracelets, necklaces and rosaries.

BUXUS SEMPERVIRENS L.
Box *
Family *Buxaceae*

height 5 (8) m, usually shrubby
crown domed
trunk divided, much ramified; twigs angular, green; bark dark grey
foliage evergreen
leaves simple, oval-elliptic, 3 cm or less, obtuse or notched, leathery; margins revolute; petiole very short; opposite arrangement
flowers in axillary clusters; flowers small, ♂ with 4 stamens which surround a ♀ flower with 3 styles; perianth yellowish-white; flowering period March–May
fruits oval capsules which open in 3 valves, each with 2 horns; dimensions about 1 cm

Buxus balearica Lam.
Balearic Box

Species similar to *B. sempervirens*, but with larger leaves (3–5 cm), which are opaque, and reddish-brown bark.

Box has a wide distribution, from the Atlantic shores of the Iberian peninsula to the Balkans. It is probably a native of southern England, which would extend to north west Europe the natural distribution shown on the map. It forms woods together with oak and beech, up to altitudes of 700–800 m, on calcareous, dry, stony soils, in sunny positions, but sometimes also in underbrush. It performs an improving and protective function where sub-standard soils are concerned.

Buxus sempervirens

Box is slow-growing and generally of shrubby habit, so that the wood is as a rule of modest proportions. It is widely planted for ornament in parks, and as hedges, responding well to pruning and retaining its shape, given the slowness of growth.

The very heavy wood, with a higher specific weight than water, when dry, is used for making small articles such as musical instruments, spindles, cutlery, buttons and chess pieces. Leaves and bark have pharmaceutical uses as purgatives and febrifuges, although the plant itself is poisonous, even to animals.

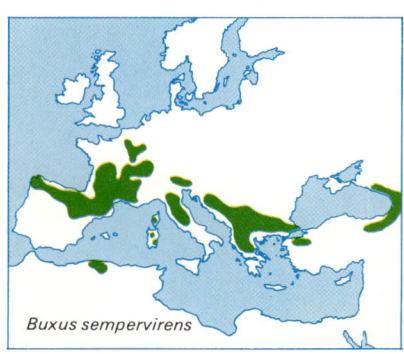

Buxus sempervirens

Paliurus spina-christi

×2

PALIURUS SPINA-CHRISTI Mill.
(= *P. australis* Gaertn.)
Christ's Thorn
Family *Rhamnaceae*

height 4 (5) m, often shrubby
crown hemispherical
trunk divided at base; branches curved and pendulous, very spiny; twigs in zigzag form; bark reddish-brown
foliage deciduous
leaves simple, oval, 2–4 cm, with 3 almost parallel veins at margins; alternate arrangement
flowers linked in small axillary corymbs, with 5 shining yellow petals

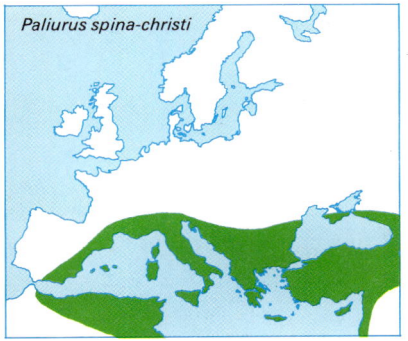

Paliurus spina-christi

and 5 stamens attached to a green disc of 8 mm ∅; flowering period May–June
fruits nuts with a disc-like wing expansion, brown and dry when ripe, 3–5 cm ∅

Christ's Thorn is a Mediterranean species, found in the maquis since it likes a very dry, warm environment; it is rarely seen in southern England. Its uses are limited because of the small trunk; it is sometimes used for hedging and to form dense thickets to keep out animals.

ZIZIPHUS JUJUBA Mill.
(= *Z. vulgaris* Lam.)
Jujube
Family *Rhamnaceae*

height up to 8 m, most often shrubby
crown domed and sparse
trunk upright and sinuous; branches spinous; twigs green; bark grey-brown, pinkish on twigs, in small plates on trunk

Ziziphus jujuba

×2

foliage deciduous
leaves simple, oval, 3–6 cm, rounded at tip; margins serrate; 3 almost parallel veins; short petiole; alternate arrangement
flowers in 2–3 globose, axillary bundles; corolla yellowish-white, 6 mm ∅, 5 petals, 6 stamens; flowering period April–June
fruits ovoid drupes of 1.5 (3) cm, reddish-brown, edible

The generic name derives from the Arabic word *zizouf*, to describe the species *Z. lotus*, common in North Africa.
　The Jujube's distribution covers eastern Mediterranean Europe, where it has been long cultivated for its fruit; it is not hardy in Britain. The hard, resistant wood is used in lathework. The fruits (jujubes) have a floury, sweetish pulp, similar to dates; they can be candied or used for their alcohol content.

RHAMNUS ALATERNUS L.
Mediterranean Buckthorn
Family *Rhamnaceae*

height up to 5 m, usually shrubby
crown domed, compact

Rhamnus alaternus

trunk ramified and divided at base; hairy twigs; bark reddish-grey, finely striped
foliage evergreen
leaves simple, varying from oval to elliptic, pointed, 3–6 cm; margins white, entire or slightly serrate; short petiole; alternate or sub-opposite arrangement
flowers in short axillary, globose racemes; flowers small, with 5 greenish-yellow petals, sometimes absent; they give out an unpleasant odour; flowering period February–April
fruits spherical reddish-brown drupes of 4 mm ∅

This species is found in the Mediterranean region, common to the calcareous or rocky terrain of the evergreen maquis. It thrives in sheltered parts of Britain but is not often planted.
　The very hard, yellowish-brown wood has a disagreeable smell; its uses are confined to the manufacture of small articles. The fruits are used in medicine for their powerful purgative properties and also produce a green colorant. Because of its compact crown, the plant is ideal for dividing and hedging.

RHAMNUS CATHARTICUS L.
Buckthorn *
Family *Rhamnaceae*

height up to 6 m, usually shrubby
crown irregular and sparse
trunk erect, branched from base; branches transformed into spines; bark reddish-brown
foliage deciduous
leaves simple, elliptic-rounded, 4–9 cm, margins toothed; veins almost parallel to margins; alternate or opposite arrangement
flowers in axillary umbels; flowers often unisexual with a tubular calyx terminating in 4 pointed parts, similar to petals, yellow-green, 5 mm ∅; flowering period April–June
fruits spherical drupes, black, the size of peas

The Buckthorn's distribution ranges over Britain and central-southern Europe, where it grows in woods and hedges, in calcareous soil. Because the bole is small, the wood has only limited use: in turnery and inlay work.

The fruits and bark are used in veterinary medicine, but because of powerful purgative effects must be treated with extreme care. The fruits, like those of related species, also produce a green dyeing colorant.

FRANGULA ALNUS Mill.
(= *Rhamnus frangula* L.)
Alder Buckthorn *
Family *Rhamnaceae*

height up to 6 m, often shrubby
crown irregularly domed
trunk erect, branched; bark smooth, reddish, with many lenticels
foliage deciduous
leaves simple, elliptic, 4–6 cm, with petiole of 1 cm, margins entire; alternate arrangement
flowers in axillary bundles, up to 10; flowers of 4 mm ⌀ with corolla of 5 oval, greenish-white petals, 5 stamens; flowering period May–July

Frangula alnus

×3

fruits spherical drupes, black when ripe (green, red previously) 8 mm ⌀

The Alder Buckthorn is found throughout Europe including Britain, in broadleaved woods, preferably in acid, wet and poor soils, up to altitudes of 1300 m.

This frugal and highly adaptable species was much used in the past and is still so today. The reddish, strongly scented wood is suitable for lathe-work, besides providing good-quality charcoal from which gunpowder is made.

The bark has medicinal applications: fresh as an emetic, dried as a laxative, but which must be used with caution, and only after a long period of seasoning (at least a year). The tree also yields dyeing colorants: grey-blue from the fruits, brown from the bark.

TILIA CORDATA Mill.
(= *T. parviflora* Ehrh.)
Small-leaved Lime *
Family *Tiliaceae*

height 20 (30) m
crown ovate, domed
trunk sturdy, branched at base; branches curving upwards; twigs glabrous; bark dark grey, brownish, divided into small plates
foliage deciduous
leaves simple, cordate with asymmetrical base, almost round, mucronate, 3–10 cm; margins sharply serrate; underside glabrous; petiole glabrous; alternate arrangement
flowers inflorescences in corymb, usually not drooping, but upright or at an angle, 4–12 flowers with 5 sepals and 5 white petals, 2 cm ⌀; flowering period June
fruits ovoid nuts, pointed at tip, 6 mm ⌀, glabrous and persistent on axis of inflorescence; the latter is furnished with a leafy bract, free at the tip, extending from the upper part of the peduncle, which thus appears winged

Key to **LIMES**

Trees growing wild
– leaves with underside blue-green, glabrous: **Tilia cordata**
– leaves with underside bright green, not glaucous
–– leaves of the same colour both sides, pubescent below; petioles and twigs pubescent: **Tilia platyphyllos**
–– leaves lighter on lower side; leaves, petioles and twigs glabrous or almost glabrous: **Tilia x europaea**

Trees cultivated
– leaves completely hairy-tomentose below, with blade of less than 12 cm: **Tilia tomentosa**
– leaves with sparse hairs below, with blade of 10–20 cm: **Tilia americana**

The generic name derives from the Greek *ptilon* (wing), because of the distinctive winged bract attached to the stalk of the inflorescence.

The Small-leaved Lime comes originally from central Europe, an area extending from the Iberian peninsula to the Black Sea. It was one of the last trees to reach Britain unaided by man. At one time more widely distributed, it is nowadays found sporadically or in small groups, in woods of broadleaved species, such as oak, chestnut and beech, on calcareous and subacid soils, up to 1400 m. It has become rarer as a result of deliberate deforestation carried out to provide more land for farming.

The tree was sacred to Germanic and Slav peoples, as a symbol of fertility, and religious rites were performed beneath its shade. Nowadays it is mainly planted for ornament.

The wood, whitish, soft, of average quality, is used for furniture, musical instruments and lathe-work, besides producing drawing charcoal of high quality. The bark provides fibres, used for mats and ropes; the flowers yield a fine, scented honey.

Tilia cordata

×1

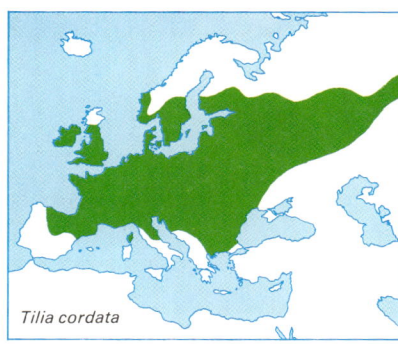

Tilia cordata

The pharmaceutical properties of the lime have long been known; a tranquillizing infusion is made from the flowers.

TILIA PLATYPHYLLOS Scop.
Large-leaved Lime *
Family *Tiliaceae*

height 30 (40) m
crown ovate, narrowly domed
trunk erect, without suckers; branches curving upwards; twigs hairy; bark dark grey
foliage deciduous
leaves simple, cordate with asym-

Tilia platyphyllos

metrical base, 6–15 cm, with mucronate apex and serrate margins; underside more or less pubescent, hairy at juncture of veins; petiole pubescent
flowers inflorescences of 1–6 flowers, pendulous; flowering period May–June
fruits as in *T. cordata*; nuts thickly hairy with 5 ridges, 1 cm ∅

The distribution of the Large-leaved Lime extends from the Iberian peninsula to the Caucasus. It is cultivated widely as an amenity tree in Britain, where it is probably a native species. It is found, infrequently, in broad-leaved woods of oak and beech, together with ash and alder, up to altitudes of 1200 m. It grows in fresh, well-drained soil and needs a fair amount of atmospheric humidity. It is very long-lived; some specimens are thought to be several centuries old.

It is often used for ornamental purposes. The wood has much the same uses as that of *T. cordata*. There are a number of ornamental cultivars, such as 'Aurea', with young yellow shoots, and 'Laciniata', with irregularly divided leaves.

TILIA X EUROPEA L.
(= *T. vulgaris* Hayne)
Common Lime **
Family *Tiliaceae*

This is a natural hybrid of *T. cordata* and *T. platyphyllos*, widespread throughout central and northern Europe and frequently cultivated in parks and avenues. Its leaves are generally very large, opaque above, with a petiole at an angle to the axis of the principal vein; the inflorescences are pendulous.

Several other species of lime may be found in parks and lining roadsides, including *Tilia americana* L., with characteristic large oval leaves (from eastern North America), and *T. tomentosa* Moench (= *T. argentea* D.C.), the underside of whose leaves

Tilia cordata

Tilia × europaea

are thickly covered by a greyish-white layer of hairs (from the Balkans, Hungary and south-western Asia).

ELAEAGNUS ANGUSTIFOLIA L.
Oleaster
Family *Elaeagnaceae*

height 7 (10) m, often shrubby
crown domed

Elaeagnus angustifolia

trunk short, erect; shoots spiny and sharp; bark greenish-brown, with long tapering scales; twigs silvery
foliage evergreen
leaves lanceolate-elongate, 4–8 cm, silvery beneath; alternate arrangement
flowers axillary in groups of 1–3, pedunculate; bell-like corolla of 8 mm, yellow, with 4 reflexed lobes; flowering period May–June
fruits long yellow drupes, 1–2 cm, floury

The generic name derives from the Greek *elaios* (olive), alluding to the resemblance of the leaves of this species to those of the genus *Olea*. The Oleaster came originally from western Asia and was introduced to Europe in the 17th century, where it later became naturalized. In Britain it is rarely grown. It is rugged and grows even on loose, poor, sandy soil, thanks to the presence of root tubercles which contain bacteria that fix atmospheric nitrogen. It is frequently cultivated for ornamental purposes because of its silvery, decorative leaves. An essence extracted from the flowers is used for making liqueurs. There is a variety *orientalis*, with larger leaves.

HIPPOPHAE RHAMNOIDES L.
Sea Buckthorn *
Family *Elaeagnaceae*

height 5 m, usually shrubby
crown irregular, loose
trunk short, ramified with stiff, spiny branches; twigs silver-grey; bark pale grey
foliage deciduous
leaves simple, linear-lanceolate, sessile, 4–6 cm, green above and silver-white below
flowers unisexual, inconspicuous, brown, 0.3 cm, ♀ solitary, ♂ in catkins; flowering period March–April, before foliation
fruits ovate-spherical drupes, 6–8 mm ∅, orange, ripening in summer, edible.

Hippophae rhamnoides

×3
Tamarix gallica

This species was once used for treating eye diseases in horses, hence its scientific name, from the Greek *hippos* (horse), and *faos* (light).

The original area of the Sea Buckthorn was from central Asia across Europe to Britain, where it grows wild in exposed river-beds, in dry, sandy places and on shifting slopes. It is a sun-loving species, extremely frugal, capable of surviving in poor, sterile sites due to the nitrogen-fixing bacteria in the root tubercles.

It usually takes the form of a very thorny shrub, cultivated for its hedging qualities and attractive berries. The edible bitter-tasting fruits contain vitamin C.

TAMARIX GALLICA L.
French Tamarisk
Family *Tamaricaceae*

height 5 (10) m, often shrubby
crown spreading, irregular
trunk short, sinuous, with branches curving upwards; bark grey-brown; shoots purple
foliage deciduous
leaves scale-like, pointed, slightly fleshy, up to 2 mm long; alternate arrangement
flowers inflorescences in dense cylindrical racemes, 3–5 cm, joined in terminal spikes, together with green shoots; flowers small, corolla with 5 petals of 1.5–2 mm, caducous, pink to white; flowering period May–June
fruits small pyramidal capsules

Tamarix africana Poiret
African Tamarisk

Similar to *T. gallica* species, but differing in having scales of 4 mm with

Hippophae rhamnoides

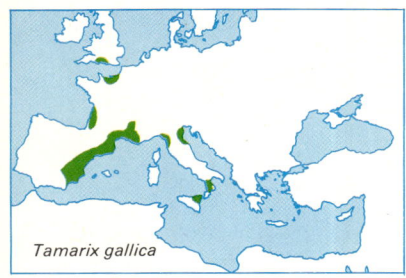

Tamarix gallica

transparent edges, longer and broader inflorescences, and flowers with petals of 2–3 mm.

The Tamarisk ranges from the western Mediterranean to the Adriatic; here, as elsewhere, a popular ornamental. It is highly adaptable to loose and sandy soils and tolerates salty coastal winds; it is widely used in consolidating unstable soils, making it possible for other, more demanding species to be planted later. In north Cornwall, it helps to stabilize stone walls between fields. The wood has no great value: yellowish-white, of limited dimensions and fragile. The bark has a high tannin content.

The African Tamarisk grows in the western Mediterranean basin, on both African and European shores, and has similar characteristics to *T. gallica* except for differences already mentioned.

LAGERSTROEMIA INDICA L.
Crape Myrtle
Family *Lythraceae*

height 4–8 m
crown domed
trunk erect and twisted, with sinuous, knotty branches; tetragonal twigs; bark smooth, light brown to pinkish-grey, with plates that flake off to leave bare white patches
foliage deciduous
leaves simple, elliptic-lanceolate, pointed, 7 × 3 cm, more or less sessile, with entire, glabrous margins;

arrangement alternate, sometimes opposite higher up; autumn colour red
flowers inflorescences in terminal spikes of 20 cm; flowers with 6 free pinky-purple or white petals; numerous sprouting stamens; flowering period August–September
fruits loculate capsules attached to axis of inflorescence

The generic name commemorates Magnus Lagerstroem (1696–1759), Swedish director of the Indies Company, and friend of Linnaeus. This small tree, of Asiatic origin (it comes from China), reached Europe in the middle of the 18th century, being planted widely as an ornamental species. It is cultivated in all mild regions, and is impervious to hazards of dust and pollution. Just hardy in southern England, it rarely flowers, but in warmer parts of Europe it is common in parks and streets.

The Crape Myrtle provides ornament in virtually any season: in late summer its flowers are a beautiful pink colour, in autumn it has crimson leaves, in winter the twisted, grey-white trunks are decorative, and in spring the new shoots are slightly orange coloured.

×1

Lagerstroemia indica

MYRTUS COMMUNIS L.
Myrtle
Family *Myrtaceae*

height 5 m, often shrubby
crown hemispherical, domed
trunk short, divided, branched; bark reddish-brown, in scales, fibrous
foliage evergreen
leaves simple, ovate-acute, 3 cm, stiff; margins entire; when crushed, they give out an aromatic scent; arrangement opposite or verticillate in groups of 3
flowers solitary or in pairs at leaf axil, pedunculate; calyx persistent, 5-petalled corolla of 3 cm ∅, white; very many protruding stamens, yellow anthers; flowering period June–August
fruits elliptic berries, up to 1 cm, blue-black, with the remains of the lobed calyces at tip

The Myrtle is found all over the Mediterranean region, especially on coasts, in hedges and on scrubland. A sun-loving species, it is scarcely hardy in Britain and rarely seen. It can survive on acid or subacid soils, but is also to be found in calcareous soil. While cultivated for ornament, it is sensitive to frost and has to be planted in sunny, sheltered spots.

The tree was sacred to Venus, symbolizing love, and was used for twining crowns and wedding wreaths; it has thus been known since ancient

Myrtus communis

times. Today it is used mainly for ornamental purposes.

Leaves, roots and bark contain tannins, used to give an agreeable odour to quality leather. From the same parts an extraction known as 'angels' water' is used in perfumery. The fruits are used for flavouring and in alcoholic beverages.

The hard, reddish-brown wood has few uses except for small articles such as tool and umbrella handles, but provides good fuel and high quality charcoal.

Numerous varieties have been selected for ornamental purposes, which differ mainly in leaf size.

EUCALYPTUS GLOBULUS Labill.
Blue Gum
Family *Myrtaceae*

height 20–40 m
crown broadly oval or irregularly domed
trunk straight, cylindrical; curved branches; quadrangular twigs; bark grey-green, flaking in spirals around trunk in form of tapering strips which leave smooth, light blue or pinkish zones
foliage evergreen

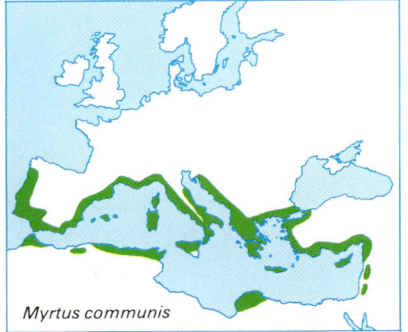

Myrtus communis

Key to **GUMS**

Flowers in groups of 1–3
– flowers and fruits sessile, usually solitary: **Eucalyptus globulus**
– flowers and fruits with short peduncles, in umbels of 3:
        Eucalyptus viminalis

Flowers numerous, pedunculate
– bark rough, fibrous, persistent; fruit cylindrical: **Eucalyptus robustus**
– bark smooth, whitish, flaking in plates; fruit hemispherical:
        Eucalyptus camaldulensis

Flowering period
– January–April: **E. robustus**
– June–November: **E. viminalis**
– June–November: **E. camaldulensis**
– November–June: **E. globulus**

leaves in adult trees, lanceolate and sickle-shaped, long, 10–30 cm × 2.5 cm, with pointed apex and smooth margins; alternate arrangement; in young trees, ovate, sessile, opposite or perfoliate, shorter; the leaves give out a characteristic aroma
flowers solitary (or 2–3), subsessile, made up of very many stamens attached to ovary; the latter is wrapped by the woody receptacle, in the shape of a top, from which the fruit develops; flowering period November–June
fruits hemispherical capsules with 4 ridges, 2 cm ⌀, grey

The flowers of the various gums are protected by an operculum, hence the generic name, from the Greek *eu* (well), and *calyptos* (covered).

The Blue Gum, originally from south-eastern Australia, was introduced to Europe at the beginning of the 19th century. In the British Isles it is only hardy in the mildest winters in Eire and Cornwall.

All the *Eucalyptus* species form part of the tropical and sub-tropical Australian forests where rainfall is at least 600 mm (23½ in) annually. They are found in countries where the climate is sufficiently warm and moist, being widely planted as forest and ornamental species. The Blue Gum is a rapid grower which needs deep, loose soil that guarantees a good water supply; it furnishes plenty of timber.

The wood of the *Eucalyptus* species

bud covered by operculum

Eucalyptus globulus

is of mediocre quality, used mainly as fuel, for paper or rough poles. The bark is processed for tannin. Bees produce a fine, scented honey from the flowers.

The leaves of the *Eucalyptus* species have medicinal properties; they provide eucalyptus oil, other ingredients used in the treatment of lung diseases and coolants.

EUCALYPTUS VIMINALIS Labill.
Ribbon Gum
Family *Myrtaceae*

This gum comes originally from south-eastern Australia. It has a fair tolerance to frost, grows well when sheltered from wind in deep, loose soil, but not clay, or dry.

The commonest gum species in Britain is the Cider Gum ** (*E. gunnii*), so called because a cider-like beverage can be made from the sap. It is distinguished by its small flat, rather oblong leaves with broad wedge-shaped bases, set on a yellowish petiole.

EUCALYPTUS CAMALDULENSIS
Dehnh.
Red Gum
Family *Myrtaceae*

Brought from its native Australia to Naples in 1803, the Red Gum was planted in the garden of the counts Camaldoni after whom it is named. Of all *Eucalyptus* species, it is the most resistant to drought and to clay and salty soil.

Together with the Blue Gum, it was formerly planted in swampy areas because it was thought to have a purifying effect on the air by dint of its balsamic emanations, helping to make the surroundings unsuitable for the development of the malaria-carrying anopheles mosquito – an unfounded belief, but one which encouraged the spread of these trees.

These species grow well in thin, airy plantations and need plenty of

fruit (capsule)

×1

buds

Eucalyptus camaldulensis

sun. The main uses are in the paper industry, and for poles and mine props.

EUCALYPTUS ROBUSTUS Sm.
Swamp Mahogany
Family *Myrtaceae*

This species was planted in Italy, France, Portugal and Sardinia during the 19th century, being particularly suited to swampy areas or brackish water. Its uses are the same as for related species.

PUNICA GRANATUM L.
Pomegranate
Family *Punicaceae*

height 5 m, often shrubby
crown domed
trunk twisted, sometimes ridged, much ramified; twigs spiny or unarmed; bark reddish-grey
foliage deciduous
leaves simple, oblong-lanceolate, 8 cm; apex pointed or obtuse, margins smooth; petiole short; arrangement opposite or verticillate, even

Punica granatum

alternate on main branches
flowers terminal, large (3–4 cm), ses-sile, funnel-shaped, coral-red, rarely white; 5–8 obovate-lanceolate petals, 2–3 cm; many (20) stamens; calyx flesh-red, bell-shaped, persistent in that it grows with operculum and ov-ary; flowering period July–October
fruits globose, large in cultivated specimens (from 6–12 cm ∅), small as a nut in wild specimens; the fruit is a particular type of berry, yellow to red, with large numbers of seeds sur-rounded by a fleshy red, translucent part; edible, it ripens in autumn

The generic name refers to its pre-sumed zone of origin, corresponding nowadays to North Africa (*punicus*, Latin for 'Carthaginian'). This small tree, however, probably came origi-nally from the eastern parts of the Mediterranean and western Asia, and already in Roman times was both cultivated and naturalized in many mild areas. In Britain it requires wall protection to produce its interesting flowers.

It is found in the Mediterranean maquis, as it favours arid ground. It grows slowly, its cultivation requir-ing no special care, but a sunny site is important.

The Pomegranate was cultivated in ancient Egypt and Greece; in Rome it signified friendship and symbolized democracy.

Every part of the plant has medici-nal properties as an astringent; the root bark provides a remedy against tapeworms, but must be used with care because of possible toxic effects.

The bark of the trunk and the rind of the fruit are used for special tanning purposes, while rind and flowers yield a red dye. The fruits, which are diuretic, are eaten raw and can be made into drinks and syrups. The wood is hard, but little used because of its modest dimensions. The Pomegranate, with its splendid flowers, is much-valued as an orna-mental tree.

CORNUS MAS L.
Cornelian Cherry *
Family *Cornaceae*

height 5 (8) m
crown domed, sparse
trunk erect, broadly branched at top; greenish twigs with 4 angles; bark grey-brown or grey, ridged and di-vided into small scales; smooth in young trees

Punica granatum

Cornus mas

Cornus mas

foliage deciduous
leaves simple, oval-elliptic, acuminate, 4–10 cm, with 3–5 pairs of veins curving almost parallel to margin; opposite arrangement
flowers inflorescences in umbels with 4 bracts at base, on branches of previous year; flowers with corolla of 4 bright yellow, pointed petals, 0.8 cm ∅; flowering period February–March, before foliation
fruits reddish drupes, elongate, 1–2 cm, pendulous; edible

Cornus sanguinea L.
Dogwood *

Similar to *C. mas*, but a shrub of 2–6 m; twigs reddish and with 2 angles; pointed leaves; flowers white in corymbs appearing after foliation in early summer; fruits black drupes of 5–6 mm ∅.

The Cornelian Cherry ranges from central-southern Europe to Asia Minor. It is sun-loving, averagely long-lived, growing in calcareous subsoils in broadleaved woods, coppices and hedges, in warm, lowland sites to an altitude of 1200 m.

The yellowish-brown wood, hard, yet elastic, needs long seasoning, tending to split; its uses are in turnery for products subjected to hard wear.

The fruits (cornels), sharp and tasty, containing saccharose and organic acids, can be eaten raw or in jams.

An oil used in perfumery and, formerly, for lamps, is extracted from the seeds.

There are ornamental varieties which differ in leaf colour and fruit size. The species is often planted in Britain for its attractive March flowers.

ARBUTUS UNEDO L.
Strawberry Tree *
Family *Ericaceae*

height 5 (12) m
crown domed, irregular
trunk erect and sinuous, broadly ramified; twigs pubescent; bark brown, rough, in soft pinkish strips
foliage evergreen
leaves simple, elliptic-lanceolate, 5–10 cm, crenate-serrate, shiny above; short pink petiole; alternate arrangement
flowers inflorescences in clusters; flowers with pinkish-white corolla;

Arbutus unedo

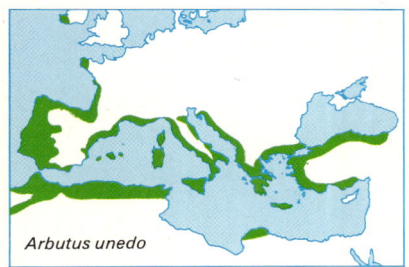

Arbutus unedo

red peduncles; flowering period October–March
fruits spherical berries of 2 cm ⌀, bright red, with grainy surface; very conspicuous, edible but tasteless

The generic name is derived from the Celtic *arbois* (rough – from the surface of the fruit), and the specific name from the Latin phrase *unum edo* (I eat only one) – despite a gaudy appearance, the fruit is insipid.

The Strawberry Tree is principally found in the Mediterranean basin, on the Atlantic coasts of Portugal and Spain, and northwards to southern Ireland. It grows together with Phillyria, Holm Oak, Mastic Tree and other members of the Heather family, forming extensive stands, adapting to a warm, dry climate as well as sandy and acid soils.

The wood is valued as fuel and produces good-quality charcoal. The branches, sprouting abundantly from the base, are made into poles.

The fruits (arbutus berries) are edible; fermented, they form the basis of alcoholic drinks.

The species is frequently used for ornamental purposes in parks and for consolidating shifting slopes in Mediterranean sites.

ARBUTUS ANDRACHNE L.
Greek Strawberry Tree
Family *Ericaceae*

A species from the eastern Mediterranean, often with a bushy habit, it occasionally grows to the size of a small tree. The Greek Strawberry Tree differs from the common species in having reddish-brown, fibrous bark, leaves with mainly entire margins, but above all by flowering in spring (March–April); the fruits, of 1 cm ⌀, are orange in colour.

ERICA ARBOREA L.
Tree Heath
Family *Ericaceae*

height 6 m, often shrubby
crown irregularly domed, loose
trunk erect, sinuous, knotty; twigs hairy; bark rough, reddish, with reticulated furrows
foliage evergreen
leaves acicular, linear, flattened, 0.8 cm; verticillate arrangement in groups of 4
flowers inflorescences in raceme at tip of branches, together with leaves; pendulous flowers with pitcher-shaped corolla of 2–3.5 mm, white or pink; the dark anthers do not protrude; flowering period March–May

×3

×5

Erica arborea

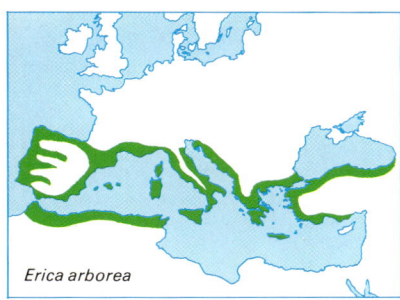

Erica arborea

fruits small loculate capsules with minute seeds

This species is found throughout the Mediterranean area, from southern Europe to the Iberian peninsula. It is commonly seen growing together with the Strawberry Tree and Holm Oak on acid soils, adapting to poor, arid terrain and tolerant of drought.

It is a very slow-growing species, used nowadays to make stiff brooms; the branches were once used to prepare the 'wood' in the raising of silkworms. It is hardy in southern Britain but rarely makes more than a medium-sized shrub.

The red wood, firm and hard, is used in lathe-work, for fuel and charcoal. From the woody root come the well-known briar pipes. Deep red in colour, the root must be boiled and cut while still wet to avoid cracking.

Honey from the flowers of the Tree Heath is of exceptional quality.

DIOSPYROS KAKI L.
Chinese Persimmon
Family *Ebenaceae*

height 4–12 m
crown domed, dense
trunk erect, then broadly branched; bark rough, brown, divided into small plates
foliage deciduous
leaves simple, oval-acute, 10–15 cm; margins entire; shiny above, hairy below, with petiole; alternate arrangement

flowers unisexual, not prominent, with 4-toothed calyx and 4-lobed, pitcher-shaped corolla; ♂ flowers yellowish, in threes, 1 cm long, with numerous (16–24) stamens; ♀ flowers of 2 cm, hairy stigma; flowering period June
fruits large berries (up to 10 cm ⌀), orange-yellow, smooth surfaced, with residues of calyx on stalk; they ripen in October and remain on tree even after leaf fall

Diospyros kaki

***Diospyros lotus* L.**
Date Plum

Similar to *D. kaki*, but with elliptic, acuminate leaves and small, spherical fruits of 2 cm ⌀, from yellow to purple.

The generic name is derived from the Greek *dios* (divine), and *pyros* (fruit), referring to the excellent fruits.

The Chinese Persimmon was introduced to Europe at the end of the 18th century from China and Korea, where it grows wild. In Britain it is rarely grown. It has become widely popular both as an ornamental and for its fruit; the handsome dark foliage is dense and the large fruits remain on the tree long after the leaves fall. Adaptable to virtually any soil, it is affected by prolonged frosts.

The fruits vary in size, and may be sweet or astringent. If the former, they are eaten soon after being picked; in the latter case they are usually without seeds and are 'over-ripened' for a couple of months before being eaten. During this time the tannins, through the action of enzymes, separate into sugars and organic acids. With the sweet fruits, this process occurs during seed formation.

There are several cultivars of persimmons, distinguished by different shapes and fruit tastes.

The Date Plum, also an Asiatic species, is a hardy, vigorous tree, used as a rootstock for the Chinese Persimmon.

STYRAX OFFICINALIS L.
Storax
Family *Styracaceae*

height 5 m, more often shrubby
crown domed
trunk erect, with broad branches; bark grey-brown, rough
foliage deciduous

Styrax officinalis

leaves simple, ovate-elliptic, rounded at base, 3–5 cm; shiny above, densely hairy below; margins smooth; petiole short; alternate arrangement
flowers inflorescences in axillary racemes, with 4–6 flowers; bell-shaped flowers with scented, 5-lobed, pointed, white corolla; 12–16 stamens, joined at base; flowering period April–May
fruits aromatic drupes of 1–2 cm ∅, whitish

The generic name in Greek means 'resin', alluding to the properties of this species. The Storax has an eastern-Mediterranean distribution and is not hardy in Britain. It is used for the production of resin, particularly in Asia Minor. This product, which has the delicate scent of vanilla, is known as solid storax and used for making incense, in perfumery and in medicine as a balsam. The seeds are used for making into rosaries and necklaces, but the wood has few uses.

OLEA EUROPAEA L.
Olive
Family *Oleaceae*

height 10 m
trunk oval, broad, loose
trunk sinuous and knotty, with age divided and hollow; bark pale grey
foliage evergreen
leaves simple, elliptic-lanceolate, about 8 cm, leathery, with short petiole, green above and silver-grey below; opposite arrangement
flowers in axillary panicles, sparse and short, flowers with persistent 4-toothed calyx, tubular caducous corolla with 4 white lobes, of about 1 cm; flowering period April–May
fruits ovoid drupes (olives), green then black, 1–3.5 cm

Olea europaea var. ***sylvestris*** Brot.
(= *O. oleaster* Hoffmg. & Link)
Wild Olive

Similar to *O. europaea*, but wild, usually shrubby, with spinous twigs;

Olea europaea

×2

leaves much smaller, oval, 1–2 cm; small fruits.

The Olive is distributed around the Mediterranean, mainly as a result of cultivation; its original distribution area probably lay in North Africa or Asia Minor. Today it is found wherever climate permits, growing in the evergreen maquis and up to a height of 600–700 m. It is a typical temperate maritime species, averse to severe frost; it can, however, withstand long periods of drought. It thrives on calcareous or clay soils, but not on sites that are too sandy or poorly drained. It is only very rarely seen in Britain.

The Olive is cultivated for its fruit, graded by size and yield for pressing, the smaller olives having a higher oil content. Olive oil is the best of all vegetable oils, with a high food and medicinal value. It is a mixture of esters of fatty acids, which include oleic acid, linoleic acid, palmitic acid, stearic acid and myristic acid. The residues of the pressing, or husks, are used as fuel and livestock fodder.

The wood, varying from brown to black, is ideal for polishing, being used in high-quality joinery, for flooring and panelling. It makes a good fuel, burning even when green.

OSMANTHUS FRAGRANS Lour.
Family *Oleaceae*

This small tree grows wild in China and Japan, and is planted in southern Europe for ornamental purposes. Highly adaptable to any soil, it is sensitive to temperature and in the open can only be cultivated in sites enjoying mild and sunny conditions. In Britain it is rarely found outdoors.

The leaves differ considerably from those of the Olive, being 8–10 cm long, 2–3 cm wide, shiny and dark above, not hairy below; the white flowers are deeply scented. The forma, *aurantiaca*, with orange flowers, is widely cultivated.

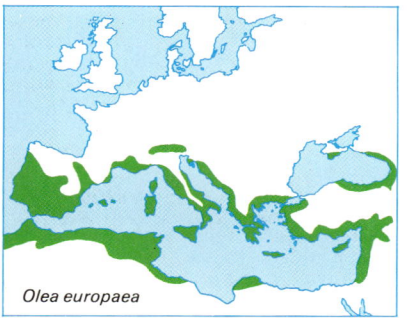

Olea europaea

SYRINGA VULGARIS L.
Lilac **
Family *Oleaceae*

height 5 (7) m
crown ovoid, domed
trunk erect, often bifurcate, broadly ramified; bark bluish-grey, ridged with age
foliage deciduous
leaves simple, ovate-triangular, 5–12 cm, acuminate, with smooth margin and cordate base, petiole about 2 cm; opposite arrangement
flowers inflorescences in terminal panicles, 20–30 cm; flowers scented, with persistent 4-toothed calyx and tubular corolla with 4 concave lobes, arranged perpendicularly to corolla; colour lilac, violet or white; flowering period late May–June
fruits bivalve, oval, compressed capsules, dry and brown, 1.5 cm

The tubular shape of the flowers determined the generic name, from the Greek *syrinx* (pipe, tube). The Lilac grows wild in south-eastern Europe, and has a wide distribution as an ornamental species, its flowers being abundant and scented. It has become naturalized in some areas.

It is slow-growing, frugal, and grows in calcareous well drained subsoils. It flowers best in sunny sites. The light brown wood is too small to be of any use, though at one time it was used for musical wind instruments, since the pith is easy to extract.

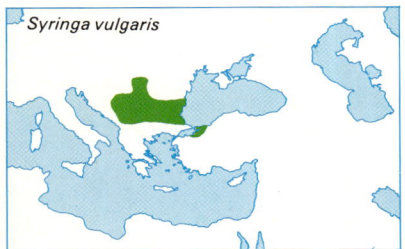
Syringa vulgaris

×3
ovary

Phillyrea latifolia

PHILLYREA LATIFOLIA L.
Phillyrea
Family *Oleaceae*

height 5 (9) m, more often shrubby
crown domed, dense
trunk sinuous, thickly branched; bark grey
foliage evergreen
leaves simple, ovate-lanceolate, more or less serrate, 4 × 2 cm, thick and leathery, with short petiole; often variable, ranging to elongate-elliptic; opposite arrangement
flowers inflorescences in axillary racemes; calyx and corolla 4-lobed, petals greenish-white; scented; flowering period March–June
fruits globose black drupes, 5–7 mm

The Phillyrea is native to the Mediterranean region, an ever-present part of the evergreen maquis. It adapts to dry, rocky surroundings and grows in almost any subsoil, apart from compact clay. It seldom reaches tree-size, is more often shrub-like and is uncommon in Britain.

The wood is very heavy, its specific weight exceeding that of water; due to its dimensions and an unpleasant smell, it has no special uses, apart from providing fuel and high quality charcoal. The leaves have certain medicinal properties.

LIGUSTRUM LUCIDUM Ait.
Chinese or Glossy Privet **
Family *Oleaceae*

height 15 m
crown domed, elongate
trunk erect, sinuous, broadly ramified; bark dark grey, opaque, smooth
foliage evergreen
leaves simple, oval-acute, 10 cm, thick and curved, with the two parts turned slightly upwards, shiny green above, pale green below; opposite arrangement
flowers inflorescences in terminal panicles, up to 20 cm long, broadly

Ligustrum lucidum

pyramidal, made up of small white flowers; flowering period August–September
fruits small black, shiny, oval berries of 1 cm, persisting until winter

The soft terminal branches of the native European privet (*Ligustrum vulgare*) were once used for binding and weaving: the generic name thus comes from the Latin *ligo* (I bind).
The Glossy Privet is an evergreen

tree originating in the Far East, growing wild in China. Imported into Europe at the end of the 18th century as an ornamental species, it is nowadays widespread throughout the temperate parts of the continent. In Britain it is grown as a bold, glossy-leaved evergreen tree.
Fairly hardy and frugal, with slow growth, it adapts to virtually any soils, standing up both to the polluted air of cities and a salty marine environment.
It is highly prized as an ornamental tree, easy to cultivate and suited to hedging and lining street display. There are many varieties, differing in leaf colour and size.

FRAXINUS ORNUS L.
Manna Ash **
Family *Oleaceae*

height 6–15 (20) m
crown hemispherical, flattened
trunk straight, broadly branched; branches opposite; bark dark grey, always smooth
foliage deciduous
leaves compound, pinnate, about 25 cm long, formed of 5–9 leaflets with short (1.5 cm) petiole, ovate-rounded, each leaflet 7 cm, toothed; terminal leaflet obovate; opposite arrangement
flowers inflorescences dense and numerous in spreading or pendulous panicles, 15–20 cm, composed of large numbers of white flowers, 7–15 mm, with corolla of 4 linear petals; deeply scented; flowering period late May

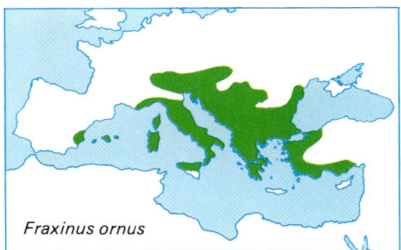

Fraxinus ornus

fruits samaras (winged achenes), lanceolate, 2–3 cm, which remain on tree even after leaf fall

Manna Ash is native to south-eastern Europe, growing on plains up to an altitude of 1100–1300 m. It is frequently found in warm woodlands on hills and mountains; undemanding as to soil, it will adapt to reafforestation on arid ground, chalk or clay. In Britain it is often planted for amenity purposes.

The wood, similar to that of the Ash, is used for poles, tool handles, and as fuel. An important by-product is the exudate known as manna; this sweet juice is extracted by making incisions in the trunk of trees from 6–12 years old. The manna congeals when exposed to the air and because of the high mannitol content is used as a mild laxative.

FRAXINUS EXCELSIOR L.
Ash *
Family *Oleaceae*

height 40 m
crown elongate, domed
trunk straight, often to top; branches turned upwards, opposite; bark grey, smooth or with thin ridges
foliage deciduous
leaves compound, pinnate, 20–30 cm, formed of 7–15 oval or elliptic-lanceolate leaflets, more or less

Fraxinus ornus

×2

sessile, 2–3 cm wide, toothed; opposite arrangement; autumn colour yellow-brown
flowers inconspicuous, hermaphrodite or unisexual; ♂ flowers formed of only 2 stamens with purple anthers, joined in clusters on branches of previous year; ♀ flowers arranged as preceding ones, purple to green; flowering period April, prior to foliation
fruits lanceolate samaras of 4 cm

Fraxinus angustifolia Vahl
Narrow-leaved Ash **

Similar to *F. excelsior*, usually shorter (up to 25 m), leaves of 15–20 cm with 7–13 leaflets 1–2 cm wide, long and lanceolate, 3–8 cm.

The dense crown explains the generic name, from the Greek *frasso* (closed, hedged in). The Ash grows wild in Britain and Europe, and in mountain habitats appears sporadically in woods of beech and spruce, up to altitudes of 1700 m. A sun-loving species, it prefers soils which are deep, fresh and loose.

The Ash is grown mainly for its timber, which is light brown with

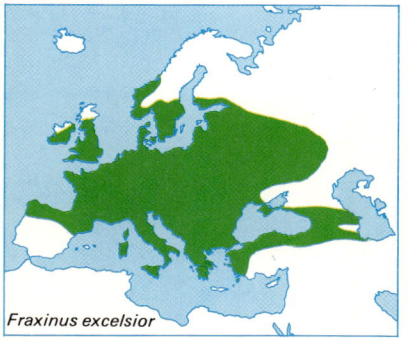

Fraxinus excelsior

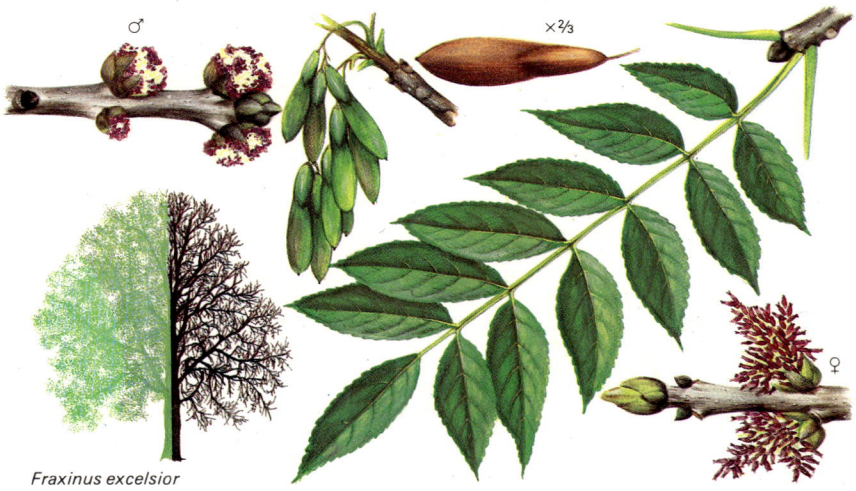

Fraxinus excelsior

bright highlights, easy to work and highly valued. It is used for furniture, sporting equipment such as skis, oars and sledges, kitchen utensils and tool handles; the roots are also valued for their dark veining.

The leaves were at one time used as animal fodder; a decoction was obtained from the bark for treating liver ailments and an extract from the ashes used for scabies. The tree is sometimes used as an ornament, especially certain varieties with a particular habit and leaf colour.

The Narrow-leaved Ash grows wild from south-eastern Europe to the Caucasus and is cultivated as an ornamental in Britain; it is found in wet deciduous woods, along river banks. Because of its elegant shape, it is often cultivated for ornamental purposes.

NERIUM OLEANDER L.
Oleander
Family *Apocynaceae*

height 4 (6) m, usually shrubby
crown domed
trunk broadly ramified, even at base; bark grey with some cracks; twigs

brown-green
foliage evergreen
leaves lanceolate-acute, 10–15 cm, with short petiole, glabrous and leathery; arrangement opposite or verticillate in groups of 3
flowers large and showy, 5–6 cm, joined in terminal corymbs; persistent 5-lobed calyx, broad 5-lobed corolla, pink or white; flowering period May–September
fruits dry and dehiscent, consisting of double, tapering capsules, 15 cm, brown; numerous seeds with pappus (tuft of long hairs) at apex, reddish

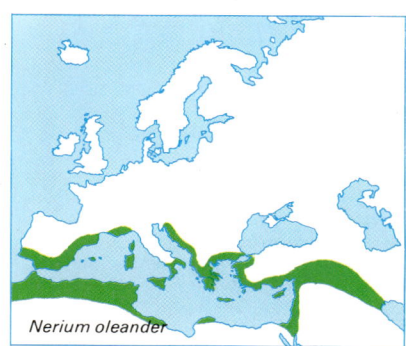

Nerium oleander

Nerium oleander

seed ↓ ×1

The Oleander grows wild along rivers throughout the Mediterranean area, hence the generic name, from the Greek *neron* (water).

This species enjoys the sun and is markedly adaptable to arid conditions, especially along river banks and in broad, dried-up river-beds. It is highly sensitive to cold and must be planted in sheltered sites, if there is the risk of frost. It is unaffected by sea winds. In Britain it is only found indoors.

All parts of the Oleander are poisonous. Its properties nevertheless include alkaloids, glucosides, tannins, sugars and other principles. An extracted substance, folinerin, rather like digitalin, is used to regulate heart conditions. Other derivatives are used in the treatment of scabies and abscesses.

The Oleander is mainly used for ornamental purposes, because of its decorative evergreen foliage and beautiful flowers which bloom from the end of spring to early autumn. Some selected varieties display single and double flowers of different colours.

CLERODENDRUM TRICHOTOMUM
Thunb.
Clerodendrum **
Family *Verbenaceae*

height 5–8 m
crown hemispherical
trunk erect, short and divided; twigs pubescent; bark dark brown, rough, slightly furrowed
foliage deciduous
leaves simple, oval-elliptic, 10–20 cm, acuminate, downy; margins smooth; opposite arrangement
flowers inflorescences with double head, forming terminal panicles; white flowers with swollen red calyx, persistent; flowering period June
fruits blue-black berries of 6–8 mm ∅, wrapped inside calyx with 5 flesh-red sepals; fruits remain on tree for a long time in winter

The generic name signifies 'tree of destiny'; the species originally came from China and is much cultivated in Britain and Europe as an ornamental for its fine blooms of scented white corollas and handsome fruits: blue berries, surrounded by the deep red calyx, which remain on the branches for a long time. It likes fertile soil and resists frosts, unless prolonged.

PAULOWNIA TOMENTOSA
(Sprengel) Steud.
Foxglove Tree *
Family *Scrophulariaceae*

height 20 m
crown domed, elongate
trunk sinuous, erect, with branches curving upwards, hairy; bark grey or slightly brown, smooth
foliage deciduous
leaves simple, oval-cordate, mucronate, large (35 × 25 cm), sometimes with 2 teeth, hairy; petiole of 10 cm, hairy; opposite arrangement
flowers erect terminal inflorescences in racemes, 20–30 cm, flowers tubular, bell-shaped, with 5 spreading lobes, purple to violet, 6 cm; flowering period May; the hairy flower buds

fruit   seed

×3

Paulownia tomentosa

are already visible from the previous autumn
fruits numerous winged, ovate-acute, bivalve capsules, 4 cm, persistent on axis of inflorescence; large numbers of winged seeds

The genus was dedicated to Princess Anna Paulowna (1795–1865), daughter of Paul I of Russia. The tree comes from central China, being imported into Europe around 1830. A very hardy species, it grows rapidly but is not very long-lived. It adapts to virtually any soil, prefers sunny sites and can hold its own against frost which, if prolonged, diminishes its flowering capacity. The Foxglove Tree is used as an ornamental species for its shade and splendid flowers. When cut at the base it coppices freely. While the wood is highly regarded, it is not widely used.

CATALPA BIGNONIOIDES Walt.
Indian Bean Tree **
Family *Bignoniaceae*

height 10 (15) m
crown domed
trunk short, stout and often inclined;

bark reddish-brown to grey, ridged
foliage deciduous
leaves simple, oval-cordate, acute and mucronate, large (up to 20 cm ⌀), hairy; petiole adpressed, glabrous, 10–15 cm; when crushed, the leaves give off a bad smell; arrangement opposite, but more often verticillate in groups of 3
flowers erect inflorescences in racemes, 15–20 cm; bell-shaped flowers of 5 cm, with 5 spreading lobes and undulate margin, white with violet and yellow spots; flowering period June–July
fruits long, cigar-shaped capsules of 15–40 cm, 0.8 cm thick, brown, pendent from branches even in winter

Catalpa is the name used by North American Indians to describe this tree. Originally from the southern parts of the United States, it reached Europe around 1730; it is cultivated in Britain for ornamental purposes and is becoming naturalized in places. The Indian Bean is a rugged species, tolerating cold with no specific soil requirements, preferring sunny, well sheltered sites.
    The timber is of mediocre quality, large-grained, tough and durable, utilized especially outdoors. The tree

Catalpa bignonioides

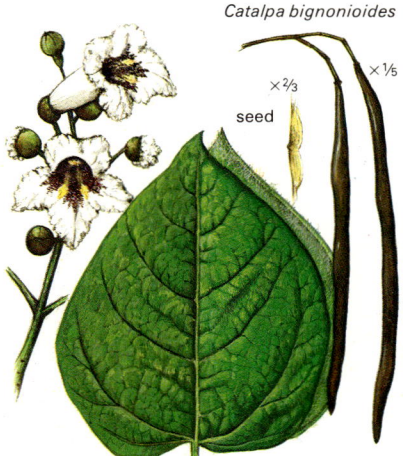

×2/3   ×1/5

seed

is chiefly interesting for its ornamental qualities: large, showy flowers and broad crown.

A similar species is *Catalpa speciosa* Engelm., or Northern Catalpa, originally from the central-northern regions of North America, also cultivated for ornament. The leaves, when crushed, give off no odour, in contrast to *C. bignonioides*.

SAMBUCUS NIGRA L.
Elder *
Family *Caprifoliaceae*

height 6 m
crown domed, spreading
trunk sinuous, bifurcate, branched; twigs with numerous brown lenticels; white pith; bark grey-brown, deeply furrowed, corky
foliage deciduous
leaves compound, pinnate, 20–30 cm, with 5 (7) elliptic, serrate-dentate leaflets, 6–12 cm; opposite arrangement
flowers inflorescences composed of umbels of terminal corymbs, 10–20 cm ∅; flowers of 5 mm ∅, corolla of 5 white, joined petals; 5 stamens with protruding yellow anthers;

Sambucus nigra

flowering period May–June
fruits black, juicy berries, 6 mm ∅, borne on red peduncles

In ancient times the branches of this tree were used in the making of the stringed musical instrument, known by its Latin name *sambuca*.

With the exception of the extreme north, the Elder grows wild throughout Europe, from lowlands up to altitudes of 1500 m. It is highly adaptable to both soil and climate, though it prefers loose subsoils with plenty of water.

The wood varies in quality according to whether it comes from the upper part of the trunk and branches, or from the lower. In the first case it is light, non-durable, with a very soft pith (which has uses in microscopy); in the second it is yellowish-white, hard and heavy, suitable for lathe-work, kitchen utensils and for fuel.

The Elder has certain pharmaceutical properties: as a sweating stimulant; the flowers in particular, together with the leaves and bark, are used not only as a diuretic but as a remedy for skin ailments and catarrh. The berries, used for making wine, jams and syrups, also have laxative properties besides producing a violet colorant for dyeing.

Sambucus nigra

×2

ANGIOSPERMS
Monocotyledons

Key to **PALMS**

Leaves palmate, in a fan
– petioles spinous
– – trees bigger than 5 m; old leaves remain stuck to trunk, becoming fibrous: **Washingtonia filifera**
– – trees seldom bigger than 5 m; old leaves drop off, so that crown consists only of green leaves: **Chamaerops humilis**
– petioles without spines, only slightly toothed: **Trachycarpus fortunei**

Leaves pinnate
– trunk horizontally ridged low down because of presence of remains of leaf petioles
– – leaves of 2–3 m, trees over 8 m, thick trunk; ovoid fruits of 1.5 cm, non-edible: **Phoenix canariensis**
– – leaves of 3–5 m, trees 8–30 m tall, slender trunk; fruits (dates) elongated, 3–5 cm, edible: **Phoenix dactylifera**
– trunk smooth low down, thickened at base, grey; tree of 8 m: **Jubaea spectabilis**

CHAMAEROPS HUMILIS L.
European Fan Palm
Family *Palmae*

height no trunk if wild; 2–8 (9) m if cultivated
crown spherical
trunk erect (in wild trees twisted and creeping) with fibrous remains of leaf sheaths
foliage evergreen
leaves fan-like, with divided and fringed blades of 40 cm; petiole of 40 cm, semi-cylindrical and spiny on edges
flowers inflorescences in erect spike (spadix), greenish-yellow, branchy, with unisexual or hermaphrodite flowers
fruits ovoid dates of 3 cm ⌀, brown and shiny, non-edible

The small size of this palm furnished the generic name, from the Greek *chamai* (on ground), and *rops* (shoot, shrub). This is the only member of the palm family native to mainland Europe, where it grows up to latitude 44°N. It is not hardy in Britain. It is found in ravines in the evergreen

Chamaerops humilis

Chamaerops humilis

Mediterranean maquis region, and along coasts, requiring sunny sites and well drained soil; it is affected by prolonged frosts.

Climate permitting, the European Fan Palm is widely grown for ornament, mainly for streets. The long fibres produced by the leaves are used as vegetable horse-hair in the making of ropes, mats and paper. The fruits provide fodder for goats.

WASHINGTONIA FILIFERA Wendl.
Petticoat Palm
Family *Palmae*

height 10 m
crown ovoid, domed at top and continuing lower down with remains of dead leaves which have not dropped off
trunk straight, squat
foliage evergreen
leaves in fan of 1–2 m ∅, with linear segments, frayed at edges; petioles of 1–2 m with backward-curving spines at margins
flowers inflorescences in spike of 2–4 m, ramified, then pendent; small flowers; flowering period June–September
fruits spherical, black, joined at axis of inflorescence

This genus of palms was dedicated to George Washington by the botanist Wendland. It originated in the western United States, in California and Arizona. It is cultivated only in the warmer southern regions of Europe, as a street ornamental and in parks, for its unusual and decorative appearance. It needs a mild climate, though tolerating frost for a short period. It is less hardy and adaptable than other palms, and does not endure prolonged periods of drought.

TRACHYCARPUS FORTUNEI Wendl.
(= *Chamaerops excelsa* Host non Thunb.; *T. excelsa* Wendl.)
Chinese Windmill Palm or Chusan Palm **
Family *Palmae*

height 5–10 m
crown spherical
trunk straight, covered with mat-like fibres
foliage evergreen
leaves in fan of about 1 m ∅, divided into 30–50 blades; petiole of 0.5–1 m with finely toothed edge
flowers inflorescences unisexual in spadix of about 60 cm, more or less erect; flowers small; flowering period March–April
fruits spherical, 1–1.5 cm ∅, blue-black

The generic name is derived from the rough surface of the fruits, from the Greek *trachys* (rough) , and *carpos* (fruit). The Chinese Windmill Palm was introduced to Europe in the 19th century from China and Japan, finding popularity as an ornamental because of its decorative appearance. It is the hardiest of palms and the only species grown outdoors in southern England. If cultivated in the open, young specimens must be protected during particularly cold periods. The tree prefers fertile, well drained, deep subsoils, having a very extensive root system.

PHOENIX CANARIENSIS Chabaud
Canary Islands Date Palm
Family *Palmae*

height 4–8 m
crown spherical
trunk sturdy, with traces of petiole bases, more or less fibrous

×½

Phoenix canariensis

foliage evergreen
leaves pinnate, 2–3 m long
flowers inflorescences in unisexual spadices; ♀ flowers branchy and pendent, up to 2 m long
fruits oval, light brown dates of 2 cm, non-edible

The origin of the name *Phoenix*, which designates various species of palms, is uncertain; it may be derived from the Greek *phoinix*, a region in the Persian Gulf, from which some of these palms originally came.

The Canary Islands Date Palm, native to this group of islands, has been cultivated in the Mediterranean region for its ornamental qualities, becoming naturalized in some places.

PHOENIX DACTYLIFERA L.
Date Palm
Family *Palmae*

height up to 30 m
crown spherical
trunk straight and slender; basal shoots present; bark shows traces of leaves as wide as they are long
foliage evergreen
leaves pinnate, curved, up to 3–5 m long; leaflets of 30–40 cm, opposite
flowers inflorescences unisexual, in spadices; ♂ flowers of about 1–2 m; ♀ flowers of 1.5–2 m; flowering period March–May
fruits ellipsoid dates, 3–6 cm, yellow to brown, edible

The specific name derives from the elongated shape of the fruits, resembling the fingers of the hand, from the Greek *dactylos* (finger), and the Latin *fero* (I bear).

The Date Palm has been widely cultivated, its range extending to the most southerly parts of Europe, notably Spain and Sicily. The species can stand strong sun and a dry climate, provided the soil holds plenty of moisture; it grows freely in African oases, where its highly developed root system probes deep down to the water-table.

Of all plant species used by man, this is one of the most famous and most ancient. The trunk furnishes building timber and, when cut, yields a sweetish, fermentable latex, from which a liquor, known in Arabic as *laghbi*, is produced. The leaves are used for making mats, but the most important product of the tree is the fruit, graded according to the consistency of the pulp, which may be soft or floury. In many tropical regions, dates are a basic source of food for both people and animals.

Dried dates contain 50% sugar and appreciable quantities of proteins, fats, vitamins and mineral salts, constituting a highly nutritious food.

JUBAEA SPECTABILIS H.B.K.
(= *Jubaea chilensis* (Molinia) Baillon)
Chilean Wine Palm
Family *Palmae*

height 10 (20) m
crown spherical; dead leaves present
trunk thickened at base (2 m ∅); lower part almost smooth or slightly ridged transversely; colour ash-grey
foliage evergreen
leaves pinnate, 2–4 m; single leaflets of 20–30 cm; petiole smooth
flowers inflorescences in spadices of

60 cm; flowering period July–September
fruits small drupes of 4 cm ⌀, yellow

This tree, originally from Chile, was introduced to Europe as an ornamental species and is found in the Mediterranean region. In South America the sugary sap is extracted and used in its natural state or, after fermentation, as an alcoholic drink.

CORDYLINE AUSTRALIS (Forst.) Hook.
Cabbage Palm **
Family *Agavaceae*

height 10 m
crown spherical, compact
trunk erect, usually undivided, sometimes branched at top; surface grey, horizontally ridged

foliage evergreen
leaves in spadix, sharp, sessile, leathery, 50–100 cm long
flowers inflorescences up to 1 m, in racemes, with white flowers of 1.5 cm; flowering period April–May
fruits bluish berries of 5 mm, shiny

The Cabbage Palm is not a true palm, belonging to the Agave family. The generic name, from the thickened form of the roots, is derived from the Greek *cordyle* (club). It came originally from New Zealand, reaching Europe around 1820 as an ornamental species, adaptable to cultivation in the open, under glass and in homes. In Britain it is mainly found in the south as it needs a mild climate and sunny sites sheltered from wind and frost. There are different ornamental varieties with diverse leaf colours.

Glossary

The explanation of the principal botanical terms used are
complemented by the morphological illustrations on pages 240–244.
Supplementary definitions will be found on pages 245–247.

Morphology of leaf

simple leaves

lamina or blade
apex

margin

toothed blade

incised blade

base
petiole
axillary bud

petiolule

leaves composed of several leaflets

rachis

petiole

pinnate

palmate

Form of blade

round

elliptic

ovate

obovate

lanceolate

flabellate

acicular or needle

scale leafed

acicular

Venation

pinnately veined

parallel veined

palmately veined

Margin

entire

scabrous

serrulate

serrate

crenate

repand

revolute

involute   sinuate

lobed

cleft

parted

septate

Apex

acute

obtuse

reniform

retuse

emarginate

acuminate

mucronate

Base

cordate

cuneate

asymmetrical

truncate

Palmate leaves

palmately-lobed

cleft or deeply lobed

parted

septate or palmately compound

Compound leaves

equally pinnate

odd-pinnate

bipinnate

tripinnate

trifoliate

petiolule rachis

petiole

biternate

thorn (hawthorn)

Modified leaves

stipule

bract

spines

aristate (leaf or bract)

tendril

stipule

Modified stems

tendril

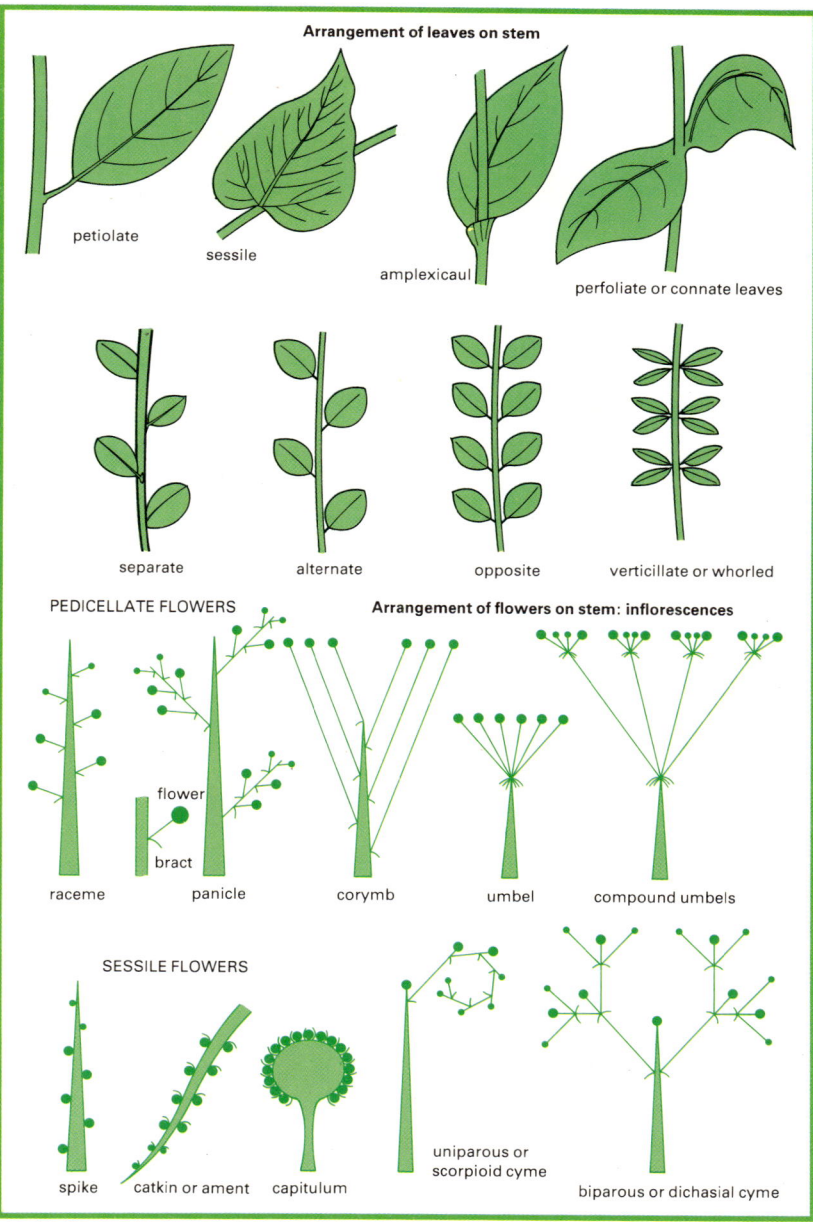

Arrangement of leaves on stem

petiolate

sessile

amplexicaul

perfoliate or connate leaves

separate

alternate

opposite

verticillate or whorled

PEDICELLATE FLOWERS

Arrangement of flowers on stem: inflorescences

flower

bract

raceme

panicle

corymb

umbel

compound umbels

SESSILE FLOWERS

spike

catkin or ament

capitulum

uniparous or scorpioid cyme

biparous or dichasial cyme

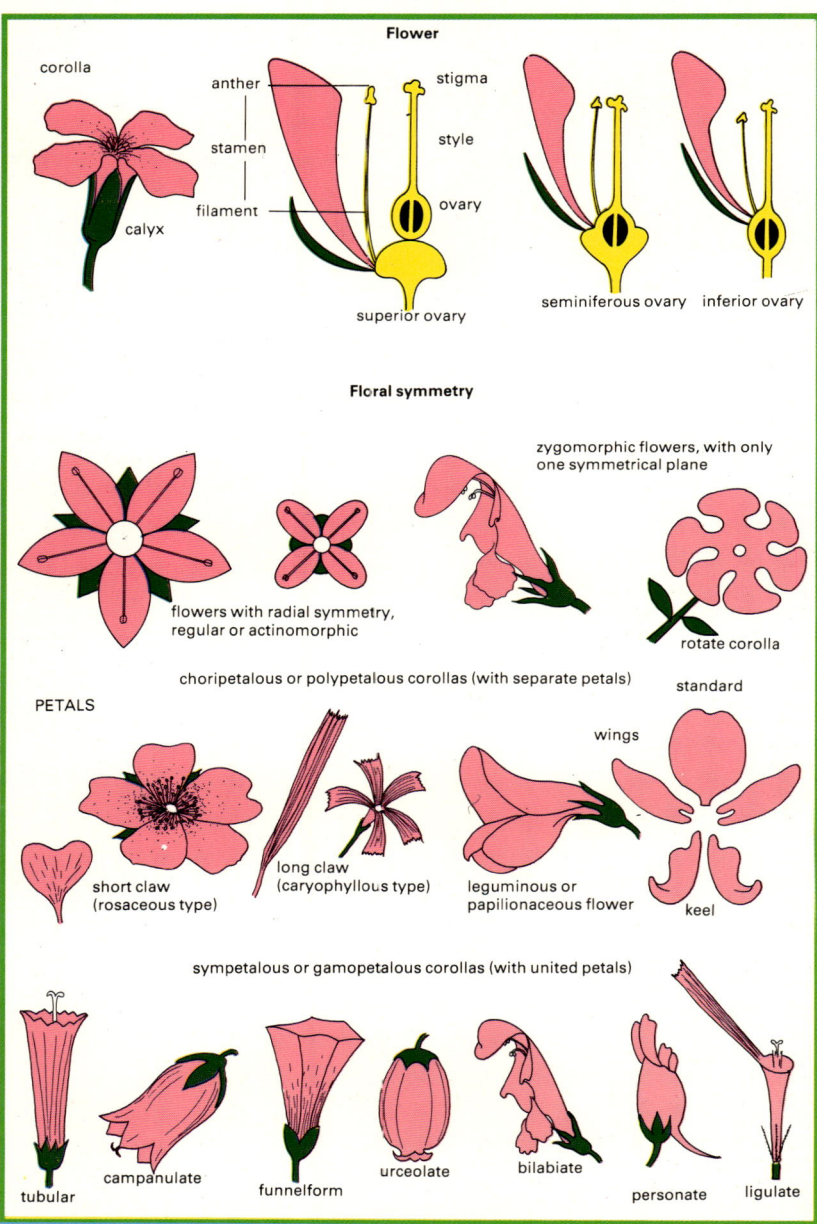

Flower

corolla

anther

stamen

filament

calyx

stigma

style

ovary

superior ovary

seminiferous ovary   inferior ovary

Floral symmetry

zygomorphic flowers, with only one symmetrical plane

flowers with radial symmetry, regular or actinomorphic

rotate corolla

choripetalous or polypetalous corollas (with separate petals)

PETALS

standard

wings

short claw (rosaceous type)

long claw (caryophyllous type)

leguminous or papilionaceous flower

keel

sympetalous or gamopetalous corollas (with united petals)

tubular

campanulate

funnelform

urceolate

bilabiate

personate

ligulate

abortive imperfectly developed, rudimentary, non-functional.

achene small, hard, one-seeded fruit.

acicular needle-like.

acidic (of soil) soil with pH lower than 7, usually lacking carbonates.

acuminate with a short tapered tip (e.g. of a leaf).

adpressed pressed closely together but not joined.

angiosperm major division of higher plants.

anther pollen producing tip of a stamen.

aphid sap-sucking insect – Blackfly, Greenfly.

auricle ear-shaped lobe at base of leaf.

berry small pulpy fruit with embedded seeds.

bifid split into two parts.

bifurcate divided into two branches.

bole lower part of a stem or trunk, free of branches.

brachblast short shoot with numerous leaf scars.

bract leaf-like appendage at base of a flower, occasionally brightly coloured as in *Cornus*.

caducous tending to drop off, as leaves; deciduous.

calcareous refers to soils containing calcium carbonate; chalky.

calyx ring of sepals beneath the petals.

capsule dry, opening seed-vessel.

catkin string of single-sex flowers, without petals, often, not always, pendulous.

ciliate with a protecting fringe of cilia, or minute hairs.

clone plant or group of plants propagated by cuttings, grafting, budding or layering, without sexual reproduction. Cultivars are clones.

columnar tall and narrow, in shape of column.

cone woody, conical multiple fruit of pine, fir, etc., consisting of scales bearing naked ovules or seeds; also strobilus.

coniferous cone-bearing, pertaining to a conifer.

continental (climate) climate with reliable and pronounced hot (summer) and cold (winter) periods, compared with a maritime climate, like Britain's, where the weather is less reliable and more switchback.

cordate heart-shaped at base (e.g. of leaf).

coriaceous with the texture or consistency of leather, as of certain leaves.

cultivar shortened term for cultivated variety.

cupule cup-like structure, woody or membranous, partially or wholly protecting the fruit of certain trees (oaks, hazels).

cuneate wedge-shaped at base, (e.g. of leaf).

deciduous tending to drop off, as leaves annually.

dehiscent process of splitting open, as of a fruit to discharge seeds.

dentate with forward pointing teeth (leaf margins).

dicot division of angiospermae with two seed leaves.

digitate with radiating lobes or leaflets, like the outstretched fingers of the hand.

dioecious having male and female flowers on separate plants.

domed roughly hemispherical, dome-shaped, as of crown of tree.

drupe pulpy fruit with hard inner shell enclosing usually one seed.

endemic peculiar to a locality, native to a zone or country.

endocarp inner of protective layers around seed, e.g. in *Prunus* the bony part of the nut.

falcate curved like the blade of a scythe, as of a leaf.

fastigiate with branches virtually upright.

filiform thread-like.

flabellate fern-shaped.

foliation process of sprouting leaves, state of being in leaf.

fruit seed and accessory parts, dry or fleshy, sometimes edible.

fusiform spindle-shaped; tapering from centre towards either end.

gabulous thickened or swollen.

glabrous without hairs, smooth, naked.

gland small organ or structure secreting liquid, usually on or near the surface of a plant.

glaucous grey-blue or whitish, often due to a wax bloom.

globose globe-shaped, more or less round, as of fruit.

glomerule inflorescence made up of sessile or very briefly pedunculate flowers, forming a spherical head.

gymnosperm major group of higher plants including all conifers.

habit bearing, appearance.

hermaphrodite plant bearing separate functional male and female flowers.

hesperidium fruit of a citrus plant, i.e. orange and lemon, with pulp and rind.

hybrid offspring of different species or varieties, as of a plant produced by cross-fertilization.

inflorescence flowering part of a plant or cluster of flowers, in form of umbel, spike, raceme, spadix, corymb, catkin, cyme, etc.

involucre collection of bracts, usually around the base of a flower cluster.

laciniate divided into narrow lobes or segments.

lanceolate lance-shaped (of a leaf).

lamina (blade) the broad flat part of a leaf, at the end of the petiole.

lateral situated at side; a side extension, as of a branch or shoot.

latex a milky liquid exuded by certain plants, coagulating on exposure to air.

legume pod or seed vessel of the pea family, which splits lengthwise into two parts to release seeds.

lenticel elliptical or round pore on surface of plant, i.e. bark, usually raised, through which gaseous exchanges take place between underlying tissues and outside atmosphere.

linear long and narrow, with parallel sides.

lobe projection or division of a leaf or petal.

lobulate bearing lobes.

loculate containing one or more loculi or cells.

loculus a small compartment or cell, specifically a cell of a flower in which

seed or pollen is contained.

loment legume contracted in the spaces between the seeds, breaking up when mature into one-seeded joints.

maquis area of Mediterranean scrubland, consisting of shrubs and isolated trees.

membranous of thin, papery consistency, resembling a membrane.

mesocarp middle of protective layers around a seed. In *Prunus* is the fleshy edible part of a peach or plum.

midrib central vein of a leaf.

monocot division of angiospermae with one seed leaf.

monopodal with a single main growing point, producing a long straight trunk as in conifers and palm.

mucronate terminating in a point.

naturalized plant species introduced to a region and eventually growing there as if native.

oborate broadest between the middle and the tip (e.g. of a leaf).

obtuse blunt or rounded (e.g. of a leaf tip).

operculum cover or lid, specifically on a seed vessel.

orbicular round in outline (of a leaf lamina).

ovoid three dimensional shape, broadest between base and middle (e.g. of a fruit or bud).

ovuliferous bearing the ovules (or immature seeds e.g. cone scales in conifers).

palmate with leaflets or lobes of the leaf radiating out from a central point, like the fingers from an open palm.

panicle compound flower structure in which the flowers are carried on pedicels branching off a rachis.

pectinate spreading either side of the shoot, like a comb.

pedicel the individual flower stalk, compared to a peduncle, which is the stalk to a cluster of flowers.

peduncle stalk of a flower or floral inflorescence.

pendent pendulous, hanging, drooping.

perfoliate leaves clasping a stem so that it appears that the stem is passing through the leaves.

perianth envelope of a flower, including petals and sepals.

perule scaly covering of a leaf bud.

persistent continuing or permanent, as of foliage.

petiolate having a petiole.

petiole leaf stalk.

pinnate compound leaf in which the leaflets arise, usually in pairs either side of a rachis or central stalk.

pistil collective term for female parts of a flower, covering ovary, style and stigma.

pith soft tissue in centre of a stem or trunk.

pollard (polliniferous) cut back to trunk to encourage vigorous branch growth.

pome fruit with fleshy body and cartilaginous core enclosing seeds, as apple, pear, quince, etc.

pubescent covered with short, soft hairs.

pyramidal resembling a pyramid, wide at base and tapering, as of crown of tree.

raceme flower string with single flowers on pedicels arising from the central rachis.

rachis axis or central stalk, of a pinnate leaf or flower.

ramified forming branches, branching out.

receptacle enlarged end of stalk bearing a flower.

repand with a slightly uneven margin.

reticulate marked with a network, as ridges of bark or leaf veins.

revolute turned down, usually of a leaf margin.

rhomboid shaped like a rhombus, lozenge-shaped.

samara indehiscent dry winged fruit.

sepal a bract-like structure, forming part of the calyx; in some plants more pronounced than the petals.

septate divided by septa (internal walls or partitions) e.g. front of an orange.

serrate saw-toothed, with forward pointing teeth.

serrulate serrate but with fewer teeth.

sessile attached by base, without stalk.

sinuate waved, as of leaf margin.

sinuous with many curves, winding.

solitary single flower to a stalk.

spadix spike with a fleshy axis.

spike a flower strung like a raceme but in which the flowers are similar, not stalked.

stamen male part of a flower, consisting of anther and filament (stalk).

stigma position of female flower on which pollen must land.

stipule leaf-like appendage at base of petiole; occasionally developed into thorns, as in *Robinia*.

sucker shoot rising from root and base of trunk e.g. limes.

sylviculture cultivation of woods and forests, growing and tending trees.

syncarp aggregate front of many individual elements e.g. mulberry, which is a cluster of drupes.

tannin vegetable principle or compound, occurring in bark of some trees, used in tanning leather.

tepal collective term for the sepals and petals of flowers like Magnolia where the calyx and corolla elements of the flower are indistinguishable.

terminal at or near tip, as of leaf or branch.

tomentose with dense, woolly covering of soft hairs.

truncate cut off at the apex.

umbel branched flower head with all the elements arising from one point.

umbo raised centre, as of scale of cone.

undulate wavy, as of leaf margin.

unisexual inflorescence of male or female flowers on single tree.

valve segment into which a capsule of fruit dehisces.

verticillate whorled.

whorl arrangement of two or more organs on same plane around stem.

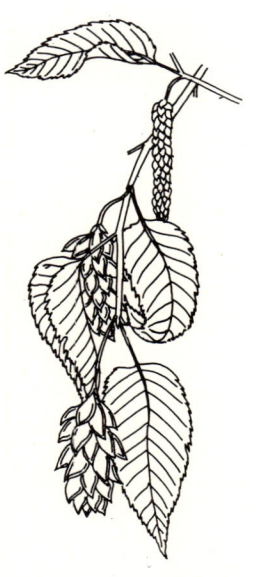

Index